LONDON TRANSPORT SERVICE VEHICLES

LONDON TRANSPORT
SERVICE VEHICLES

A history by Kim Rennie and Bill Aldridge

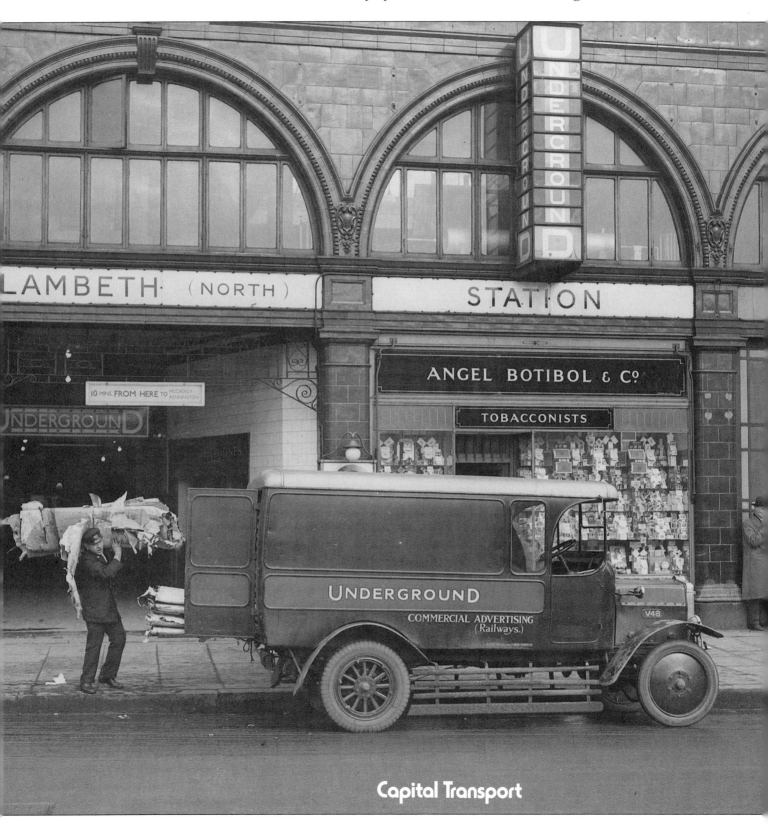

Capital Transport

FOREWORD

In October 1999, (Central) Distribution Services celebrated 50 years since its inception in 1949. Upon creation, it brought together under one centralised organisation all miscellaneous transport allocated to the many departments then forming London Transport. Until the start of the break-up of LT in the early-1980s, it was a division of the centralised supplies organisation; which had responsibility for procurement, storage, distribution and disposal of all material and services required to support LT's road and railway operation. CDS's remit was to provide transport services as efficiently, economically and safely as possible, whilst ensuring compliance with all relevant legislation. Throughout the years, it has worked in conjunction with and in competition with outside industry, concentrating in-house services on core essential transport and contracting out other work where appropriate. The shape and size of CDS has of course changed continually to meet the ever-changing requirements of the customer. However, it says much for the sound organisation that was established, and the many dedicated staff who have worked for the department over the years, that it still exists today with the same broad responsibilities.

Kim Rennie's and Bill Aldridge's book provides a good historical record of the department's services and vehicles, and has been compiled as a tribute to the work done by many 'unsung heroes'.

Michael Clark
Distribution Services Manager
1977 – 1993

Peter Forsdick
Distribution Services Manager
Since 1993

INTRODUCTION

The vast majority of bus operators have always included within their fleets a number of vehicles whose sole purpose was to help to maintain the passenger-carrying rolling stock in running order. In general terms, the most common vehicle would be the fitters' run-about van and then perhaps a breakdown truck able to rescue recalcitrant buses. However in the case of London Transport, the largest passenger transport undertaking in the world, the standard rulebook was 'thrown to the wind'. There were few organisations that had to cope with fleets composed of buses, coaches, trams and trolleybuses; alongside a comprehensive network of railway lines that relied on the generation of either steam or electric power, and all this over a 'Special Operating Area' of some 2000 square miles.

Because the LT undertaking was so large, the service vehicle fleet was designed to cover virtually every eventuality, including even that of nuclear war! In general terms, the overall capability of LT was such that it was almost self-supporting and the service vehicle fleet reflected this ability. From re-railing trains and repairing buses, policing its premises, to clothing and feeding staff, LT was probably the most self-sufficient transport operator in the world.

To many, the archetypal LT service vehicle is the ex-bus converted to a lorry or breakdown tender, and whenever the support fleet is mentioned, these types spring to mind. But, they were only a small proportion of the fleet. Just as important in their own way were the signal engineers' vans which helped keep the trains running, the road inspectors' radio-cars controlling bus routes and the canteen vans supplying food to employees. Without ticket delivery vans fares could not be collected, nor could vehicle batteries be maintained in the absence of the distilled water carriers. All these vehicles were part of a complex web of operations, which the authors hope this book will help to explain.

At the most basic interpretation, Central Distribution Services was a transport and delivery service. However, there can be few delivery services that had to transport their goods daily through what was once the most densely-populated conurbation in the Western World.

There are even fewer that have to serve such demanding customers as the travelling public, and fewer still that had to serve a road and rail network with all its consumables and equipment. The men and women of CDS service deserve a special dedication, and we hope that this book will be a suitable tribute to them.

Acknowledgements to: Peter Forsdick of Distribution Services, Nick Agnew, Paul Blackwell and Chris Edney of London Buses, Jim Blake, Ian Blee, David Bosher, Julian Bowden-Green, Michael Clark, David Corke, Barry Coward, Maurice Doggett, Ian Dyckhoff, Derek Fisk, the late J. Graeme Bruce OBE, John Gillham, Robin Hannay, Brian Hardy, Fred Ivey, Colin Lloyd, Ivor Norman, Peter Rothschild OBE, David Rowe, Steve Smith, Les Stitson, Alan Toomer, Jim Wright; also publications of the London Tramways Historical Group, London Transport, LOTS, the Omnibus Society and PSV Circle.

We very much appreciate the help given by Mr J. C. Gillham in thoroughly reading the text and offering a large amount of additional material that has filled in numerous gaps in the story.

The reader will understand that in a fleet that has included nearly 5000 commercial vehicles, cars and light vans it is not possible to identify every single one that has operated in London. The authors have tried to cover the most interesting vehicles, as well as some of the more mundane ones, but it is inevitable that some operations and types will have been omitted. It will also be appreciated that the service vehicles of London Transport and its predecessors have never been as well documented as the bus and rail fleets. Because of this, we have attempted to give an overall impression of the background to and operation of the service vehicle fleet, rather than concentrating on a detailed appraisal of the vehicles themselves. Current and former members of CDS have given much of the information within this book, and we are very grateful to them for sharing their memories with us.

Kim Rennie
London

Bill Aldridge
Stockport

First published 2003

ISBN 185414 274 7

Published by
Capital Transport Publishing
38 Long Elmes, Harrow, Middlesex

Printed by CS Graphics, Singapore

© Kim Rennie and Bill Aldridge 2003

CONTENTS

A FLEET WITHIN A FLEET

The London Passenger Transport Board (LPTB) assumed control of the vast majority of bus, coach, tram, trolleybus and Underground railway operators within a 30-mile radius of Charing Cross on 1st July 1933. The organisation had actually been formed on 13th April 1933, but naturally a certain amount of background work was required before operations could commence under the LPTB banner. The overall concept was to ensure that the capital city was given a comprehensive and co-ordinated public transport network. The bus operators involved varied in size from the mighty London General Omnibus Company (LGOC), to small partnerships running one or two vehicles. Amongst the better-known operations taken over were Birch Brothers and the London-based operations of Thomas Tilling. The compulsory take-over of the independent bus operators did not start until November 1933 and continued right through 1934 to early 1935.

The railway lines owned by both the Metropolitan Railway and Underground Group were also to become part of the new organisation. The Underground Railway Group had owned the LGOC from 1912, and also operated the District Railway, plus all the deep tube lines except the Southern Railway's Waterloo & City. The Under-

ground Group also owned three tramway companies: London United Tramways (LUT), Metropolitan Electric Tramways (MET) and South Metropolitan Electric Tramways (SMET).

In addition, a total of fourteen council-owned tramway undertakings also came into the LT fold. These ranged from the London County Council Tramways system (LCCT), to municipal concerns like Croydon and West Ham, as well as operations existing only 'on paper' such as the City of London's trams (actually worked by the LCCT). Even the early trolleybus operations were acquired through the absorption of the fledgling LUT fleet. Although the Underground Group owned the Associated Equipment Company (AEC), this traditional 'Builder of London's buses' was not included in the amalgamation, and became an independent company.

The LPTB was organised into four main operating departments: Central Buses, Country Buses & Coaches, Trams & Trolleybuses and Railways (i.e. the Underground). Though the Underground Group had a large element of standardisation, many of the smaller concerns had no more than one or two service vehicles. What the fleets did bring was a multiplicity of bus chassis and body-types, many of which were not really required by their new owners and some of which were quickly converted into support vehicles. Initially each former operator retained its own service vehicles numbered in its own series, and their operation remained much the same as before the takeover. Several different fleet numbering schemes were in use pre-war. The simplest was just a numerical series, whilst the LGOC had a 'class' letter prefix in the style used on its buses since the early years of the 20th Century. Some vehicles were not numbered at all, or retained pre-LPTB numbers throughout their very short new life with the Board. Others were re-numbered in theory, yet continued to display the earlier number. The Board's first Annual Report was published in 1934, and listed the following non-passenger carrying road vehicles among its assets:

Breakdown tenders	…	…	…	…	25
Lorries	…	…	…	…	111
Vans	…	…	…	…	156
Miscellaneous	…	…	…	…	250
Total	…	…	…	…	**542**

In October 1939, the LPTB renumbered all its service vehicles in a common series beginning at '1', followed by a suffix-letter denoting chassis make (e.g. 'A' Albion, 'B' Bedford, 'C' Leyland Cub, 'Q' AEC Mercury, etc). These vehicles had previously been listed in the LPTB's hand-written 'Register of Miscellaneous Vehicles' in alphabetical order, according to manufacturer. The list started with ADC/AEC and finished with Vulcan and the miscellaneous vehicles, and the list was used as the basis for the renumbering. Consequently, the vehicles were not renumbered in age order, but simply by their position in the register. This explains why the oldest vehicle in service, 157D, an ex-LCCT 1907 Foden steam wagon, became numbered in the middle of the series. The same numerical system continues in use today, though in 1983 a series beginning at 3000 commenced to identify leased vehicles. The latter was up to 5400 by 2002, whilst the original range had got as far as 2577. In keeping with the bus fleet, vehicles were given body numbers until 1964. In fact, few service vehicles actually exchanged bodies on overhaul, but the numbers were useful in the case of apparently identical-looking trailers.

After the Second World War, the 'powers that be' at 55 Broadway became concerned at the enormous prolifer-

The men who made it work. Central Distribution Services has been a classic example of the traditional LT principles of centralisation, standardisation and fitness-for-purpose. Throughout its existence, day-to-day operations have been supervised from the Chiswick/Acton Works site, and rely on the close co-operation of management and staff. This photograph was used to illustrate an article on CDS published in London Transport Magazine, and shows the driver of an AEC Matador loaded with vehicle axles being briefed before departure. The young man with the clipboard is Michael Clark, later to become Distribution Services Manager from 1977 to 1993.
LT Museum

ation of miscellaneous vehicles owned by various departments of LT and the duplication of work. Vehicles were required to service not only the railway depots and permanent way establishments, but also bus garages, trolleybus and tram depots, stations and offices. On 1st November 1946, 'miscellaneous vehicle' users of the LPTB were organised as follows (numbers of vehicles shown in bold):

Department of the Chief Engineer

Distribution Engineer (Trams & Trolleybuses)
Northern Division – various depots ... **(27)**
Distribution Engineer (Trams & Trolleybuses)
Southern Division – various depots ... **(26)**
Mains Engineer
– Lillie Bridge ... ... **(1)**
Permanent Way Engineer (Railways)
– Brockley Hill, Chalk Farm,
Lillie Bridge and Neasden ... ... **(16)**
Permanent Way Engineer (Trams & Trolleybuses)
– Rye Lane, Deptford Wharf and
Walthamstow ... ... **(38)**
Signal Engineer
– Lillie Bridge ... ... **(15)**
Wiring Section
– Thornton Heath ... ... **(1)**
Works & Building Engineer
– Parsons Green ... ... **(38)**

Railway War Damage Plant Vehicles [operated by Works & Building]

– Hammersmith [Plant] ... ... **(15)**

Department of the Chief Mechanical Engineer (Railways)

Assistant Mechanical Engineer
(Lifts & Escalators Division)
– Griffith House ... ... **(2)**
Mechanical Engineer – various railway depots **(11)**

Department of the Chief Mechanical Engineer (Road Services)

Miscellaneous vehicle control pool
– Chiswick ... ... **(20)**
Redundant vehicles not in service
– stored at Chiswick and Walthamstow **(7)**
Rolling Stock Engineer (Buses & Coaches)
– various garages ... ... **(88)**
Rolling Stock Engineer (Trams & Trolleybuses)
– various depots ... ... **(21)**
Technical Officer (Fulwell) ... ... **(2)**
Works Engineer (Charlton) ... ... **(13)**
Works Manager (Chiswick) ... ... **(16)**

Department of the Chief Public Relations & Publicity Officer

Commercial Advertising Officer
– Turnham Green ... ... **(7)**
Publicity Officer – various garages ... ... **(13)**

Department of the Chief Commercial Officer

Chief Stores Superintendent
– Chiswick ... ... **(20)**
Fares & Charges Officer
– Chiswick and Rye Lane ... ... **(7)**

Department of the General Manager (Road Services)

Operating Manager (Central Buses)
– Turnham Green and Old Kent Road ... **(2)**
Operating Manager (Country Buses & Coaches)
– various garages ... ... **(5)**
Operating Manager (Trams & Trolleybuses)
– various depots, plus Vauxhall and
Shoreditch ... ... **(7)**

Department of Executive Officer for Staff and Staff Welfare

Welfare Officer
– various garages and roadside locations
[mobile canteens] ... ... **(21)**

The fleet ranged from private and chauffeur-driven cars used by senior managers to motorcycles, small vans, large vans and heavy lorries, not to mention specialised vehicles like tankers, tower wagons and mobile canteens. In an attempt to bring some semblance of order to the situation, a committee was established, chaired by the Chief Civil Engineer, Mr Cedric Dunton, with the intention of rationalising the support fleet. As a consequence of this, a decision was made by the Executive to establish a central pool of commercial vehicles under the overall control of the Chief Supplies Officer, Mr Eric C. Ottaway. The somewhat fragmented service vehicle fleet was thus reorganised in November 1949 to form Central Distribution Services (Freight), whose sole purpose was to offer an extensive back-up service to the main passenger-carrying fleet.

The first Superintendent (General Manager) was Geoffrey Fernyhough and the basic organisation he developed remains in operation. The aim was to 'provide support transport, as efficiently, economically and safely as possible', a statement which still holds true today. The fleet initially operated under a 'C' licence issued by the Ministry of Transport. This style of licence meant that CDS could carry its own goods without restriction, but was unable to offer services for 'hire or reward' to any other company, not even to other nationalised concerns like British Railways, British Road Services or other members of the British Transport Commission. Today, in line with all transport companies, the fleet has an Operators Licence and also holds a Waste Carriers Licence – the latter enabling the movement of rubbish. CDS Management reported to the Chief Supplies Officer, whose department was responsible for the purchase of everything from trains to ticket rolls. This department was also charged with the storage and distribution of supplies, and the eventual disposal of buses.

Under the reorganisation, the fleet was split into three distinct categories:

Group 1 vehicles were designated as 'special purpose' types such as the breakdown tenders, tower wagons and ambulances (i.e. those incapable of carrying out any other type of work). Although these came under CDS for administrative purposes, staff from the departments they served – e.g. the Rolling Stock Engineer (Buses), Chief Signal Engineer, Distribution Engineer (T&T) – actually manned them. These employees were not on the CDS payroll, and were paid directly by their own departments. Most vehicles in this class were in red or red & cream livery – red for tram & trolleybus and motor bus breakdown tenders, plus tower wagons; red & cream (divided horizontally) for railway breakdown tenders and emergency vans. Group 1 types in green livery included specialised tram & trolleybus or railway vehicles such as those involved in permanent way or electrical power distribution, but not in an emergency-response role. The need for many of the more unusual Group 1 vehicles later diminished following the end of the trams in 1952, and was reduced still further when the trolleybus system closed ten years later.

Group 2 vehicles operated where a department had a full-time need for a vehicle, but the driving of it was subsidiary to the employee's normal occupation: e.g. billposting, catering, gully emptying or building repair. These were also driven by staff from the user section, which also allocated the work. Although these vehicles could be specialised, (e.g. pole carriers for the overhead wiring of the trolleybus fleet), under certain circumstances, they could also be used for general haulage. They were maintained

Parsons Green Works & Building Department Depot was one of the main hubs of CDS operation for over fifty years. In this 1955 view, Bedford 'OSS' tractor unit 953B and its associated Eagle trailer are being loaded with a recently repaired Green Line coach stop shelter. The solid-tyred crane, complete with a 'BUILDING DEPT' bullseye, was one of a number of vehicles regarded as 'plant' and thus not included in the CDS fleet number series. The structure in the background was the principal Works & Building Department manufacturing shop and backed onto the eastbound District Line. Vauxhall Motors

and replaced as necessary by CDS, and the user departments charged for their use. If CDS needed to use one of these vehicles, the department concerned would be recompensed for its 'hire'.

Group 3 vehicles were the 'maids of all work' and their drivers (over 200 in all in 1956) were directly employed by CDS. Types varied from small vans to full-size articulated combinations. They were totally under CDS control, and staff at the headquarters in Chiswick Works allocated their work. Examples of this included the ferrying of bus engines and other chassis components from the ninety-odd garages then operational to and from Chiswick Works; and the movement of rail wheel-sets, electric motors and equipment between rail depots and Acton Works. Other tasks were the transfer of passengers' lost property to the Baker Street office, and the supply of provisions to canteens from the Food Production Centre at Croydon.

Both Groups 2 and 3 were painted a dark green until about 1960, when *Cargo Grey* was progressively introduced on new deliveries, and then to older vehicles through repaints. In 1972, the colour red was extended from Group 1 vehicles to small vans (and on inspectors' cars from 1967). This hue later spread to most saloon and van based designs, up to and including Transit-size. From 1990, virtually all vehicles (of all three groups) have appeared in LUL white & blue livery.

The use of Group 3 vehicles was split into two further sub-categories: Regular scheduled services and non-regular or 'ad-hoc' work. Within the first category was the collection and delivery of engines, motors and other equipment to the main works. The supply of tickets, ticket machines, destination blinds, batteries and tyres was also carried out to a regular pattern. The scheduled, regular services were not time-critical, the only requirement being that the work was completed on the day promised. The work might be daily, weekly, monthly or even run on alternate months. Only one job ran to a specific daily timetable, this being the internal mail service. The central mail room was on the ground floor of 55 Broadway, and as an example of the extent of its operations, the early-1980s saw it able to distribute letters to any part of LT and

LCBS, the BR main termini, New Scotland Yard and the GLC at County Hall. All the regular services (of which there were once about 40) were given 'route numbers'. These included the distilled water and canteen delivery runs and the lost property collection service. Amongst the 'ad-hoc' work were jobs such as plant and equipment delivery, transformer/rectifier movements, bridge section transportation, and the supply and installation of bus washing machines. To some extent, this part of the fleet could be described as a rather specialised and up-market general haulage firm. This group of vehicles, whilst nominally allocated to one depot or one type of haulage work, could easily be transferred to alternative tasks. Although many vehicles carried 'allocation plates' in the 1940s and 1950s indicating their home base, they might not always be working for that particular depot.

Any application or 'bid' for the movement of goods on an 'ad-hoc' basis was submitted on a 'TRDN' form (Transport Requisition & Despatch Note). The person concerned had to specify if the job could be done on an 'as and when' basis, or if it had to be carried out on a specific day. The ad-hoc jobs all helped to make up loads on the scheduled services, and it was in the interests of drivers to help with these, since a bonus scheme was based on weight carried and distance travelled. Interesting jobs included the movement of museum artefacts and vehicles from the Museum of British Transport at Clapham to Syon Park and, more recently, to the LT Museum at Covent Garden. There were also various moves to and from the Museum's reserve collection stores (principally Ash Grove Garage and the Acton Town site). One job even involved the delivery of an AEC RT engine to the crypt at St Paul's Cathedral for an exhibition. Another oft-quoted job was the removal of some Plane trees from the Embankment opposite Scotland Yard. The roots of the trees were penetrating the brickwork of the Underground tunnel. As the trees were under a preservation order they had to be re-planted elsewhere, and CDS carried out the work in conjunction with Beck & Pollitzer.

Other examples of ad-hoc work involved the movement of office furniture and fittings. The arches under Putney Bridge Station acted as a furniture store, and it was the job of CDS to move these items throughout the LT

operating area. CDS staff even undertook full office moves when departments changed location. There was also the work of clearing the leaves and dead animals from the screens that filtered the cooling water from the Thames at Lots Road Generating Station.

To give an idea of the scope of the CDS operation in the 1950s, there could be 1,000-1,500 ad-hoc requests per week, and the distance covered by the whole fleet at its maximum was around 5 million miles a year. CDS was a 24-hours a day operation, seven days a week, and all this in the biggest and busiest conurbation in the country. There was even a certain amount of 'out of town' mileage, when spares had to be collected from provincial vehicle manufacturers like Guy Motors in Wolverhampton or Daimler at Coventry. Some other very regular work in the 1980s was the delivery and return of rail motor alternators for modification at Mawdesley's in Warwickshire. When small consignments of goods required returning to manufacturers, CDS made use of the National Carriers parcels delivery service.

To put the service fleet size in context, in 1954 LT owned nearly 11,000 passenger road vehicles, in addition to almost 4,000 Underground cars. The CDS total fleet in the same period numbered about 500. In one year, the amount of goods moved totalled 400,000 tons. When one considers that the majority of the fleet carried loads of less than one ton, the fleet was certainly worked hard. Throughout the period under review, the railway network was to provide well over 50 per cent of the work for the department. CDS always charged for the work they carried out, and the charges made reflected the contribution required by the Board. Initially the aim was to just cover the costs of the operation, but later there was a need to meet profit targets. Latterly under the aegis of London Regional Transport and now TfL, CDS has been a separate 'cost centre' altogether, having to pay rent for its offices and depots.

As with any haulage fleet that has to earn its living, the aim of the CDS Department was to ensure that all vehicles were loaded at all times and kept rolling. Many of the vans delivering advertisement posters, publicity and stationery to garages and depots would return with lost property for the Baker Street store. Those ferrying

Top: Vehicles allocated to the Works & Building Department helped maintain road and rail premises and infrastructure throughout the huge LT 'Special Operating Area'. Although the Bedford 'O'-series tended to be the preferred breed for CDS in the late-1940s and mid-1950s, a batch of broadly similar-looking Austin 'K4' 5-ton lorries saw service with the Building Department. Dropside lorry 902AS was built in 1948, and here carries a mixed load, which includes wooden planking, scaffold poles, bricks, plus archetypal LT vitreous enamel signs. The driver wears a uniform derived from Central Bus practice. LT Museum

Centre: This highly evocative official LT view shows the 'morning run out' at Parsons Green Depot in its late-40s/early-50s heyday. From left-to-right can be seen 839B (KGK 999), a 1949 Bedford 'KZ' box van; 369A (FJJ 589), an Albion 'KN127' open lorry from 1938; to 369A's nearside sits 820B, a 1948 Bedford 'OLBD' open lorry. In the centre, 1949 Austin 'K4' dropside bolster lorry 908AS stands ready to depart with concrete castings which have been made on site, whilst ahead lies an unidentified Bedford 'OLBD' dropside equipped with half-tilt. LT Museum

Right: The scene from further inside the Parsons Green Depot yard. Though open drop-sided Austin or Bedford lorries predominate, also visible is a step-frame trailer carrying a cement mixer. Prominent too are pitched-roofed wooden 'Country Area' shelters, plus a concrete bus stop post, all of which were made at Parsons Green. The Bedford 'O'-series full-tilt passing the entrance gates is not a CDS vehicle, but shows how ubiquitous the marque was in the mid-1950s. LT Museum

Concrete casting was a major activity at Parsons Green. Here, the finished product has been loaded onto the trailer hauled by AEC Matador 603P. The latter had been supplied to Clifford's of Fulham in 1938 and was acquired second-hand by LT in 1941 to assist with the repair of bomb damage. The trailer's twin axles and wheels could be removed, or 'knocked-out', if need be, to facilitate end-on loading. The trailer also had the benefit of a winch. The location is the north end of the Parsons Green yard farthest from the road.
LT Museum

engines would be fully loaded each way, as would the battery-carrying lorry. However, stores lorries delivering parts and components to garages could not guarantee return loads, and this is where the 'ad-hoc' arrangements proved a major revenue earner. In earlier years there were few 'motor factors', so spare parts for the buses had to be purchased direct from the manufacturers and held in a central store awaiting use. It was not until the late 1950s that this situation altered, when more factors entered the market, and not until the end of the 1970s that the supply of 'impressed stock' was readily available. This term meant that though kept in the user's stores, the manufacturer retained ownership of parts until they were required. The major advantage was that they were immediately available to the user, and without having to send out for them. The supply of uniform clothing to staff was a major undertaking in itself, and was carried out on a programmed garage-by-garage basis using specially adapted vehicles serviced from the clothing store in Chiswick Works.

CDS management could also offer 'day work hire' for specific jobs or regular work. For example, although the main depot of the Works & Building Department was at Parsons Green, a number of 'District Sub-Offices' existed across the system. In 1982, these were situated as follows:

Area	Location
No. 1	Gray's Inn Road
No. 2	Neasden Lane
No. 3	Junction Road N19 (including locksmiths)
No. 4	Bow Road
No. 5	Oval
No. 6	Chiswick Park
No. 7	Chiswick Works
No. 8	Gray's Inn Road (nights)
No. 9	Hammersmith (plumbers)

There were also 'Area Inspection Offices' at Hammersmith, Northwood and South Woodford, together with 'Major Works Offices' at Clapham Common, Edgware Road, Hammersmith and Willesden Green. Building materials destined for these locations might be brought from Parsons Green as a part-load, or a vehicle hired from CDS just for the one job. Often these sub-depots would have a Works & Building vehicle based on site, these being known as 'section-vans' or 'section-lorries'. If there was a large quantity of material to be moved, tipper trucks from the CDS Group 3 fleet could also be hired-in for the job.

The in-house building department had been started by the LGOC, and its transfer to the railway side of the organisation under the Chief Engineer caused some resentment in bus quarters during the early days of the LPTB. Among its varied duties was the repair and re-decoration of premises, covering everything from roofs to door locks, the construction of new buildings (e.g. signal relay rooms), sign-writing, and even major rail bridge reconstruction for the Civil Engineer (more usually carried out by contractors). Other work included bus garage modernisation, one aspect of this being the replacement of underground fuel tanks by surface installations surrounded by 'bund walls' to contain spills. In 1960, sixty men were involved in the modernisation of the Metropolitan Line, whilst another hundred and fifty were engaged in alterations to Chiswick Works. This was after the move of vehicle bodywork overhaul to Aldenham, allowing the old west London site to concentrate on electrical and mechanical component repair.

A once-yearly operation was the erection of large signs and queuing pens for racegoers attending the Derby. The pens were manufactured from tubular steel and bolted together at Epsom Town Station and on Epsom Downs in such a way as to funnel passengers onto the special route 406F buses. The involvement of Works & Building in such diverse projects as signal replacement, bridge construction, garage upgrading and special bus services shows just how totally-integrated the operations of LT then were. The department also provided an out-of-hours service, and from 1974, the 'emergency men' were available via a new 24-hour Works & Building Report Centre situated at Parsons Green.

It is important to reiterate that the Underground system as a whole was CDS's largest customer. Much of the work was routine repair and replacements of equipment. Unlike the road services, LT in all its guises was totally responsible for the railway infrastructure. There were no local councils who would repair the right-of-way or replace light fittings as there was for the buses, so it was the responsibility of LT to undertake many more diverse functions than would be expected with a road-bound fleet. The Underground operation at Lillie Bridge covered virtually every aspect of the infrastructure maintenance, with the exception of building large structures. For instance, senior signal engineers had small vans, both for emergency repairs and for the routine work of changing relays and signalling equipment; and larger vans for the delivery of bigger items undergoing routine

planned replacement. The Clocks Section had two dedicated vans just to maintain all the network's timepieces. These could cope with the usual work, but twice a year the section had to hire extra vehicles and drivers to alter the clocks backwards or forwards. All the electricity sub-stations received supplies and replacement equipment on a regular basis. From the point of view of the passengers, one of the most important functions was to ensure that all the escalators and lifts remained safe and in working order. This work could involve anything from a 5-cwt van to a 12-ton capacity articulated low-loader combination. Within the depot at Lillie Bridge, tippers were permanently engaged for many years in moving equipment from the stores to ballast trains. Coal was another commodity transported by CDS tippers, with regular deliveries made to the LT power stations at Lots Road, Greenwich and Neasden, plus the remaining steam engine fleet at Lillie Bridge.

In the 1950s, the fleet of CDS vehicles operated from at least 32 different locations within the LT area, in addition to being based at most garages and depots. The major locations were Chiswick Works, Parsons Green, Lillie Bridge, Charlton (tramway works) and the sub-depots at Croydon (Food Production Centre), Effra Road (tickets) and Bowles Road (tramway permanent way yard). Some locations were small, e.g. the Works & Building depot at the Oval, whilst others were far more important such as Glenthorne Road, Hammersmith, where the Chief Electrical Engineer's and Works & Building departments shared the same premises.

One of the biggest developments in CDS was the introduction of a staff bonus scheme in 1959. This reduced staff numbers from a high of 234 in 1949, to 166 in 1966. The scheme was only one of the factors that assisted in reducing the driving staff level. Another point worth mentioning is that many of the drivers were older staff who had transferred to CDS after a long stint driving buses. Consequently, there was a constant flow of drivers retiring, and this enabled the number of employees to be reduced without compulsory redundancies. The effect of natural wastage, the close co-operation of the drivers themselves and their trade union officials (from both the TGWU and the NUR) managed to achieve this without any compulsory redundancies. The management was fortunate in having exact records of what had been done in 1956. They were able to convert this knowledge into a 'points' scheme, and compared the number of points accumulated set against the hours worked in following years. They also had a stroke of luck in being able to show the staff some real advantages in the early days of the scheme. This good fortune occurred in an area designated to become a car park at Epping Station. Here a considerable amount of spoil had to be removed, and in earlier times, a fleet of tippers, each with its own driver, would have been necessary. Under the bonus scheme, the tippers were supplied, but with only one or two drivers. These men drove all the time, changing between tippers as they were loaded, and leaving the unattended vehicles to be filled by workers. The extra points accrued in this procedure resulted in every man directly on the CDS payroll earning an extra £1 the following week (and in 1959 this sum was worth a lot more than today).

The underlying principles of the scheme were the idea of Mr Peter Rothschild, with the 'nuts and bolts' of the scheme the work of CDS chief clerk Mr Charles Coleshill and his assistant Mr Absalom. At 31 years of age, Mr Rothschild was the youngest-ever Superintendent of CDS. This was considered a ridiculously young age to be in charge by many of his contemporaries at the time, but he was to prove a success. He received full support from central management in the form of Chief Supplies Officers Eric Ottaway and later Alan Shave. Once, during a dispute with drivers, Mr Ottaway said to Mr Rothschild: *'Don't ever come to me with a problem which you know I can't solve'*. This meaningful phrase demonstrated the

confidence held in the CDS Superintendent by the LT Board.

The bonus scheme 'experts' said the idea was unorthodox and not within their normal policies. However, the scheme proved to be of great advantage to LT, not to mention the drivers themselves. These bonuses were paid to drivers who were directly employed by CDS, but as the organisation also supplied staff to departments such as Works & Building and Lifts & Escalators, these employees received it too. The bonus scheme ran for approximately 10 years, after which it was replaced by a full work-study scheme. The earlier 'Standard Performance Bonus Rate' was absorbed into the basic rate of pay over a period.

Another positive development affecting employees was the introduction of crew-cab-fitted lorries in the 1959–1961 period. This allowed management to do away with the dangerous habit of gang members riding in or on the rear of vehicles when travelling to jobs requiring three or more men. This was of benefit to the management as 'Health & Safety' issues came to the fore, and also to workers, who could now travel to and from their place of work in relative comfort, dryness and safety.

As LT changed, so did CDS. In 1967, the word 'Central' was dropped and soon afterwards, the operation became 'Distribution and Advertising Services' when it took over the responsibility for the posting of adverts. By 1976, it had forgone the advertising business to a new 'London Transport Advertising', reconditioned and was simply renamed as 'Distribution Services'. However, the abbreviation 'CDS' (with the obsolete letter 'C') remained in colloquial use for many years afterwards.

1st January 1970 saw the Country Bus & Coach Department devolved to National Bus Company subsidiary London Country Bus Services under the Transport (London) Act, 1969. LT continued to provide many LCBS support services, including provision of stores from Chiswick and Aldenham, reconditioned parts from Chiswick and destination blinds from Aldenham. Certain service vehicles were transferred to LCBS, whilst others were loaned to the new regime at Reigate. It is doubtful that many senior managers mourned the loss of the green bus services. Of the 1267 PSVs passing to LCBS, 89 per cent were more than 4–5 years old, and most were unsuitable for one-person operation. The Act drastically reduced the LT operating area, and withdrew most of the organisation's operations to within the Greater London Council (GLC) administrative region,

Works & Building were responsible for the cleanliness of most of LT's road and rail premises, both in and out of the public domain (though stations were swept by local staff). This photo shows how 'cleaning van' 1051AS, a standard Austin/Morris 'LD' 1-ton dating from 1957, was fitted-out to safely carry ladders, brushes, buckets and other appropriate equipment.
LT Museum

Although supporting the day-to-day operation of LT's services was CDS's primary concern, there has always been scope for the occasional 'special' duty. One of the more unusual occurred in 1974, when the body of an ex-City & South London Railway car was transferred to Ruislip Depot on behalf of the London Underground Railway Society. Ford 'D600' prime mover 1665F was used together with a step-frame trailer and the combination is seen here entering the depot's driveway upon the completion of the move.
R.J. Greenaway

but gone were the unprofitable rural bus services and cross-London Green Line coach routes, increasingly plagued by traffic congestion.

In 1978, LT set up 'Cleaning Services', initially under the auspices of the Chief Civil Engineer, with the intention of introducing the concept of 'heavy cleaning' to premises using industrial-type washing and polishing machines. To quote from an internal advertisement for staff which appeared in the May of that year: '*The purpose of the new Cleaning Organisation is to bring together the various aspects of cleaning that take place in those static areas where the public are concerned, on both the road and rail side, i.e. railway stations, bus stops and shelters. The staff that will fulfil these functions will be classified as Cleaning Operatives, and a new grade has been created with this title. All staff joining the Cleaning Organisation will be both flexible and interchangeable; flexible with regard to the areas they clean within a station or on the roadside, and. interchangeable with regard to working on both road and rail.*' The department operated from several bases around London and a number of standard vehicles were allocated to it as 'cleaning vans'. Cleaning Services seems to have had some difficulty in finding a home, and in 1987 its report centre moved first from Grosvenor Gardens to 20 Wood Lane, W12; and then to the old Recruitment Centre at Chiswick Works.

The main LT organisation had undergone a number of changes over the years. The LPTB gave way to the London Transport Executive in 1948, the London Transport Board in 1962, and back to a London Transport Executive again under the Greater London Council in 1970, when the Country Bus services were divested. Throughout this time though, the organisation had continued to provide a public face as 'London Transport', and for most passengers and staff, it appeared that little had altered (Country Area apart). This settled state of affairs was later to change radically. Dissatisfied with the Labour GLC's overall control of LT, the Conservative Government effectively 're-nationalised' it on 29th June 1984, just short of the organisation's 51st birthday. Now renamed as 'London Regional Transport', it initially seemed no different from its predecessors. But on 1st April 1985, the direct operation of the bus and train services was placed in the hands of two new LRT subsidiaries: London Buses Limited (LBL) and London Underground Limited (LUL). The two bus maintenance works were transferred to a third new subsidiary – LRT Bus Engineering Limited (BEL). Distribution Services was retained as a central LRT department, an appropriate decision given that it still served all areas of what

was to become an increasingly-fragmented 'London Transport'.

Under Section 6 of the London Regional Transport Act 1984, the new organisation was obliged to seek competitive tenders for suitable in-house activities. In time, the most economic course deemed for many departments was complete closure, and the buying-in of their former services from outside contractors. After the demise of Aldenham and Chiswick Works, the Parsons Green-based Works & Building Department and numerous other former internal operations, the need for such a large service vehicle fleet diminished. Activities like installing bus shelters and stops, cash handling, catering, cleaning and general property maintenance were transferred to private contractors. Distribution Services itself had to justify its own continued existence, though happily the LRT Board accepted their 'business case'. Naturally, this contraction of the LT 'empire' reduced the requirement for certain types of vehicle.

Conversely though, the decision to devolve Underground train overhaul to individual lines meant that road vehicles were now required to play a greater role in this process. Though regular maintenance work was undertaken at ordinary train depots, items like compressors, motors and seats were refurbished in Acton Works, and were transferred to and from depots by Distribution Services.

In some cases, there were short-lived attempts by LRT subsidiaries to operate at 'arms-length' from the main organisation in slimmed-down form and in competition with outside firms. None of these was ultimately to prove a success, and such entities as BEL, Cleaning Services and Work Force (a.k.a. LRT Builders, and originally Works & Building) disappeared from the scene. Though the Building Department dated back to LGOC days, BEL and Cleaning Services had only been established in recent years.

By the late-1980s, Distribution Services was operating from Acton under a standard 'Operator's Licence'. It had to compete for the remaining LRT business existing after privatisation and outsourcing, however it now had the ability to sell excess capacity, as long as it did not conflict with the parent organisation's interests. The economics of the distribution service had been under study a number of times in the last 15 years. Although certain jobs could be carried out more cheaply by outside contractors, overall, the department remained cost-effective. The restrictive licensing system for goods vehicles had altered in 1968. Gone were the old 'A', 'B' and 'C' licences. In their place were 'O' for Operators' licences, where the operator could carry goods for anyone without let or hindrance. Some of

Distribution Services' spare capacity was later sold to British Rail/Railtrack, with a little work also being done for supermarket group Sainsburys, plus the airline British Airways. There was also some contract work on behalf of the new bus companies, and crane-fitted vehicles were supplied to Hammersmith Council to assist in the clear up after the 'Great Storm' of 1987. Work was also undertaken for engineering company Frontsource (which had acquired both the LRT and LCBS bus engineering operations).

On 1st April 1989 Distribution Services was transferred from direct-LRT control to became a wholly-owned subsidiary of London Underground Limited, a move which reflected what was now the core business for the department. In spite of this, vehicles continued to be supplied to the bus units and the inner-area Central Traffic Division. At about the same time, the head office vacated Chiswick and transferred 'over the bridge' to the old canteen building in Acton Works, with an official address of 130 Bollo Lane, W3. This was just one example of the central LRT departments that left the long-used Chiswick site during the run-up to its complete closure in September 1990. Further changes occurred in September 1999, when LUL was split into one Operating Company ('Opsco') and three Infrastructure Companies ('Infracos'). This was part of the Labour Government's public-private-partnership (PPP) plan for securing funding for the Underground. Distribution Services was placed within 'Infraco JNP' (Jubilee, Northern & Piccadilly lines). All three InfraCos were established as separate LUL legal companies on 1st April 2000, with the intention that they be sold to private sector bidders in the future.

'Transport for London' took over responsibility for most LRT activities from 3rd July 2000. The new organisation was designed to oversee not only the existing spheres of 'LT' interest, but also take responsibility for the Docklands Light Railway, Public Carriage Office (taxis), Traffic Control Systems Unit (traffic lights) and the Traffic Director for London. In preparation for the establishment of TfL, London Transport Buses was renamed 'London Bus Operating Services Limited' on 1st April 2000 (trading as London Buses). LRT remained the parent company for LUL (and thus CDS) until the part-privatisation was completed, when control of the Underground was ceded to TfL and the Mayor of London.

Today's work is planned by the Dispatch Department, which allocates the tasks and ensures resources are used as efficiently as possible. Administrative staff check that drivers do not exceed the legal limit of working hours, and have sufficient time to load and unload vehicles safely. New routes are timed to ensure that breaks are taken after set periods of driving. All large vehicles (over

3.5-tonnes gross) are fitted with tachographs. In addition, the heavier vehicles (over 12000kg gross) are equipped with 'speed-limiters', restricting their top speed to 56mph (80kph).

The maintenance of CDS vehicles was originally the responsibility of the Chief Mechanical Engineer (Road Services), but transferred in the 1980s to the Distribution Services Manager. Routine servicing was once often carried out at the nearest local bus garage to save unnecessary mileage, though was charged to CDS. The regular overhauling of vehicles was carried out at various premises over the years. Originally performed at Chiswick Works, some of the work was passed to Nunhead, a former garage that had also built bodies for the 'J', 'W' and 'P' classes of service vehicles. Other sites carrying out maintenance were Riverside and Thornton Heath garages. Some work was handled at the Aldenham bus overhaul works. Maintenance work later moved to the old Chiswick Tram Depot (now London United's Stamford Brook Garage) and then to Stockwell Garage in south London. The former Chiswick Tram Depot had long been used for non-standard activities. It was used to overhaul the small GS and RLH classes, which did not change bodies in the process, and therefore did not need to visit Aldenham. Later it provided a home for the LT-operated BEA, and later British Airways, London – Heathrow coach fleet. Small vans up to (and including) Transit-size were serviced by outside contractors from the mid-1960s onwards.

One hire involved this white-painted Fiat '170' tractor unit registered CAB 402S, here paired with York step-frame trailer YT 28 in the yard of Victoria Garage. The connection with Fiat would be revived in 1993 when CDS began to obtain lorries from the merged Fiat/Ford 'Iveco' operation.
Jim Wright

A Foden tractor unit and trailer was supplied on hire by the well-known firm Godfrey Davis in the 1980s and used for carrying chaired sleepers. The unit is in white and blue, of interest because in 1990 the same two colours formed the basis of a new livery for most of the service vehicle fleet.
Michael Clark collection

Although the vehicle purchasing policy of the LPTB, its constituent companies, and indeed LT after 1948 is covered in detail within the following chapters, it is appropriate that the subject is summarised at this stage. It was the LGOC and LCCT who had the most standardised purchasing policies, with the LGOC naturally choosing vehicles built by another member of the Underground Group, in this case AEC. The LCCT on the other hand had a much more open mind, purchasing quality heavy vehicles from Albion and Karrier, whilst also converting petrol-electric buses into service vehicles.

After the establishment of the LPTB, the link with AEC was lost, but this company continued to supply medium-duty vehicles in the 3- to 7-ton capacity range. Equal opportunity was given to Albion and Leyland to supply 4-ton trucks under a tendering process for the Tram & Trolleybus Department. The LGOC had used a number of rebuilt time-expired buses as the basis for a small fleet of commercial vehicles, and the LPTB continued this policy for use with the bus and Underground fleets. Under the Lord Ashfield/Frank Pick era at 55 Broadway, the London Transport of the 1930s was a tightly-run, highly cost-conscious organisation. This practice of keeping expenses down had led to the continued use of second-hand bus chassis, with the occasional purchase of equivalent high-quality heavy-duty vehicles occurring only as funds and new vehicle availability allowed. In any case, the relatively low mileages operated by some of the converted bus chassis would not have justified the expense of buying brand new vehicles.

The Morris and Morris Commercial Companies had been regular suppliers of small and medium size vehicles to the LGOC. Once the LPTB was able to take measure of its overall requirements, a large fleet of both types was purchased. The publicity, signs, stationery and maintenance departments' requirements (amongst many others) were met with a fleet of Morris Motors 10-cwt vans, whilst 1-ton and 30-cwt Morris Commercial models were used to strengthen the garage 'runabout' and spares delivery fleet. The smaller vehicles were made by Morris Motors

Limited at Cowley, while the larger ones came from Morris Commercial Cars Limited of Adderley Park, near Birmingham. Though Morris Commercial was a wholly-owned subsidiary of its parent Morris Motors, the two existed and were run as separate concerns.

During the war, the LPTB was faced with the need to acquire a large number of second-hand tippers to help in the construction of deep-level tube shelters. A wide range of unusual makes entered the fleet in 1941, mostly Bedford, Dodge and Ford, plus a few examples from Austin, Commer and Morris. Tippers were also bought new from Ford in 1942 to assist with bomb damage clearance. The latter were grouped in a sub-class under the Works & Building Engineer and referred to as 'Railway War Damage Plant Vehicles'. After the war, the Ford and Bedford marques took precedence over other manufacturers, with delivery of fleets of Ford 10-cwt vans to replace the Morris light vans, whilst Bedford was chosen as the standard medium-weight truck. Although the choice of Ford for the vans may seem a little perverse, since the design dated back to pre-war days, there was little else on the market, and the side-valve engine was relatively indestructible. In the case of Bedford, the alternative from Ford was the '7V' truck with its cramped cab and fuel-thirsty V8 engine. The Bedford, with its powerful and war-proven 6-cylinder petrol engine, fitted the bill exactly for an up-to-date 5-tonner.

Whilst LT had continued rebuilding old buses into service vehicles, by 1956 CDS management was seriously questioning this practice. The converted bus chassis had a high tare weight compared with their carrying capacity, which restricted their legal payload. The vehicle taxation system at the time based charges on the unladen weight of the vehicle. Unlike today, when the gross plated weight is the basis for tax, the older system penalised heavier, longer-lasting vehicles. This system added unnecessary expense to the CDS operation. Additionally, the older AECs were costing, in the words of the contemporary management, 'a fortune to maintain and overhaul'. Part of the problem was caused by the design of the lorries con-

Although LT had standardised on Bedford chassis for much of the early postwar period, a small number of Austin K4 chassis had been purchased in the late forties and a reasonable number of Austin LD vans were purchased after 1955. To complement the LDs a total of five Series III Austin 5 tonners were purchased, four as tippers, including 1068AS, and one as a van. The Series III model was a descendant of the earlier K4 model, but was able to boast a three seater cab and a much modernised bonnet arrangement. At the time LT possibly considered the Series III model a more satisfactory design than the equivalent Bedford normal control model. LT Museum

verted from buses, where the minimal rear overhang, combined with a relatively long wheelbase, produced high loadings on the front axle. Not only did this cause very heavy steering for the drivers, but also disproportionate wear and tear on steering components, adding additional repair and servicing costs.

With the rapidly-ageing fleet, the whole of the old Chiswick Tram Depot had become devoted to overhauling service vehicles. Because of the age of some of the vehicles and lack of parts, overhauls could take up to six weeks each, leading to an increased number of spare vehicles needed to cover those under repair. This in turn meant that all of the depot overheads were charged to CDS, instead of a proportion being charged to the bus fleet, again increasing CDS's costs. It was the idea of Superintendent Peter Rothschild to update the fleet with new vehicles. With help from Ted Bonny and his boss, the Chief Mechanical Engineer (Road Services) Kenneth Shave (brother of Chief Supplies Officer Alan Shave and both sons of George Shave, LGOC Chief Engineer in the 1920s), a recommendation was made for the 'non-replacement' of the old bus chassis and instead to purchase new vehicles. The Ford Company now had a long association with LT, and their new Thames Trader haulage model was introduced at an opportune time for the organisation. For the first time in many years, Ford could offer an up-to-date vehicle able to gross over 11-tons on the heaviest rigid model. Whilst there were broadly-equivalent models on offer from other manufacturers, the Trader was considered the most suitable 'off the shelf' vehicle. There was the added bonus that the vehicles were built at Dagenham, thereby employing Londoners who may well have made use of London Transport's services!

The major advantages of new vehicles over the former practice of converting buses were the need for less maintenance, spares readily available from main dealers, and there was even a guarantee period. In part, this reduction in maintenance requirements was to lead to the closure of Chiswick Tram Depot as a CDS maintenance site. The new Ford fleet proved successful from all points of view, and the ability of outside coachbuilders to fit 'crew-cabs' to lorries proved to be of great benefit to employees. Service vehicle general maintenance was later carried out using excess capacity at the large Stockwell bus garage, though the fleet was concentrated on Chiswick Works by the late-1980s. Formal 'overhauls' had ceased by the late-1970s and servicing was progressively transferred to main dealers. The introduction of the grey livery for CDS vehicles came about because Ford would not supply vehicles in primer, and it seemed wasteful to repaint vehicles into Chiswick Green livery over a high-quality factory stove-enamelled finish. New vehicles would therefore be delivered in Ford *Cargo Grey*, a standard colour in the manufacturer's range.

LT was to remain faithful to Ford for light and medium vans right through to the new century. For heavier vehicles they continued with the Ford range, although by the late-1970s a much broader purchasing policy came to the fore with Bedford, Commer, Dodge and Leyland vehicles all seeing use. In line with many transport operators, continental vehicles were to be found in the fleet with the purchase of Mercedes '308'/'408' vans and some full-size trucks from the 1980s. There was also a move to purchase Leyland/Freight Rover Sherpa vans, followed by Volkswagens. Details of many of these vehicles will be found within the text.

The basic design of body set by Thornycroft Cygnets 334T and 335T was adopted for the T-class AEC Regals converted to lorries in 1939-40. This is 396W (ex-T 279), carrying a low floor body, with a central hinged dropside section for ease of loading by hand from the roadside. The disadvantage of this type of body was severe wheel arch intrusion into the load space. The majority of bus to lorry conversions were fitted with a higher floor space to ensure a flat loading platform from front to rear. The cream cab roof and full size fleetnames would disappear in later years. *LT Museum*

In the earliest days of the Underground train, maintenance was carried out by individual companies at depots spread across London. As most of the network had come under the Underground Group umbrella by 1913, certain activities were concentrated at individual sites (e.g. District Railway traction motors were repaired at Golders Green). In 1920, a decision was reached to centralise the major overhaul of the stock in a new factory at Acton. Regular servicing was still carried out at local depots, but rolling stock would visit Acton for major overhaul and repair. Within Acton, cars were lifted off their bogies and all the component parts overhauled in different parts of complex. This style of depot servicing and main works overhaul continued until the mid-1980s.

Having to maintain its own infrastructure and rights-of-way, the Underground has always been a major user of service vehicles. This 1947 Morris Commercial 'PV' was utilitarian in the extreme, despite being a post-war design, even down to its 'artillery-style' wheels and flat panelling with minimal curvature. The only obvious advance was the ease-of-entry facilitated by a low step behind the front axle and the sliding cab doors. 'Parcel Van' 686M was allocated to the Chief Engineer, Lillie Bridge Depot. LT Museum

The railway depots were fed with reconditioned and repaired spares from Acton Works. Most went by road, as many lines had been built separately with limited transfer points for goods trains. For example, what was to become the Northern Line remained isolated from the rest until linked to the Piccadilly via the King's Cross loop in 1926. The Bakerloo Line was also difficult to access, prior to being linked with the Metropolitan at Finchley Road in 1939. In other cases, delivery of components by rail would be too slow, and with track maintenance taking place at night it would often be the case that no routes would be available for trains. The main depots on each line (i.e. Golders Green, Lillie Bridge, London Road, Morden and Wood Lane – also Neasden and Northfields in later years) would receive spares and components on a twice-weekly lorry delivery service. Items carried included pairs of wheels that had been turned on the lathes at Acton, compressors and traction motors. There were also many additional journeys made to the more important depots on an ad-hoc basis carrying urgent spares. The vehicle drivers were permanently allocated to this work, and became conveyors of messages and even instructions between various sections of Acton Works and local depot staff. They became an integral part of the maintenance team even though they received their pay from CDS. The District Railway made less use of road transport as it could utilise its own fleet of self-propelled electric engineers' wagons, and it was easy to operate journeys from Ealing Common Depot to Acton Works and East Ham (later Upminster) Depot.

With the introduction of wartime restrictions on fuel, some road journeys from Acton Works had their functions transferred to rail. The Northfields trip used a flat wagon marshalled between two converted driving motor cars, whilst the Ealing Common journeys made use of what were virtually electric powered open wagons. Each was the equivalent of a large lorry, but with driving cabs at both ends. Originally built as battery locomotives in 1909 by Renshaw & Co for engineering work on the District Railway, what became L 8 and L 9 were converted to mains current operation in 1924 (i.e. solely powered by conductor rail). Engineers' trains were also used to deliver supplies to Queen's Park and Croxley Green depots on the Bakerloo Line, neither of which were designed for road vehicle access. Prior to the opening of the Central Line extensions in both east and west London in 1947-48, two new depots came into operation at Ruislip and Hainault. This increased the road vehicle mileage considerably, and the operations in general became less parochial in character as more vehicles and drivers became involved. Following a reorganisation of Distribution Services in 1969, it was found more economical to revert to road transport for the Acton to Ealing Common deliveries, and locos L 8 and L 9 were scrapped at Ealing in September 1969.

After the control of LT passed from the GLC to the DoT (administered via LRT) in 1984, there was a greater overall emphasis on costs rather than levels of service to the public at any cost. Amongst the changes proposed were plans for streamlining the rolling stock overhaul procedure. Coincidentally, the need was identified to carry out major refurbishment at Acton Works, the majority of buildings by then being over 60 years old. The revised overhaul procedure recognised that most of the local depots had been built to cater for much heavier maintenance than was required with modern stock. Acton Works itself had been designed to undertake the heavy overhaul of 30 cars a week, but by the mid-1980s, improvements in equipment meant that only nine cars per week were being handled. The new process resulted in cars being overhauled at the running depots using components such as motors, compressors, electronic equipment and wheel-sets repaired in new premises built on the site of the old seat-trimming shop within Acton works.

The change in arrangements did not cause any significant increase to the requirements made on Distribution Services. Most lines already had a 7-ton lorry allocated for their use in transporting defective equipment to Acton. These lorries had not been overworked in recent years, usually undertaking just one round trip per day between Acton Works and the major depot on a line (for example Northfields), so visits could be slotted in to the subsidiary depot (in this case Cockfosters) as required. Although articulated vehicles enabled a reduction of vehicles in this group of lorries, the depots' priorities of maximising the number of trains in service meant that a reduction in the number of vehicles of other types could not be achieved. Equipment would often be despatched from Acton in the late-morning to be fitted to a car, enabling one more train to operate in that afternoon's peak service. This higher level of service and requirement for the urgent delivery of spares became more critical as the Underground enjoyed success in increasing the numbers of passengers carried.

There was always a continuing discussion between the Supplies Department and depots as to the level of stores kept locally, since the depot management always wanted maximum spares in stock, whilst purchasing always desired the exact opposite! There was a limit to the extent to which articulation could be used to its fullest extent. The ideal situation was to have three trailers dedicated to each depot trip (one being loaded, one in transit, and one being unloaded). Unfortunately, space for leaving trailers at the older depots was at a premium, and CDS could not use the trailers as hoped. This shortage of space and lack of room for manoeuvring, means that CDS still have to operate short single-axle articulated trailers to LUL sites.

The revised procedure also included the need for a dedicated articulated lorry to move mini-containers between Acton and the depots undertaking overhauls. Each train under overhaul requiring separate containers for seats and electrical/mechanical components. All other equipment continued to be moved on the original lorries, with some vehicles being dedicated to moving wheel-sets. Although there were wheel lathes at Ealing Common, Golders Green and Neasden, two thirds of the lines had no lathes and needed to transfer wheels for turning. The movement of wheel-sets was carried out on scheduled services using dedicated vehicles. These trucks (later trailers) had cradles, wheel chocks and chains to ensure loads could not move whilst in transit. The sets needed to be returned to the main works for either skimming or re-tyring after developing a 'flat', this was normally caused by it snatching whilst braking, and having the tyre surface worn away in one spot. When a lot of wheel-sets needed turning or replacement at the same time, arranging the routing of these lorries became a logistical nightmare. Fortunately, there was spare capacity between lathes, although their reliability became another factor to contend with!

Just as necessary are the other aspects of the Underground that have involved CDS: The lifts and escalators at stations needed constant maintenance and repairs, the ticket machines required refilling and servicing. Every station had to be cleaned and repainted regularly, and supplies made available for staff. Every light tube and bulb would need replacing at regular intervals, with signal lamps in particular requiring scheduled changing. Though maintenance of lifts and escalators was under the control of the Chief Mechanical Engineer's Lifts and Escalators Division, it became the responsibility of CDS to transport their requirements. The most common items repaired and replaced were escalator chains, gears, motors and steps. The machine shop at Acton manufactured these chains, and delivery and replacement would be carried out at night. The escalator chains manufactured at Acton were long-lasting and of high precision, and nothing since has ever matched their quality. All the heavy trucks involved with the repair of escalators (also Austin van 979AS) were fitted with winches to enable the crews to move escalator components safely into station premises. The modern vehicles allocated for this work had hydraulic cranes fitted to lift heavy components safely. Also needing regular attention were Interlocking Machine Room (IMR) equipment, control room equipment, ticketing and accounting machines, clocks, train describers and platform public address equipment, all requiring the services of CDS vehicles.

Most of the background work for the rail network was carried out at Lillie Bridge, which was a very compact site. Located here were permanent way workshops with an open storage area. The signal overhaul workshop repaired relays, train-stops and manufactured racks for the IMR's. The works also repaired ticket machines and assembled signal equipment.

A box-van van from Group 3 was permanently allocated to Lillie Bridge for delivering and collecting

relays between signalling depots, and also available for signalling emergencies. The body featured padded racking for the relays, which were very delicate. The Signal Department also made great use of the tail-lift vehicles once these had become established within the fleet. They would often hire three vehicles a day, but their utilisation was poor, due to the time they had to spend at Lillie Bridge waiting to be loaded. Eventually the CDS management (Michael Clark and David Corke) arranged for the Signal Department to request specific stores the day before so that loads were ready when the CDS vehicles arrived.

To give two other examples of CDS's work on the Underground, when the Victoria Line was being built the major stores were based at Walthamstow and Northumberland Park, and CDS delivered virtually all materials apart from the tunnel segments. For surface lines, the concrete cable-run posts were manufactured in bulk at Lillie Bridge and transported by CDS to various sites for storage. This caused some difficulties later on when the Willesden Green storage yard was sold for redevelopment, but no one advised the operators that the site was absolutely full of heavy concrete posts. CDS were given just 24 hours to clear the site, which held wedges and anchor parts, in addition to the 6ft posts!

Top: The Lifts & Escalators Department maintained a base at LT's Griffith House offices and operated this 1957-built Austin 5-ton '503' van. The vehicle was winch-fitted and could tow a mobile generator normally kept at Chalk Farm. Note the hinged flaps on the body above the cab, allowing the transit of long items, and the 'LIFTS & ESCALATORS' allocation plate. LT Museum

Above: The 1990s saw LUL make widespread use of crew-cabbed drop-side Ford Transit lorries. One of the reasons for this was the need to carry staff and equipment to worksites following the withdrawal of the converted ex-Tube Stock 'Personnel Carrier' cars. In June 2001, the Metropolitan & Circle Lines' 4961F was in use by their track section and engaged in delivering sleepers to Neasden Depot. Behind it can be seen redundant units of 1983 Tube Stock. Kim Rennie

The large number of Morris Commercial 30-cwt trucks were either inherited from the Underground Group or bought new by the infant LPTB and used by such diverse departments as advertising, catering, publicity, tramways and railway permanent way, and Works & Building. No.310M was a 1937 acquisition (as M 116) and operated as Leyton Garage's engineers' runabout and stores vehicle, though appears to be visiting Upton Park on this occasion.
D.W.K. Jones

The garage 'runabout' took various guises during the years of direct LT bus operation. Between the late-1940s and early-1960s, they were provided by the 30-cwt Bedford 'KD'-type bodied in half-tilt form. This is 872B, seen here at Chelverton Road garage in the company of RTW 397.
Kim Rennie collection

Within the grounds of Chiswick Works were a number of important separate departments essential to the smooth running of LT. Though this book is mainly concerned with the service vehicle fleet, it is only correct to outline some of the more important functions of what was the original bus overhaul works.

The LGOC established their main works at Chiswick in 1921 to build and overhaul bus bodies, as well as repairing mechanical components. Overhaul work involved the separation of bus body from chassis, and both were repaired to a high standard. After the Second World War, with passenger numbers increasing, it was assumed that Chiswick would not be able to cope with overhauling a larger fleet. The intended Northern Line railway depot in Hertfordshire was thus converted to the Aldenham 'production line' bus body overhaul works to deal with the highly-standardised new fleet of RT and RF classes.

Because the overhaul period of the bus body did not always coincide with the need for the engine or other major mechanical component replacement, the repair and overhaul of engines, gearboxes, steering gear or axles remained at Chiswick. Mechanical component replacement was normally carried out at garage level, and again the service vehicle fleet would be called upon to move the components between the garages and Chiswick Works. Aldenham also produced spare body parts for the whole fleet for fitting at garages and these too required transportation.

The large 'Plant Workshops' at Chiswick repaired fuel-dispensing pumps, hydraulic pumps, cranes and lifting tackle, as well as bus-washing machines. The Training School for drivers and conductors was also established at Chiswick, along with its famous skidpan. The Bell Punch Company at Uxbridge supplied bus and coach tickets and punches, and a fleet of vans operated from Chiswick to facilitate their collection from the manufacturer and subsequent distribution to garages.

The laboratory at Chiswick undertook all Research & Development work for the road and rail network, and other parts of the 32-acre site were responsible for all uniform and stationery issue. All the scheduled delivery services operated from Chiswick, including bus units, batteries, general stores, plant material for garage maintenance and the regular component ferry service to and from Aldenham. Chiswick held the 'Bill Store' or Advertising Store during the period 1967–1976, a time when CDS had responsibility for posting material on behalf of both LT and private advertisers. This included delivering carriage cards to the depots for the tube cars, fitting adverts onto escalators, passageways, platforms and bus stations; and lastly the delivery of material to garages.

Unlike either the Railway or Tram & Trolleybus departments, Central Buses did not have the burden of having to maintain the thoroughfares its fleet traversed. However, items like bus stops and shelters still had to be provided and serviced, this being carried out by the 'common user' Works & Building Department. On 2nd November 1960, Thames Trader 1138F visited Uxbridge Road, Hillingdon to install a new combined bus & coach request stop. The period 1959–61 saw the changeover from green to grey liveries, but this Trader was one of a number delivered in the old colour. *John Gillham*

This advert-placing work was previously undertaken by the Publicity Department, but passed to CDS and then later transferred to private contractors.

Alongside the overhaul work, a major delivery task was the distribution of all tyres used by the bus, coach and lorry fleet. Tyres were supplied by the manufacturers on a 'mileage charge' basis and distributed from Chiswick on a scheduled delivery system, with the serial numbers of all tyres recorded as they were removed from and fitted to buses. The AEC 'YC'-Tylor, 'J', 'P' and 'W' class stores lorries undertook this regular work, which was later done by Thames Trader and 'D' series articulated vehicles. This work had for a short time been temporarily and partly handled at the former Colindale trolleybus depot, but later returned to Chiswick.

Below: The Effra Road Ticket Machine Works was once responsible for the repair and servicing of most fare collection equipment used on London's buses. Among the many vehicles allocated to Effra Road over the years was this Ford Escort van numbered 3232F. What is interesting about this view is that it was taken at Dorking Garage in 1988 and shows that London Country (South West) was still reliant on LT for certain core functions some 18 years' after the 'split'. *David Rowe*

Below right: The concept of the 'radio car' was introduced in 1967. By the mid-1980s, London Buses was specifying a van-based format for its mobile inspectors, as opposed to the earlier estate car configuration. Retained throughout though were the roof-mounted roundels, which were transferred between successive batches of vehicles. No.3268B was a Bedford Astravan, a model derived from the Vauxhall Astra car and designed as a successor to the 'HA' van. The cab door legend 'General Manager Buses' is interesting, as no such position existed when the photo was taken in 1986. *Colin Lloyd*

BREAKDOWN AND TOWING

Vehicles designed to attend emergencies and breakdowns can be divided into three groups: Firstly, box-bodied vans and lorries used to convey equipment and spares (naturally, this varied between road and rail). Next come the large and specialised recovery tenders, fitted with cranes, and able to haul broken-down or seriously damaged road vehicles on suspended-tow. All such vehicles had red-based liveries, and the use of this colour had originally been chosen so that such vehicles 'can easily be recognised by road users and the police' and might 'accelerate their passage through congested streets when engaged on urgent work'. Originally, the railway did not use Bus Red on vehicles, but a slightly different shade called Signal Red.

The third and most common category was that of the towing lorries, which used a steel tow-bar or chain to assist defective buses and coaches (and indeed fellow service vehicles) back to garages for repair. This was the standard practice of LT throughout most of its years of direct-involvement with bus services. It was the problem introduced by more modern buses with set-back front axles (and expensive front body panels) that prematurely ended the lives of the last batch of towing lorries. This led to both recovery and towing duties being carried out by Leyland Freighters (q.v.).

Trams & Trolleybuses existed as a separate operating department between 1933 and 1950, after which merger with Central Buses took place. During this time, and until the end of trolleybus operation in May 1962, a totally different range of recovery and maintenance vehicles was in use supporting electric traction, most of which are detailed separately later.

RAILWAY BREAKDOWN VEHICLES

Following the creation of the LPTB, the new Board began a programme of integrating the previously separate breakdown arrangements maintained by the Metropolitan Railway and the Underground Group. The Chief Mechanical Engineer of the Underground, Mr W. A. Agnew, was now in charge of all LPTB rolling stock requirements. On 12th March 1934, the Superintendent of Rolling Stock, Mr E. T. Brook, assumed responsibility for the clearance of breakdowns on all sections of London Transport's railways. The breakdown section of his department was under the control of Mr S. J. Hubbard, the Assistant Depot Engineer at Ealing Common; with Mr L. R. Cotton, Sectional Assistant, Morden-Edgware Line, assisting him. Two rolling stock breakdown teams were then in existence, titled as the 'Metropolitan' and 'Underground' gangs, and composed of men from the workshops. The former was under the control of Foreman T. Hyde at Neasden, the latter by Assistant Foreman Preston at Golders Green. If a breakdown occurred, the Traffic Controller would advise Mr Hubbard, or in his

Above: An early LPTB railway breakdown truck was this 1926 example built by the Star Engineering Company of Wolverhampton. The vehicle had originated with the Underground Group and remained in service until 1938. Its red & cream livery was to be a distinguishing feature of LT railway breakdown tenders for some thirty years.
Arthur Ingram collection

Facing page: The first specially designed railway breakdown tender was 110J, an AEC Regent dating from 1931. It was joined by 111J seen here when new in 1935. This vehicle carried LT fleetnames from new, but the 'Urgent' sign had yet to be fitted when this view was taken outside Neasden Depot's North Lodge entrance. The buildings in the background are part of the 'Neasden Estate' built to house workers of the Metropolitan Railway. LT Museum

Left: Two of the 1937-intake of Albion 'KN127' trucks were assigned to railway breakdown duties. Vehicle AN 27 was used by the Wood Lane Depot rolling stock gang, later moving to Ealing Common along with AEC Regent 110J. The vehicle is seen here some years after delivery and carries its 1939 number of 130A and has lost its cream roof. Albion Motors advertised their trucks 'as sure as the sunrise'; a claim alluded to by the motif on the radiator header tank.
LT Museum

Two further AEC Regents numbered 417J and 418J entered stock in September 1939 and continued with the style of body pioneered by 110J and 111J. No.417J was initially allocated to Golders Green Depot but was operating out of Hainault by the time this post-war view was taken at Whitechapel. The prominent 'Urgent' sign is clearly visible, but one wonders just how effective it was in practice?
Arthur Ingram

absence, his deputy Mr Hyde. If one of the gangs was required, the Traffic Controller of the line concerned would contact the Wood Lane Depot Gatekeeper, who would himself call either the Metropolitan or Underground gang 'in accordance with the instructions posted in his office'.

The majority of call-outs were the result of problems caused by shunting incidents involving trains at depots, especially derailments. The less regular calls would be to trains that had 'stalled'. This happened if an electric traction motor failed, a brake connection pipe were to rupture and leak, or through minor electrical control equipment defects. Another regular fault was the loss or breakage of collector shoes. The breakdown gang would need to locate and identify the fault before the train could move, and the knowledge of the gang members gained from working in the lifting shops and in overhauling the equipment was invaluable.

Although a number of AEC Regents were subsequently converted by LT for use as road or rail breakdown vehicles, what were later to be known as 110J and 111J were bought new for the task in January 1931 and September 1935. The former was based on the ST chassis, the latter on the longer STL chassis. Their official description was as 5-ton 'Railway Master Breakdown Tenders'. Livery was red with cream above waist level and black wings (all inherited from the Underground Group), and distinctive 'URGENT' warning signs were soon fitted.

Each vehicle carried a standard set of equipment that was the responsibility of the Assistant Breakdown Engineer. Since the earliest heavy tenders were limited to 12-tons gross weight, it was necessary to monitor carefully the tools and equipment carried. Both vehicles were later equipped with short-wave transportable transmitters and receivers to advise management of progress or problems. Vehicles 110J and 111J proved good value for money, lasting until September 1964. There was also the breakdown train and crane based at Neasden, but this required a locomotive to be kept 'in steam' for 24-hours a day. The rail breakdown crane was also steam-powered, and the locomotive could, if need be, help in raising steam for the crane.

Special arrangements were made for the Coronation of Their Majesties King George VI and Queen Elizabeth on 12th May 1937. The Rolling Stock Superintendent's Department's breakdown vans were manned continuously from 11th May to 17th May. Although the Neasden vans and men remained at that location, the Wood Lane vehicles and staff were transferred to the Bakerloo Line's London Road Depot from 11th May to 13th May. As much of the centre of London was closed to normal road vehicles, the Board received dispensation from the police to allow its breakdown lorries to enter this area, should they be required. In addition, if the police wished to make use of LT's railway breakdown vehicles, this could be arranged via the Traffic Controller at Leicester Square. For the Permanent Way and Signal Departments, a joint breakdown lorry was on stand-by at Lillie Bridge from midnight 11th/12th May to midnight 12th/13th May, plus a 'special lorry' loaded with permanent way material, and these were also authorised to enter the closed area. LT virtually dusted off the 1937 plan for the Coronation of the present Queen in June 1953. By this time however, there was an additional rolling stock gang in Hainault Depot, and it was the Ealing Common squad which migrated to London Road (though now only for a 48-hour period from start of traffic on 1st June to its close on 2nd June). Again, LT had permission to enter the central area, and its vehicles were once more available for use by the police.

Returning to September 1939, an additional pair of purpose-built AEC Regents was delivered using a brand new STL-type chassis as a base. Perhaps ordered in response to the worsening international political situation, and with thought of future conflict, they became another long-serving duo. 417J and 418J were also classed as 5-ton master breakdown tenders, and complemented the earlier two. The same red & cream colour scheme as 110J and 111J was employed, and they also remained in use until 1964. The four were shared between the railway depots at Ealing Common, Hainault and Neasden (Neasden having the extra vehicle).

The pre-war Albion 'KN127' 4-ton forward-control chassis was bodied in a number of forms for LT, and although only four of these were to be found in emergency roles, one was to last until the early-1960s. 130A and 131A entered service in February and April 1938 as breakdown tenders liveried in red & cream. 132A was a March 1938 4-ton breakdown van for Lifts & Escalators at Baker Street with a sliding steel rear roof allowing conversion to half-tilt (it towed a trailer from December 1946). A fourth Albion, 382A, was in use from April 1939 as a 4-ton Signal Department breakdown lorry.

The Albions had a separate box-body wider than the

No.AN 27's twin was AN 28. This Albion attended signal and permanent way emergencies and was kept at Lillie Bridge Depot. Much of the equipment carried could be accessed through a series of doors on the nearside, as demonstrated here. Visible inside is a steel keg lettered 'Calcium Carbide', a substance used to power the lamps carried by staff undertaking night or tunnel working. Pristine AN 27 (later 131A) is pictured here as delivered with a cream roof. It would later be fitted with a short-wave radio-telephone and remained in service until 1962. *LT Museum*

cab, as was often the case, and heavily-radiused corners and cove panels. Of the four, 130A and 131A are known to have carried the then-standard design of illuminated warning sign. Vehicles 130A, 131A and 132A were originally numbered AN 27, AN 28 and AN 29 in the pre-1939 numbering series. The Albion Company supplied a number of vehicles to LT and the 'K'-series trucks all had 4-cylinder 3.9 litre engines. The 'KL' had a 14ft wheelbase, the 'KN' 12ft and the 'KS' 10ft 9in.

Albion 382A was transferred to the Catering Department in June 1942, exchanging red livery for dark green in the process, and fulfilled its new task until withdrawal in August 1957. 130A went out of stock in April 1957, 132A followed it in February 1958, whilst 131A hung on until June 1962. The latter was still at the forefront of technology in the June of 1956. When allocated to the Signals Department, Lillie Bridge, it was one of a number of breakdown vans fitted with short-wave radio-telephones.

The Morris Equiload was mainly used by the LPTB in dropside truck format, the exception being 416M, a 30-cwt railway breakdown van delivered in 1939. Though many members of the pre-war breakdown fleet were destined to have long lives with the organisation, 416M was withdrawn in 1950, being replaced by one of the new Bedford 'KZ' vans. *LT Museum*

Fordson 'AA' 1934-built 30-cwt van F 8 formed part of the Neasden breakdown fleet and became 166F in 1939. In February 1946, it was repainted into standard Chiswick Green livery and transferred to Country Buses & Coaches, whom it continued to work for until withdrawal in May 1947.
LT Museum

The main receiving and transmitter mast was positioned on the tower of 55 Broadway, whilst calls from outlying areas used regional base stations. The radios communicated to the Chief Signal Engineer's Report Centre at Earl's Court (Acton Town from 14th March 1965), which used the call sign of 'Transport Base'. Call-signs used by the rolling stock breakdown lorries in the early-1960s were 'Transport Peter' (Neasden gang), 'Transport Easy' (Ealing Common gang) and 'Transport Queen' (Hainault gang); none of which gives any clue how these seemingly random names were arrived at. London Transport Magazine reported at that time that messages from the Executive's breakdown tenders 'can be fed into the private telephone system at the flick of a switch'. Quite some feat, considering that the internal phone network then covered not only head office and the Underground, but also Central Area bus garages, trolleybus depots and roadside locations.

The Second World War put an ever-increasing strain on LT's emergency engineering activities, and August 1940 saw three bus-to-lorry conversions produce 7-ton railway breakdown tenders 441W, 442W and 443W (ex-T 203, T175 and T206). The 1938 delivery of new coaches and the cessation of Green Line services in 1939 had rendered these AEC Regals redundant at the commencement of the war. A standard LT full-fronted 'goods' cab was provided, whilst the separate box-body fitted behind was not unlike those carried on the Albions, though longer. Livery variations had 441W first in green, then khaki and to Chiswick Green in November 1944. Vehicles 442W and 443W also started off in khaki, but all three were in the more traditional red by 1952, after which they saw about a ten years use. They were all equipped with an internal rear gantry and 'blocks & falls' to allow the lifting of very heavy equipment into the body. At one time or other, all three carried a roof-mounted spotlight, plus a painted 'L.T. URGENT' sign crudely formed from an upright metal plate.

Another vehicle to undergo various changes of livery was 625J. Formerly 'Tilling' ST 937, it was reconstructed as a 5-ton Permanent Way breakdown tender from January 1942. It too began its new life in wartime khaki, becoming green in April 1946, and finally appeared in red in the March of 1953. Typical of the long service given by many breakdown lorries, it did not retire until the October of 1963. This was the only ex-Tilling ST to be converted into something other than a canteen or tree lopper for LT (though twenty of the type had been fitted with Chiswick-built steel armoured-car bodies between December 1940 and February 1941 before being transferred to the Home Guard). After disposal, 625J came into the ownership of Prince Marshall, who acquired it for spares to facilitate the restoration of 'Tilling' ST 922 (ex-canteen 693J).

Smaller motorised types also formed part of the breakdown fleet of the Underground. Fordson 'AA' 30-cwt breakdown van 166F (ex-F 8) was a one-off in red and cream new in November 1934 and based at Neasden Depot from March 1935. The vehicle was too small for the customary 'URGENT' sign, so the legend 'LONDON TRANSPORT EMERGENCY EQUIPMENT' was sign-written on the body above the cab. It was later painted green and used by Country Buses, though oddly allocated to Catford Garage. Withdrawal was in May 1947. The Morris Commercial 'Equiload' was another pre-war design, and one numbered 416M was in use between July 1939 and July 1950 as a 30-cwt railway breakdown van at Neasden. Livery again was red and cream.

One consequence of the Second World War was the 1940 conversion of three ex-Green Line T-class coaches into 7-ton Permanent Way breakdown tenders 441W–443W. The cabs were of the standard LT 'goods' design, whilst the bodies gave a low loading height for the heavy equipment carried. All were in khaki livery at one stage or other, as in this wartime view of tender 442W (ex-T 175) in the shadow of Lillie Bridge's 'Goliath' overhead crane. The sign on the front of the cab roof reads 'repair party' and was of a type used on a number of service vehicles during the war.
LT Museum

The 1949 additions to the rolling stock breakdown fleet continued the use of a red-cream livery and included 924F, a small Ford Thames 'E83W' van based at Neasden. It remained in service until 1962.
Arthur Ingram

The war years presented the road and rail breakdown gangs with their greatest challenge. For the Underground, seven breakdown lorries and the breakdown train were allocated to this important task. Neasden had two breakdown lorries, each with a crew of between five and seven men. Golders Green and Wood Lane Depots also had two lorries and two crews apiece, whilst a seventh lorry and crew was based at Morden. The railway's road vehicles performed most of the work, since the breakdown train was not able to operate in 'tube' sized tunnels, and air-raid damage often blocked its passage from Neasden over sub-surface lines. What was to become known as the 'London Blitz' began on 7th September 1940, after just over a year of the so-called 'phoney war'. LT's rail breakdown lorries went into action that night at Plaistow on the District Line, where a bomb had thrown one 35-ton railway car on top of another. Five other trains were also stalled within one mile of the area due to damage, but in every case, the site was clear for services to run within 24 hours. The cars at Plaistow had to be split into hundredweight pieces using oxyacetylene cutters whilst bombs were still falling. During other incidents, breakdown crews were lowered to working sites in the buckets of cranes, there being no other means of access. At other times, they were forced to work in two or three feet of water, or by the light of blazing gas mains. On one night, there were major jobs at Aldgate, Baker Street, Bow Road, King's Cross, London Road and Neasden. All were tackled successfully within 24-hours. As might be expected, the main duty of the rail breakdown gangs was to clear lines as quickly as possible to enable services to resume. This was carried out in three stages: Firstly the removal of debris from the immediate area, secondly the cutting away of items likely to fall onto the track, thirdly the repair of the train sufficiently enough for it to be moved under its own power (if possible), and fourthly the repair or relaying of the track.

The Board's 'Air Raid Precautions – Operating Instructions (Railways)' dated 20th March 1940 listed breakdown gangs at Cockfosters, Golders Green, Lisson House (today's Griffith House), Morden, Neasden and Wood Lane. The Lisson House squad was stationed at Marylebone 'until further notice' and was for use by the Lifts & Escalators Department. Later that year, an item in the Traffic Circular (Railways) for 3rd August 1940 gave the following vehicle locations and types: Golders Green (Regent and Morris), Morden (Regent), Neasden (Regent and Ford) and Wood Lane (Regent and Albion). Reading between the lines, it is obvious that the 'Morris' was Equiload 416M, the 'Ford' 166F, and the 'Regents' 110J, 111J, 417J and 418J. In 1940, 'Rescue and Demolition Gangs' of the Permanent Way Department were available at Baker Street, Lillie Bridge and Whitechapel and provided with 'breakdown or other lorries'. These were made up of a Ganger, Sub-Ganger and four men (including a first aid man), plus a lorry driver. The Permanent Way Department supplied 'decontamination gangs' in case of gas attack, and these were based at Lillie Bridge and Parsons Green using lorries. Meanwhile, Neasden and Northfields depots both had one relaying gang, one 'contact rail' (conductor rail) gang and one sewer gang, each provided with full equipment, tools and lorry transport.

Post-war rolling stock breakdown developments included a change of location, with what was now being called the White City gang moving to Ealing Common Depot from November 1948. In addition, the third gang had been introduced at Hainault. Hainault Depot had been completed in 1939, but was handed over to the American Expeditionary Force for use as a maintenance base during the war years. It did not return to LT use until 1946, when the 1935/40 New Works Programme recommenced. Rolling stock stored outside during the presence of the Americans had deteriorated badly, and CDS helped transfer rehabilitation materials between Hainault and Acton.

In 1949, three Bedford six-cylinder petrol-engined 'KZ's were delivered as 30-cwt recovery breakdown vans. Nos. 836B, 925B and 926B were normal-control vehicles with a curved roof profile, whose design was more appropriate to the 1930s than the 1940s. The continued use of red and cream, plus the usual warning sign, complemented their flamboyant body-style. The same year 924F, a single Ford Thames 'E83W' van, was dedicated to breakdown use as a replacement for 416M. The normal uninspiring green van livery gave way to red and cream. The Bedfords themselves were eventually withdrawn between 1962 and 1964.

Between 1948 and 1950, John Chalmers Ltd of Reigate rebuilt a number of earliest petrol-engined STL buses into service vehicles. Of these, seven were reconstructed as 'Auxiliary Breakdown Tenders' for use by the road

According to 'Section 6 of Appendix to Working Timetables 1948', the breakdown section of the Chief Mechanical Engineer's Department was controlled by the Rolling Stock Divisional Depot Engineers. They in turn delegated its supervision to three Breakdown Engineers and three Breakdown Foremen (later re-titled Assistant Breakdown Engineers), who were on duty or call on a rotational basis throughout 24-hours. The method of call-out varied over the years. At that time, the Traffic Controller of the line requiring assistance would notify the Neasden South Lodgekeeper, who would contact the Engineer and Foreman on duty/on call and dispatch the appropriate gang depending on location. In later years, this arrangement was changed, and calls were made to a Rolling Stock Engineer's Report Centre at Neasden. From Monday 1st May 1972, this office was closed, and Line Controllers would inform the Headquarters Controller in Room 222 at 55 Broadway, who then co-ordinated the response to any incident.

A snapshot of the breakdown arrangements as at 25th July 1962 saw the fleet distributed as follows: AEC Regents 111J and 418J were radio-equipped and based at Neasden, as was 832J, the converted ex-STL. Also at this site was Bedford 'KZ' van 836B, and a standard green-liveried Ford Thames '100E' 7-cwt box-van 1091F, plus of course the breakdown train. Allocations at the subsidiary bases were Regent 110J (radio-fitted) and Bedford 'KZ' 926B at Ealing Common, and Regent 417J (radio-fitted) and 'KZ' van 925B at Hainault.

In the hard winter of 1962–63, Regent 832J attended an incident near Amersham. The weather had deteriorated during the day, heavy snow covered the ground and all Country Bus services had been withdrawn. On the way back to Neasden, the breakdown gang came across a schoolteacher and a number of children standing helplessly at a bus stop. 832J was then pressed back into passenger service for the first time since 1950! The children were put into the rear, whilst the teacher occupied the crew compartment, from where directions were given as to when to pull over. Thus, the pupils reached their destinations safely.

During this same period, the Lifts & Escalators Department kept two vehicles at Griffith House for emergency use, one being Thames Trader 3-ton open lorry 1127F. This was the lowest numbered Trader in the fleet, and in stock from December 1959 (though not the first in use, this honour going to 1134F and 1135F in September of that year). Trader 1127F was fitted with a 2-ton Burtonwood tail-lift and available to tow a mobile generator

services, being based at both bus garages and trolleybus depots (see also next section). Three were subsequently used as breakdown tenders for the Underground: 738J (ex-STL 169) was at Lillie Bridge between 1963 and its sale in 1971, 833J (ex-STL 159) was based at that location from 1960 to 1966, after which it too was disposed of.

Perhaps the most famous of the railway 'J's was 832J (ex-STL 162), which joined the Chief Mechanical Engineer's breakdown fleet at Neasden in 1955. Unlike the other 'J's, 832J gained full red & cream Underground livery, complete with gold 'EMERGENCY EQUIPMENT' sign-writing applied each side above the underlined LT fleetnames. Another change involved the 'BREAKDOWN TENDER' glass panel, which was altered to read 'EMERGENCY EQUIPMENT' in white-on-black Johnston, the two words separated by a light blue roundel which bore the abbreviation 'LTE' in red (later just 'LT'). 832J did not replace an existing lorry, rather being regarded as an 'auxiliary' vehicle available to transport miscellaneous equipment. The 'J's, like the Master Breakdown Tenders, had a specific allocation of tools and equipment and vehicles carried a diagram showing the exact location of each item.

based at Chalk Farm. The generator could also be hauled by 979AS, a 1957 Austin 5-ton '503' van with winch normally allocated to the Lifts & Escalators Department. The other vehicle at Griffith House for L&E duties was 1048AS, a standard Austin 'LD' 1-ton general freight van dating from 1956. Drivers for the L&E fleet were provided by CDS during the early-turn of Mondays to Fridays, outside these hours, the department made use of its own staff. Unlike the Rolling Stock Engineer's lorries and vans, the L&E's vehicles were in standard green.

As a number of trucks were fitted with winches, the obvious conclusion is that these were used to extricate bogged-down buses from the mire. In fact, they came to be fitted to some quite lowly vehicles, and their function was involved with the on-site movement of escalator components. If necessary, they could also pull power cables through underground ducting, rather like the similarly equipped GPO Telephones' vehicles. In LT's case, the power cables could belong to the tram, trolleybus or Underground systems.

Top: Three of Central Road Services' 'J'-type AEC Regent 'auxiliary breakdown tenders' were later transferred to the Underground. 833J (ex-STL 159) was one such vehicle, being used by the Signal Department from 1960 until 1966. The sign-writing on the door of the crew-compartment indicates that its base was Lillie Bridge Depot. This was the only breakdown 'J' to carry a roof-mounted traditional 'Urgent' sign, a fitting that may well have been taken from Albion signal van 131A. *John Gascoine*

Centre: The practice of HGV/PSV vehicle preservation by individuals was not widespread when the AEC Regent railway breakdown fleet was retired in 1964, and the scrapyard was the inevitable destination. 111J (left) and 418J (right) were first moved to North's of Sherburn, later being transferred to Arthur Hepworth's yard at Norton, near Doncaster. They were still there on 2nd January 1970, though in the process of being dismantled. The 'Urgent' sign of 111J has been altered at some point, losing the upper half-circle of its roundel, presumably the result of damage. *Leo Pratt*

The new face of the railway breakdown fleet was provided in 1962–63 by a fleet of specially-bodied Leyland Titan 'PD3A/1' bus chassis. The first four were allocated to the Permanent Way Department as 1273LD–1276LD and could be differentiated from the Rolling Stock Engineer's version by a lower roofline and the absence of a nearside sliding door on the body. *Fred Ivey*

The interiors of the Permanent Way Department 'LD's were equipped to deal with most eventualities and were lit by a translucent roof. A Burtonwood tailboard-loader was fitted, but unlike today's modern tail-lifts, this was sited within the van body, and part of the mechanism can be seen to the extreme right. LT Museum

At this time, some of the major problems associated with the existing 'Master Breakdown Tenders' were the sheer weight of equipment carried, the age of certain vehicles and their appallingly high fuel consumption. Indeed, they could only 'trundle' along at a legal maximum of 20 mph, and with ever-increasing traffic congestion, a new fleet was urgently required. Therefore, replacements for the increasingly aged railway breakdown fleet began to enter stock from December 1962. Between then and May 1966, nine specially-bodied Leyland PD3A/1 bus chassis entered service as the 'LD' class. Although it was now deemed more cost-effective to obtain vehicles new rather than convert ex-PSVs, these purpose-built Leylands sported a standard PD3 'St Helens' cab front and appeared as if they had been former buses. Early drawings show an original proposal to use a 'Birmingham' tin-front design, though in any case it seems odd that LT did not make use of a standard plain radiator. No fewer than three different body-styles were devised, with each batch being tailored to fit its specific field of work. Common to all was bodywork by Mann-Egerton of Norwich, a crew-cab behind the driver, Burtonwood tailboard-loaders and typical London bus-type trafficator 'ears'.

The first four were 1273LD to 1276LD, allocated to the Permanent Way Engineer. These carried separate box-van bodies topped with distinctively curving roof cove panels, and hinged double-doors giving access from the rear. In later years, some of the Permanent Way batches were given two 'Half-Royal' advertisement panels on each side to display LT publicity material. The quartet were based at Baker Street (1274LD), Lillie Bridge (1273LD and 1276LD) and Whitechapel (1275LD), and were called out via the Permanent Way Emergency Inspector, one of

whom was constantly on duty at the department's 'Emergency Headquarters' at Chalk Farm. The Permanent Way 'emergency desk' was later relocated to Pelham Street, South Kensington, from 4th May 1976; and moved again in October 1987 to the 5th floor of Ashfield House (adjacent to Lillie Bridge). It finally closed from 0700 hours on 22nd March 1993, following the inception of the Emergency Response Unit (q.v.).

Next came 1277LD to 1280LD, designed for the Chief Mechanical Engineer (Railways) as breakdown tenders, and allocated to the traditional locations of Ealing Common, Hainault and Neasden. In order to carry large items of equipment, these bodies were around 1ft taller and had a sliding door on each side. Other differences between the two types were in the cab area. 1273LD to 1276LD had radiused lower corners to the cab door windows and shallow lip over the front windscreen. On 1277LD to 1280LD however, the window corners were right-angled and there was no slight overhang at the front. Another variation involved one of the Permanent Way lorries, which had glazed windows fitted into the normally plain rear doors.

Both types were received in stock between December 1962 and March 1964, but May 1966 saw a third and final development of the concept with the arrival of 1416LD. Instantly recognisable from the others, 1416LD's cab and body were constructed as an integral unit, and was for use by the Chief Signal Engineer's Department at Lillie Bridge. In this case, the attendance of emergency men was arranged via a Chief Signal Inspector. The inspectors were based at Acton Town, later relocating to Griffith House in April 1987. The post was abolished when maintenance was devolved to individual Underground lines circa-1993.

All three variations carried a simpler red-lettered design of illuminated warning panel. These were fitted to cab roofs, except on 1416LD, which had the sign set into the front dome. In later years, the LDs had these signs altered, and they received a Johnston-lettered panel with the large white-on-black word 'URGENT' topped by a white strip containing an LT roundel plus the title 'LONDON TRANSPORT' in black. One suggestion for this change was the realisation that it was illegal to display a forward-facing red light. Other modifications saw the replacement of the trafficator 'ears' by wing-mounted fittings as used on modernised RF Green Line coaches. As legislation altered, some vehicles gained double orange flashing lights either side of the roof sign, whilst 1278LD had its sign replaced by a single orange light when transferred to Cricklewood Garage in March 1979.

This was not the first such move, as 1416LD had been used by the Chief Mechanical Engineer (Road Services) at Camberwell Garage since May 1974, during whose tenure it acquired black mudguards, one of only a few LDs to do so. The two 'bus' LDs were operated in conjunction with the AEC Militant master breakdown tenders, and replaced the bus engineers' ex-STL 'J's (further detailed later).

The LDs used on railway breakdown duties featured in the London Transport Magazine of May 1966. At that time, vehicles were based at Ealing Common, Hainault and Neasden (plus one spare at Neasden) and were available on a 24-hour basis (Hainault only from 07.00 to 23.00). As well as replacing the pre-war generation of Regents, they had also allowed the withdrawal of the old 1925-vintage ex-Metropolitan Railway 50-ton Neasden breakdown steam crane C 604 and its associated tool vans BD 700, 702, 703 and 704 in 1965. Again, the crews of these LDs were drawn from existing employees, who continued to perform routine maintenance tasks on rolling stock when not being called out for emergencies.

Former-STL 832J was not replaced, but retained at Neasden as a 'special equipment' vehicle. It was to become unique in a number of ways. It was LT's last ex-LGOC vehicle, the last service vehicle in red & cream, the last with semaphore 'trafficators', the last with a 2-letter, 4-figure registration number; the last service vehicle with rear wheel discs and the last without a cab heater!

With the scrapping of C 604, LT no longer had a dedicated breakdown crane, but provision was made for the utilisation of the Permanent Way Department's 1931-built ex-District Railway 30-ton crane C 606. Disadvantages associated with this vehicle were that it was neither manned nor kept in steam throughout 24-hours. It was also restricted to travelling at between 5–10mph. C 606 was converted to diesel operation between 1976 and

Being required to deal with rolling stock as opposed to track, the inside of the RSE 'LD's presented a quite different appearance from the Permanent Way batch. In the generally cramped conditions of the Underground, LT avoided the crane-lifting of derailed trains in favour of 'jack and pack', and examples of both types of equipment can be seen here. One unchanging principle of the Underground's breakdown vehicles is that tools and equipment are always stowed in predetermined places, so to speed their location and retrieval by crews in an emergency.
LT Museum

Four further LDs were provided for use by the Rolling Stock Engineer as breakdown vehicles and numbered 1277LD–1280LD. The body is clearly higher than on the Permanent Way version, a sliding door allows nearside access and the cab door windows have non-radiused lower corners. The LDs carried the so-called 'St Helens' cab front, but initial proposals suggested using the 'Birmingham'-style tin-front.
Jim Wright

1978 (i.e. two years in the making), yet withdrawn in February 1986. Though the LT crane was specifically prohibited from being used on BR, the opposite was not the case. The BR travelling cranes at King's Cross, Stratford and Willesden were authorised for use on the Metropolitan Line north of Willesden Green and east of Leyton on the Central Line (excluding the Hainault Loop). In addition, the Old Oak Common crane could attend the City Widened Lines, being transferred via Kentish Town (LMR) Sidings. In fact, due to the generally restricted nature of the Underground environment, LT's rail breakdown gangs have traditionally used the procedure of 'jack and pack' in preference to crane lift, with such materials to effect this being carried to site by road.

Paired with the RSE LDs were Ford Thames Traders 1281F, 1282F and 1283F. Classed as 'Auxiliary Breakdown Tenders', they were based on the 3-ton Trader chassis and had crew-cabs, box-van bodies and radio-equipment. Their primary use was in carrying out on-the-spot repairs to Underground trains. All entered stock in September 1963 and carried the normal roof sign (and later, two orange lamps). 1281F and 1283F lasted until January 1981 and March 1981 respectively. Middle vehicle 1282F had a more interesting career, subsequently being converted into the Underground's first communications vehicle. Stored in the former breakdown garage at the north end of Neasden Depot, 1282F contained the following fixed equipment:
 2 post office telephones,
 3 LT internal telephones,
 1 field telephone and
 1 radio transmitter/receiver.
Portable equipment included:
 1 spare telephone,
 1 field telephone,
 2 radio transmitters/receivers,
 1 loudhailer and
 linking cable-drums of telephone wire.
The vehicle also carried high-visibility clothing, torches

and stationery for use during incidents. To reflect its revised status, the title 'COMMUNICATIONS VEHICLE' was applied in white to body sides, just above the full-size gold LONDON TRANSPORT fleetnames. Following its replacement by Ford 'A'-series 2086F in the early-1980s (q.v.), 1282F was repainted into the old Chiswick Green colour to represent a general-use CDS delivery truck of the early-1960s. Its first public appearance was at the 1983 LT Golden Jubilee Gala at Chiswick and Acton Works, and has continued to make occasional appearances for Distribution Services ever since.

The Rolling Stock Engineer's Department acquired 1491LR, a long-wheelbase petrol-engined Land Rover in April 1968. It was based at Ealing Common Depot until its demise in December 1976, and was employed as a mobile workshop. The standard Land Rover 'hard-top' had a hinged flap on the nearside, which opened upwards to allow access to (and cover for) a workbench fitted inside the vehicle. Livery was non-standard army bronze green body with an off-white top.

A report dated 29th April 1970 shows the rolling stock breakdown gangs' fleet now organised as follows: At Neasden were 1278LD and 1279LD, AEC Regent 832J, communications Trader 1282F, and grey-painted Land Rover 12-seat personnel carrier 1291LR dating from June 1963. Ealing Common held 1277LD and Trader 1281F, whilst Hainault was host to 1280LD and Trader 1283F. Radio call signs were still in use at this time, and were now listed as 'Isaac' (1278LD), 'Henry' (1279LD), 'Yellow' (1282F), 'Kenneth' (1277LD), 'Easy' (1281F), 'Jack' (1280LD) and 'Queen' (1283F). As in earlier years, no obvious theme explained the origin of the names. Land Rover 1291LR was for the Breakdown Foremen, who later made use of several generations of Morris Marinas and Ford estate cars. An item published in the Traffic Circular for week commencing 29th April 1972 revealed that by this time, the Ealing Common and Hainault gangs had been reduced to being staffed early and late, Mondays to Saturdays only.

The most traumatic incident attended in the 1970s occurred at 08.46 hours on Friday 28th February 1975. The 'Moorgate Crash' involved the entire rail breakdown organisation at one time or other, and such was the difficulty of the work, the site was not cleared until almost a week later. Despite this event demonstrating the importance of the teams, a reduction in their capability took place around this time, when the Hainault gang was disbanded (by 10/75) and resources concentrated on Ealing and Neasden. This decision was influenced by the improvement in build-quality of the trains and the lesser frequency of breakdowns. Equipment failures had also decreased, since vulnerable aspects were being 'designed out' in the light of experience.

In July 1977, a Ford 'A0609' 4-ton van registered TVT 834R was on hire for evaluation purposes. The Ford 'A'-series was introduced in an attempt to fill a gap between the Transit and 'D'-series models, but was to prove under-engineered and became one of the manufacturer's less-inspired designs. Apparently considered a success by London Transport, it later entered the fleet as 2062F in September of the same year. LT took a further three examples new in November and December 1977 as 2086F, 2087F and 2088F, supposedly to replace the Transit '290' parcel van design (though in the event, use of the Transit range continued). The 'A'-series vans were in normal grey livery, and engaged in day-to-day distribution work, but in 1982, 2086F was converted to a new communications unit designed to replace Trader 1282F. The most noticeable difference was a change from grey to red livery, an orange flashing roof light and the insertion of a small window near the roof on each body side. As well as carrying the equipment previously contained in 1282F, a collapsible booth was introduced for use as a temporary office, should no suitable facility be available on site. The booth carried the legend 'LT INCIDENT REPORT CENTRE', and housed a seat and desk, plus an 'internal' Auto telephone for connection to the nearest fixed LT line. Like its predecessor, it was based at Neasden Depot.

A Leyland Terrier was acquired second-hand via Mann Egerton of Norwich in February 1978. No. 2091L combined a grey-painted cab with a ribbed unpainted box-body, and was considered as a potential replacement for the LD-class of breakdown tenders. It was based at Baker Street, and occupied the same front-of-station

The RSE LDs and Thames Trader vans were eventually replaced by six Ford D0710 box vans delivered between 1976 and 1980. 2140F exhibits the Locomotors modified crew-cab provided and the painted warning sign that took the place of the illuminated 'Urgent' panels.
Colin Brown

parking space normally reserved for an LD. No. 2091L's cab roof had an illuminated headboard ideal for the 'URGENT' display traditionally used, but this was in fact left blank. Reports at the time suggested that spares for the old LDs were now becoming a problem, and they suffered the disadvantage of requiring HGV-licensed drivers. In contrast, the Terrier was a modern design and light enough to be driven on a normal car licence.

In the event however, the Ford 'A'-series was used to replace the Permanent Way Department's LDs from 1979. Nos. 2135F, 2136 and 2137F were three 'A0609' 4-ton breakdown vans with extended crew-cabs and tail-lifts. In at least one case, a glass 'Urgent' panel from an LD was mounted in a new frame and attached to the front of an 'A'-series body. With the combination of new and existing Transit components, plus the very long wheelbase, the three vehicles presented a very ungainly appearance (the AA used similar-length platform-bodied beaver-tailed vehicles for its 'Relay' recovery service). One month later they were joined by 2138F, a shorter wheelbase Ford 'A0609' 4-ton box-van. The rear of this was fitted with seats, although the body had no side windows. Like the previous three, the only clues to its function were the words 'PERMANENT WAY ENGINEER' in white below the standard cab-door gold LT transfer.

As regards the Rolling Stock Engineer's Department, the heavier Ford 'D'-series was chosen for a new generation of vehicles. This type had already been used for emergency work, with Ford 'D0710' 5-ton box-van 1759F of 1972 later being repainted from grey to red (gaining an orange flashing light) and allocated to the Chief Signal Engineer's Department at Acton Town. 1759F almost certainly replaced 1416LD as the signals emergency vehicle, as the Leyland moved to Camberwell Garage around the same time.

The next use of this model was with 1986F. This Ford

'D0710' 3½-ton capacity box-van with crew-cab and Ratcliff tail-lift was a direct replacement for Regent 832J (sold 6/78). Indeed, 1986F even received some of the interior racking formerly fitted to the ex-STL (later re-fitted to 832J when in preservation). It may well have shown the way regarding future orders, arriving in October 1976 and initially operating alongside the existing LDs for the Rolling Stock Engineer (Railways). As well as the now customary orange warning light, the box sides were lettered 'EMERGENCY VEHICLE' in white. Instead of the usual illuminated warning sign on the cab roof, a large rectangular plate was riveted to the front of the body, bearing the words 'L.T. EMERGENCY VEHICLE' sign-written white-on-black in upper case Johnston.

Between 1978 and 1980, six more similarly equipped 'D0710' box-vans were delivered for use as breakdown lorries. November 1978 saw the first two, and comprised numbers 2139F and 2140F. Livery and signage followed that applied to 1986F, but with the addition of the words 'LONDON TRANSPORT' displayed under the 'EMERGENCY VEHICLE' lettering in same length and style. A further four completed the replacement programme between November 1979 and February 1980. Nos. 2199F, 2200F and 2201F (and 2217F q.v.) differed from the previous vehicles by having the white-painted lower cab front common to most 'D'-series replaced by a matt-black finish (a late-1978 re-vamp of the model by Ford). By this time, the part-time Hainault gang had been disbanded, and the RSE vehicle fleet was now distributed as follows: 1986F, 2199F, 2200F and 2201F (Neasden), 2139F and 2140F (Ealing Common). Apart from 1986F, the five main RSE 'D'-series were kitted-out similarly, and there was no longer a split between 'Master' and 'Auxiliary' roles. Most if not all of these 'D'-series were delivered with rear-facing crew-cab bench seats. Unpopular with staff, delays in commissioning occurred whilst these were reversed.

Vehicle 2217F was allocated to the Chief Signal Engineer's Department at Acton Town and lacked the 'emergency' lettering carried by the others (replacing 1759F). The only clue to its response role was red livery, the now ubiquitous orange flashing roof light and the words 'SIGNAL ENGINEER' in white on cab doors. Following the arrival and commissioning of these new types, the Permanent Way LDs were sold between May 1976 and April 1980; whilst the Rolling Stock Engineer's LDs and Traders departed from January 1980 to July 1983 (1278LD was in bus engineering use by this time).

From 1986 to 1990, a long-wheelbase Ford Transit numbered 3393F was in use by the Permanent Way Manager's Department. Livery was the standard manufacturer's red of the time, but with certain unusual additions. The words 'EMERGENCY RAIL UNIT' appeared in yellow on the sides, together with red/blue LUL roundels contained within white squares. The front had the reversed word 'EMERGENCY' in white, and all was in upper case New Johnston Bold. An orange 'beacon bar' was fitted above the cab, and an orange/red reflective strip adorned the vehicle's sides fire service-style.

Left: Ford designed its 'A'-series trucks to fill the gap between its Transit and 'D'-series range, but the model did not prove to be a success. CDS obtained three 'A'-series box-vans in 1977 as a possible alternative to the Transit '290' parcel-van and in 1982, one of these, 2086F, was rebuilt to replace Thames Trader 1282F as a new Railway Communications Vehicle. As well as the obvious change to red livery, another external alteration was the provision of a small window high up on each side of the body.
Colin Lloyd

Below: The Permanent Way LDs were replaced by a trio of Ford 'A'-series lorries numbered 2135F–2137F. No.2137F shows off their extremely long wheelbase and the very ungainly appearance this presented. As might be expected, this resulted in a turning circle capability that was nothing short of appalling! At least one of the three had an old LD 'Urgent' panel remounted on the front of the box.
David Rowe

London Transport turned away from the almost exclusive use of Fords for the provision of large vehicles at the beginning of the 1980s, and this was reflected when consideration came to replacing the 'D'-series breakdown lorries. LRT Vehicle Specification No. 683A of December 1987 shows a red-liveried Ford Cargo '0811' with removable body for the 'Railway Engineering Emergency Unit'. An earlier drawing, No. 683, clearly illustrates an intention to use a Leyland Terrier chassis and cab.

However, the Mercedes-Benz firm was eventually chosen. Initially it had been intended to use the Mercedes-Benz '814' and '1114' chassis, with five for the RSE and one for Permanent Way use. The former were specified as 7500kg gross, whilst the latter was rated at 11000kg gross, and all employed a de-mountable concept. One reason for this was to avoid the need to completely empty a vehicle before servicing. Instead the chassis could be separated for this work, whilst the fully equipped body was remounted on another vehicle and immediately available for use. The new bodies were built in a box form, and included a crew compartment, flashing orange lights and external equipment lockers.

The de-mountable equipment consisted of self-supporting van bodies on a strong sub-frame fitted with folding and extending legs. To de-mount the body it would be lifted by either an on-board air bag, or utilising the vehicle's own air suspension. With the body in the raised position, the legs would be unfolded and some of the air released. This allowed the legs to touch the ground. With the air fully released, the chassis could be driven out from under the body. As well as being de-mounted and left on site, the system allowed different 'DB'-prefixed bodies to be exchanged between vehicles.

Unfortunately, it was realised that when fully loaded, the MB '814' chassis would be overweight, partly since de-mountable equipment is much heavier than a conventional body. In view of this, the originally ordered vehicles delivered as 2486M to 2490M were re-deployed for other purposes within the main Distribution Services fleet (detailed later). Replacement vehicles were quickly ordered, and entered stock in 1990 as Mercedes-Benz '1114's 2491M (Permanent Way) and 2492M to 2496M

(RSE). Together, they carried bodies numbered DB 1 to DB 6. Body DB 1 on 2491M was substantially different from the other five, being required to carry permanent way material.

For the first time, the use of red or red-based livery was abandoned in favour of the new white/blue London Underground scheme, with the addition of distinctive red/blue chevrons on the box front and lower cab area. The vehicles entered stock between August and October of 1990. Before the establishment of the ERU (q.v.), the Mercedes were stationed as follows: For the RSE breakdown gangs, 2492M, 2493M and 2494M were at Neasden; whilst 2495M and 2496M resided at Ealing Common. 2491M was used by the Permanent Way Emergency Squad, and kept at either Baker Street or Lillie Bridge. The vehicle spent a week at each site in turn, depending on which Permanent Way gang was on stand-by.

LUL's 'Company Plan' was published in November 1991, and envisaged fundamental and far-reaching changes into the way the Underground was organised and staffed. One of these was the concept of multi-functionalism, whereby long-standing demarcation lines were removed and employees trained to perform a much wider variety of tasks. One example of this was the establishment of the 'Emergency Response Unit' (ERU) from 1992. This combined elements of the RSE breakdown gangs and Permanent Way Department emergency squads, and was established as a full-time organisation. The new ERU inherited all six of the MB '1114's, but once the formerly separate activities were fully integrated, it could no longer justify use of the whole batch. Vehicle 2491M thus became redundant, and transferred to other duties within the main haulage fleet. In any case, it had a much higher mileage than the others, and its ex-Permanent Way body would have required major rebuilding to match the rest of the ERU's vehicles.

At first, the ERU based their vehicles at traditional locations, but in time, new bases were opened. Ealing Common was closed in January 1993, and staff transferred to Neasden to cover the multi-functional training programme then beginning. The first new ERU site was in the old station building on South Harrow E/B platform,

Two of the later Ford D0710 box vans, 2199F and 2200F, showing the black lower front panels fitted to 2199–2201F. Colin Brown

the second in the former Permanent Way emergency squad accommodation at the end of Baker Street platform 3 & 4. Non-railway buildings were then utilised, with industrial premises occupied in Tottenham Hale and Vauxhall. The next development was the vacating of South Harrow and Baker Street in favour of Acton (inside the works) and Camden Town (industrial lock-ups again). As far as possible, the MB '1114' lorries were attached to specific sites, these being: 2492M/DB 2 (Camden), 2493M/DB 5 (spare and training), 2494M/DB 3 (Tottenham), 2495M/DB 6 (Vauxhall) and 2496M/DB 4 (Acton)

A consequence of the Fennell Report into the King's Cross fire was the commissioning of a new state-of-the-art control and communications unit. The Mercedes-Benz '814' chassis and de-mountable body concept was used, and the vehicle arrived as 2488M in September 1991. This was the most extensively-equipped such unit yet, with body DB 7 having a range of radio and telephone systems, mess facilities and a small conference area. When on site, a telescopic pole-mounted illuminated LUL roundel could be raised for identification. The latter made use of one of the frames formerly used on the roof of London Buses radio-cars/vans. The now-standard 'emergency' livery was employed, but with the addition of the title 'Emergency Control unit'. The vehicle was later named 'Jim Winters MBE' after the manager responsible for combining the various part-time breakdown teams into the permanently-staffed ERU. Usage of 2488M has included attendance at derailments, multi-agency training exercises, the Jubilee Line Extension 'safety case' detrainment at North Greenwich, and even the 1995 VE-Day celebrations in Hyde Park. This vehicle is often driven by 'on call' emergency drivers from CDS, whilst Network Services supply a 'loggist'. Although capable of being transferred, the control unit body has remained on the same chassis throughout, though was de-mounted on-site when deployed at White City following a terrorist explosion in March 2001. Given that the vehicle sees little use, the M-B '814' chassis/cab unit was not replaced along with the rest of the ERU's main fleet in 1999.

Four additional vehicles joined the ERU fleet between July and August 1993. 2529M to 2532M were small Mercedes-Benz '410D' box-vans with crew-cabs and tail-lifts, and often operated in tandem with the larger Mercedes. As delivered, they were not given the special

Top: One of the smaller vehicles used by the Permanent Way Department was Ford Transit 3393F. This long-wheelbase van, which operated from 1986 to 1990, featured a standard red Ford factory-finish, augmented by a flashing beacon-bar, specialised lettering and the type of horizontal yellow stripe more usually associated with the fire service. This sort of 'customised' livery was swept away by the advent of the corporate LUL white/blue livery in 1990. Crew accommodation was provided behind the front seats.
Colin Lloyd

Centre: The 1990 Mercedes-Benz '1114' lorries introduced the demountable principle to the breakdown fleets and were used by both the Rolling Stock and Permanent Way gangs. Although the Emergency Response Unit was later to establish new bases for their combined teams, the vehicles were originally operated separately from their departments' traditional locations. Nos. 2495M and 2496M replaced a pair of Ford 'D'-series at Ealing Common and introduced a new white-blue based livery relieved by red and blue chevrons. The words 'Passenger services' were later replaced by 'Response unit'. Kim Rennie

Right: Volvo 'FL6' demountable chassis/cabs 2566V–2570V replaced the ERU's Mercedes-Benz '1114' units in 1999 and box-bodies DB 2–DB 6 were transferred onto the new vehicles. Shortly before the changeover, the bodies had received a modified livery, with the front repainted Underground Red and a red-white chequered band added to the sides. 2568V shows the present-day combination of new Volvo chassis/cab and re-liveried box DB 2. The Volvo chassis was chosen in preference to Mercedes due to a higher specification braking system. Kim Rennie

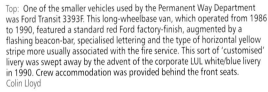

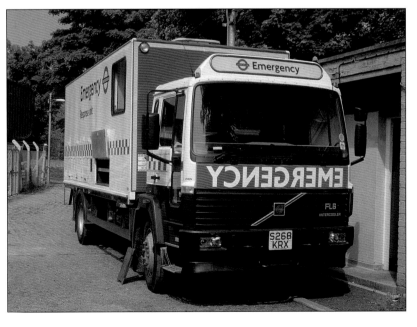

Right: The box-bodies of both the Rolling Stock and Permanent Way Mercedes-Benz '1114' lorries were capable of being de-mounted and left on site. Although this has rarely occurred in practice, an open day at Ruislip Depot provided an opportunity to demonstrate the procedure. Permanent Way body DB 1 is standing on its four support legs after chassis/cab 2491M has been driven out from underneath. Also illustrated are the external lockers, crew-cab at the leading end of the body and original lettering.
David Rowe

Below: Four Mercedes-Benz '410D' crew-cabbed vans were acquired in 1993 and twinned with the larger Mercedes at the new ERU bases of Acton, Camden Town, Euston and Vauxhall. The miniaturisation of tools and other equipment meant these could be much smaller than those provided in the past. 2532M is effectively in 'as delivered' condition, i.e. before the application of red/blue chevrons.
Kim Rennie collection

ERU chevrons, but 2530M and 2531M had these applied retrospectively.

The ERU's Mercedes-Benz '1114' chassis saw considerable use attending incidents on both the Underground and the main line railways, and in 1999 five replacements arrived in the guise of 2566V to 2570V. These were Volvo 'FL6' units, the first vehicles from this manufacturer since 2455V, the second-hand Volvo 'F717' articulated tractor acquired in 1986, and appeared in a revised ERU livery. The existing ERU 'DB' bodies were remounted on the new trucks, and had themselves received the modified livery in the months before transfer. For the first time since 1985, the opportunity was taken to match fleet and registration numbers. Like the 1114's before them, the Volvo units are sited strategically around London at the four ERU bases: 2566V/DB 4 (Camden), 2567V/DB 6 (Tottenham), 2568V/DB 2 (Vauxhall), 2569V/DB 3 (Acton) and 2570V/DB 5 (spare and training). They were used in rotation after the 1999 Ladbroke Grove train disaster, when ERU teams assisted the London Fire Brigade with carriage stabilisation and other work in the days following the crash. Other non-

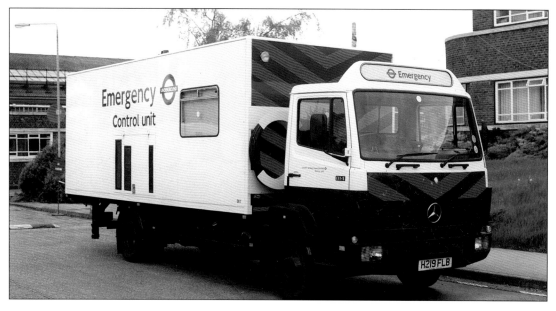

Right: The 1987 King's Cross fire led to a substantial review of the LUL safety culture and incident management procedure. Associated with this was the commissioning of a much larger, state-of-the-art, 'Emergency Control Unit' to replace Ford 'A'-series 2086F. 2488M paired one of the lighter-weight Mercedes-Benz '814' chassis/cab units with demountable body DB 7. The unit has a wide-variety of communication systems, plus separate conference and mess areas. Events attended have included the White City bomb blast, derailments at Piccadilly Circus, the 1995 VE Day Celebration in Hyde Park, and the 2002 Queen's Golden Jubilee Parade (as a participant).
Colin Lloyd

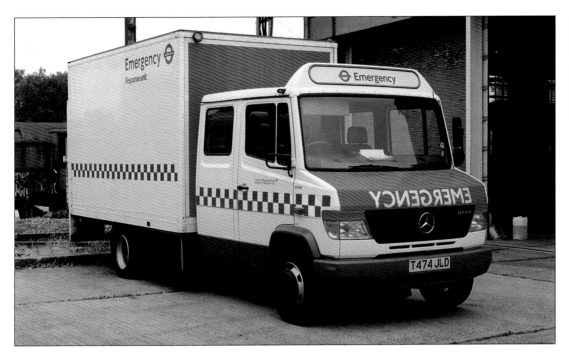

New in 1999 were four, much larger, new-style Mercedes-Benz '814D' models finished in the ERU's revised livery. One subtle difference from the livery carried on the Volvos is that the word 'EMERGENCY' on the bonnet is depicted in reflective silver characters. No.2574M stands outside the ERU's Acton Works base. Kim Rennie

LUL incidents attended have included the Clapham and Watford rail crashes, and even the Marchioness riverboat sinking (when the ERU supplied lighting to illuminate the Thames).

In 1999, the smaller ERU vehicles were also supplanted by new deliveries. The model chosen was the new Mercedes-Benz '814D' box-van, a design significantly larger than the '410D' type used previously. All were given full ERU livery from new and fleet numbers 2572M to 2575M again matched with registrations.

In addition to those vehicles already mentioned, both the bus and rail emergency breakdown departments have used a number of ordinary small vans. Most were in the standard red or grey fleet livery of the time and were effectively indistinguishable from hundreds of other similar types in use by LT. However, a small number of vans and minibuses have received the LUL 'emergency' livery, and are thus readily identifiable from the rest of the fleet.

BUS BREAKDOWN VEHICLES

The LGOC had been the first company to build and operate a successful petrol-engined bus suitable for the difficult conditions in London. The first were known as the X-type, and the famous B-type bus soon followed the earlier prototypes. Both models were built at Vanguard's Walthamstow Works, which by this time was under LGOC control. In addition to supplying chassis for bodying as buses, some were built as lorries or vans. From 1911, the majority of LGOC garages were allocated their own open-cabbed, open-backed B-type lorry for stores and recovery

Centre: The LUL central signals store is situated within Acton Works, and the ERU is responsible for the delivery and collection of both urgent and non-urgent items to and from the worksite. High-top Ford Transit 4852F was one vehicle used to convey delicate equipment like relays and was classified as the 'Black Van' for ERU movement logging purposes. It is one of a number of vans and minibuses to have carried the 'Emergency' variant of the Corporate livery. Kim Rennie

Right: The latest signal courier 'Black Van' is 5119F. This high-top Ford Transit arrived in 2001 and was the first vehicle of this size to carry the new ERU livery. The management and operation of the ERU and its vehicles, together with the rest of the Distribution Services' fleet, was transferred to Infraco JNP in September 1999. Kim Rennie

The conversion of the four 'London Six' LS-class buses to 'master breakdown tenders' meant they had a multi-purpose role to play and the amount of equipment carried resulted in them being very slow and cumbersome. This view of 219U (ex-LS 6) shows the shortened chassis, plus the numerous side lockers containing items such as jacks, tow chains, ropes, skid-plates, wooden packing, pinch bars and a first aid kit. The circular disc in front of the leading rear wheel concealed a capstan winch and there was a similar winch on the offside.
LT Museum

duties; recorded examples being: B 75, 114, 201, 389, 436, 437, 725, 727, 752, 1184, 1374, 1387, 1391, 1393, 1398, 1399, 1400, 1404, 1721, 1728, 1758, 1831, 2296, 2530, 2570 and 2622. Fitted with a very basic crane, they were capable of hauling disabled buses using an early form of 'suspended tow'. Other LGOC trucks were based on Straker-Squire or Milnes-Daimler chassis, and there was a certain amount of body and even registration plate transfer between these marques and the B-type lorry fleet.

In 1919, a number of AEC solid-tyred 'YC'-type trucks were acquired by the LGOC. Four of these were crane-fitted and designated as 'Master Breakdown Tenders'. The vehicles operated on trade plates 015 GH, 016 GH, 087 XY, 069 LM and carried standard Chiswick Green livery. These lasted until sale in 1937–38, by which time four former LS-class 6-wheel double-decker buses had been converted to 9-ton bus heavy breakdown tenders. The LS-design had been the first LGOC double-decker to

be equipped with pneumatic tyres from new, and was the ADC '802' model. ADC stood for Associated Daimler Company, the short-lived and unsuccessful liaison between AEC and Daimler lasting from 1926 to 1928. Author Alan Townsin has suggested that the 'London Six' LS-class had been '*designed in haste by AEC to compete with the pneumatic tyred 6-wheelers offered by Guy and Karrier*'. Only 20 of this chassis were built, all as 'Associated Daimler' vehicles, and twelve of these came to the LGOC.

What became breakdown tender number 219U was the first to be modified in 1936. Originally LS 6, it was rebuilt by the LPTB at Chiswick. The conversion to service vehicle status included chassis shortening, installation of new bodies and the fitment of twin winches to enable them to pull upright overturned buses. The new body was of integral construction (i.e. van and cab combined). The conversion incorporated a full-front cab, rather than the original half-cab with no windscreens, and provided a number of external equipment lockers. Once converted they looked nothing like the buses they had been. They still lacked cab doors, canvas sheets sufficing instead. The body colour remained red.

A further three conversions took place in 1938, when LS 8, 3 and 10 reappeared as 220U to 222U. The initial vehicle had retained its ADC radiator, but the subsequent three were given the more modern AEC design used on the LT, ST and STL classes. The second conversion, LS 8, had operated as a demonstrator bus for the Greenock & Port Glasgow Tramway Company for a short period when new, prior to returning to service in London. Though all four chassis were shortened by LT, the bodies of 220U to 222U were provided by Eagle of Warwickshire, The breakdown lorries were based at Hammersmith (219U), Dalston (220U), Cricklewood (221U) and Camberwell (222U) garages. Withdrawal of the four occurred en-masse in April 1951, and they had at least fared better than sister vehicle LS 1, reduced to the ignominious status of a temporary waiting room at Sevenoaks Bus Station. One assumes that as winch-equipped vehicles they were invaluable during the war. All four operated on trade plates, three of which had been carried by their 'YC'-type lorry predecessors.

A 'London Six' breakdown tender in action in the September of 1945. 'Pre-war' RT 18 has overturned in Chelsea after colliding with a coach and Hammersmith (Riverside) Garage's 219U has been called to the rescue. The tender's nearside capstan winch has been pulled out ready for use and can be seen protruding just in front of the rear wheels. Julian Bowden-Green collection

The ex-LSs carried enough equipment for virtually any emergency, but this made them heavy and slow. After the war, their function was to be split between breakdown trucks (with cranes and winches) and lighter breakdown tenders. From December 1947, eight AEC Matador gun tractors were acquired second-hand from the War Department and fitted with recovery crane equipment. These ex-Army and RAF vehicles were described as 5-ton 'Master Breakdown Tenders', and had been new between 1943–1945. Most operators using Matadors as breakdown vehicles opted to keep the large section military tyres, allowing a good cross-country ability. LT however decided to alter the tyre specification to a more mundane 9.00–20 size, in view of the infrequent need for their vehicles to go off-road. One has to assume that the differential ratios were altered to ensure that the Matadors retained an adequate road speed. Like many major bus operators, LT altered the cab and body design before they entered service, resulting in probably the most unassuming-looking Matadors ever to do duty as breakdown vehicles. The fact that 219U to 222U also remained in operation alongside the Matadors probably had more to do with the poor state of the post-war bus fleet, rather than the suitability of the ex-London Six buses themselves.

Top: After the war, recovery duties were split between crane-fitted breakdown trucks and lighter breakdown tenders. Eight former Army and RAF vehicles were acquired from the War Department and rebuilt as 5-ton 'master breakdown tenders'. West Ham Depot's 747P had been new in February 1945 and lasted until January 1977. On this vehicle, the side valance covers half the rear tyre, most of the batch had this area cut to form a normal wheel-arch. LT Museum

Above: Tender 748P demonstrates the late-1940s method of righting an overturned LT-class bus. This rear view shows the small stores/workshop area behind the cab, as well as the conventional semi-circular rear wheel-arch. This particular tender did not enjoy the longevity of some of the batch, being sold out of service in December 1956 after just nine years' use. The white rear trade plate figures and numerals have been painted directly onto the red bodywork. LT Museum

Right: Two of the AEC Matador breakdown tenders remained active until well into the 1970s. In April 1974, Leyton Garage's 746P still had a few years' service left, ultimately becoming the last ex-WD tender to leave the fleet upon withdrawal in July 1978. It is unclear if it was actually towing the following RM. Certainly, the bus's radiator grille has not been removed, which rules out the use of a fixed tow-bar. The tender's typical LT trafficator 'ears' are an early addition; another alteration is the application of a white LT 'open' roundel. Jim Blake

Seven ex-STL buses were converted to 'auxiliary breakdown tenders' between 1948 and 1950 and worked alongside the 'P'-class Matadors. Rebuilding included the provision of a sliding nearside door, hinged rear doors and a crew compartment behind the driver's cab. One of the most familiar types of LT service vehicle, the last 'J'-class tender did not to retire until July 1978. Jim Blake

As 746P to 751P, 753P and 754P, the Matadors were strategically-allocated to Central Area bus garages (and trolleybus depots); and after the demise of 219U to 222U were the sole performers of this role until 1966. (The gap in the number sequence oddly being filled by film unit 752F.) Painted red, the only relief was provided by a glass panel above the full-width cab displaying the words 'BREAKDOWN TENDER' in white Johnston-style letting on black. Additions in later years included a single roof-mounted flashing orange light, trafficators, plus a slot-in plate offside of the radiator which could be reversed to exhibit the word 'TOWING' in red on white. Fleetnames were originally smaller versions of the style used pre-1970, though survivor 746P gained a pair of the large white 'open' roundels used on the DMS-type bus and a number of Routemasters from 1971 to 1973. Withdrawal started as early as October 1956, but 746P was still in stock as late as July 1978.

Despite the diminutive image of the AEC Matadors, they played a major part in keeping London moving in the post-war years. The vehicles were amongst the heaviest breakdown trucks readily available to the police, and were often used to right overturned lorries and vans not belonging to LT. Until the mid-1980s at least, the Metropolitan Police still relied on LT to clear breakdowns likely to affect the flow of traffic (e.g. in one of the Thames tunnels). This was recalled in an article on traffic congestion published in the April 1966 issue of the London Transport Magazine: *'When a breakdown occurs the [bus] controller frequently learns of it through bus officials before the police. He passes the information to Scotland Yard, with the invitation: 'Do you want one of our master lorries?' These are based at Camberwell and Cricklewood Garages . . . if the police are not making their own arrangements . . . the controller contacts our engineers, who order a lorry to the scene.'* The report added that the

Bus Controllers maintained contact with their opposite numbers at Country Buses, the Underground and on British Railways, and 'are ready to offer assistance in the event of any incidents'.

Although many fire brigades have today adopted the title of 'Fire & Rescue' services and attend road accidents, their primary (and only statutory) duty is fighting fires. Up to the 1960s however, the police would often call on the services of the local breakdown garage in the case of a serious 'RTA' (road traffic accident). To allow for the freeing of persons trapped under vehicle wheels, LT provided 'Emergency Bus Lifting Gear' at certain garages and depots. The equipment came in two parts: a long A-framed jack; and a box containing tools, scotches and packing blocks. The box fitted on top of the jack, but the two could be separated to allow for transportation to an incident inside an open-platform bus, on a lorry, or in the luggage compartment of a (pre-war) taxi. If the equipment was required near to a garage, it could even be pushed to site using the wheels on the jack. The equipment was not just confined to road service premises, and in 1948 was available at Finsbury Park, Golders Green, Goodge Street, Kilburn Park and Notting Hill Gate (Central) Underground Stations.

Instructions for obtaining lifting gear were printed in the Central Bus, Country Bus, Trams & Trolleybuses and garage staffs' rulebooks, and remained the same for some 50-odd years: *'The Conductor will first call a Police Constable or an Official of the Board (whoever is nearer) to take charge of the vehicle, and then accompany the Driver to the nearest Emergency Station (as published from time-to-time in the Traffic Circular), collect the jack and tackle, and return to the scene of the accident.'* The equipment was in use from the 1930s at least, and locations were still being listed in the bus inspectors' 'red book' timetable well into the 1980s.

Above: The J-class service vehicles became a vital component within the bus breakdown service, and as a result were to be a familiar sight throughout the LT operating area. At one time, the 'J's were used as 'anchor vehicles' for the ex-LS and Matador tenders when they had to winch upright overturned buses, and had a special bracket at the rear provided for this. Initially, the vehicles retained petrol engines, but diesel replacements were later provided. Three J-class tenders were transferred to railway duties in later years, detailed earlier.
LT Museum

In May 1936, ST 61 has overturned after a collision with a lorry in Leatherhead. It is seen being prepared for lifting.

As mentioned earlier, Chalmers converted seven STL buses into breakdown vehicles between 1948 and 1950 to work in conjunction with the 'P' class Matadors. Originally, all were for road service use, and the details are as follows (with the initial allocation shown in brackets):

737J (ex-STL 197)   (Cricklewood 9/49)
738J (ex-STL 169)   (Dalston 1/50)
739J (ex-STL 175)   (Camberwell 2/50)
828J (ex-STL 43)   (Reigate 7/50)
830J (ex-STL 390)   (Riverside 3/50)
832J (ex-STL 162)   (Merton 7/50)
833J (ex-STL 159)   (Chiswick Works 9/50)

Their official designation was as a 7-ton 'Auxiliary Breakdown Tender', and the rebuilding provided a square body with a nearside sliding door and hinged rear doors. The bus-style half-cab was retained and the crew rode in accommodation provided just aft of the front bulkhead.

Livery was all-over red with a black coach-line, and an illuminated glass panel above the cab carried the words 'BREAKDOWN TENDER' in a similar arrangement to the 'P' class Matadors.

During the 1950s and 1960s, the weight of the average bus progressively increased again as new widths and lengths were legalised. In order to improve on the 5-ton capacity of the Matadors, a pair of huge ex-Ministry of Defence 1964-built 6-wheeled AEC Militants were obtained in October 1966 and numbered as 1456MR and 1457MR. These were described as 'Master Breakdown Tenders' and were fitted with 10-ton cranes, towing equipment and hydraulic outriggers/stabilisers that could be deployed outwards and downwards during lifting operations. The revised design of 'Urgent' panel was installed (as used on the railway LDs), atop which sat a single orange warning light. Both operated on trade plates throughout their time with LT (1456MR – 559 LB,

1457MR – 587 LB), but had previously been registered in the Army series as 36-BM-73 and 36-BM-12. As well as the application of black mudguards, extensive use was made of diagonal black and yellow hazard markings on the front, sides and hook of the vehicles. Allocation was to Camberwell (1456MR) and Cricklewood garages (1457MR), the respective head offices of the South and West Divisions. Despite their impressive and rugged looks, the MRs were found to be sluggish performers, far too big for use in London, and thus not ideally suited to the demands of their new job. The end came in May 1981 and April 1983 respectively, but both continue to exist in private ownership. No. 1456MR later earned its keep with Brooklands-based recovery firm National Rescue, whilst its sister vehicle 1457MR entered the ownership of Essex bus operator Blue Triangle.

A new and ultimately final development in bus recovery commenced in April 1982, when the Leyland Freighter was adopted as LT's standard road service breakdown tender. The Freighter was part of Leyland's 'T45' range introduced in 1980, and LT later used examples with platform or dropside bodies. First in stock was 2372L, with a second example arriving in February 1983 as 2391L. Another four were delivered in October 1984 as 2415L to 2418L, and together, all six allowed the remaining Matadors, Militants, Regents and LDs to be progressively retired. The Freighters were of the '16.13' and '16.18' 16-ton chassis variant, and some had detail differences in body layout and crane/lifting apparatus.

The procedure of hauling defective buses using a rigid towing bar or chain required a second member of staff sitting in the bus cab to brake (if possible) and steer. With the introduction of buses with front entrances and set-back front axles, the safest method, and that least likely to cause additional damage, was the modern 'spectacle lift', which elevated the front (or rear) axle. At least one of the Freighters, 2415L, was fitted with this equipment instead of the usual crane. It consisted of two hollow adjustable metal rectangles carried on a transverse bar, which itself was affixed to a hydraulic ram projecting rearwards from the lorry's body. Straps on the 'rectangles' could be tightened around the wheels of a bus, the main bar then raised, thus lifting the vehicle into a position for towing. By raising the wheels of buses off the ground, the 'second man' could be dispensed with. (It is unlikely that any reduction of tender personnel actually occurred, but the 'raised lift' form of recovery was now deemed a safer method to use.)

The Freighters carried a unique livery, combining the usual Bus Red plus a white-painted front roof dome. The normal illuminated headboard option available on such commercial vehicles was exercised, and used to carry the 'LONDON BUSES' title in black upper case New Johnston on white. The use of this name as far back as April 1982 is interesting, since the LRT subsidiary London Buses Limited was not formed until 1st April 1985 (though the name 'London Buses' had been utilised for publicity purposes since at least 1979). Standard bus-size plain white roundels were initially applied to cab doors, but the vehicles became increasingly customised with District/Unit symbols and names in later years. Though registered from new, they originally operated on trade plates; but revised legislation led to them being licensed normally in 1988 using their original marks. In order to achieve London-wide coverage, the trucks were distributed between the operating districts. In May 1987, the allocation was as follows: 2372L (Cricklewood), 2391L (Camberwell), 2415L (Merton), 2416L (Wood Green), 2417L (Victoria) and 2418L (Upton Park).

Once LBL had been privatised in the period 1994–95, there was no longer a need for such types to remain in the service vehicle fleet. Vehicle 2417L passed to bus operator BTS in April 1991, whilst 2418L departed for an unknown destination in August 1992. London General and Cowie Leaside both bought the Freighters then in use at their

garages (2415L and 2416L). No. 2372L was returned to the parent Distribution Services' fleet at Acton Works and gained the new 1990 white & blue LUL colour scheme, whilst another Freighter found a use by specialist Essex recovery firm T&J Motors. All had left LT stock by 1992, though the pair sold to the former LBL units could still be seen around the capital even into the 21st Century.

Also worthy of note is 2473F, a Ford Transit dropside lorry with crane for London United. Delivered in November 1989, it was the last red-painted vehicle added to the 'owned' fleet, thus ending a tradition dating back to 1933. Carrying dedicated 'London United – Hounslow Bus Engineering' lettering and logos, it was allocated to 'AV' garage and transferred to that company upon its privatisation in November 1994.

TOWING LORRIES

Although the various generations of breakdown tenders were among the most impressive and important-looking types in the service vehicle fleet, plain and simple towing lorries attended the vast majority of defective buses. Unless a vehicle had turned over, was disabled in some

Top: Based at Wandle District's Merton Garage, Leyland Freighter 2415L passed to London General upon the creation of the bus units in 1989 and was retained by them upon privatisation. Over the years, the vehicle has undergone a number of changes in appearance. In this 1992 view, it carries a mix of LBL and LG insignia. The single orange roof light has been replaced by a pair; and the illuminated headboard, which once read 'LONDON BUSES', is now left blank.
Colin Lloyd

Above: Freighter 2372L was later returned to Acton Works, where it spent some time supporting the main CDS fleet. It was the only heavy breakdown vehicle to appear in the new LUL white/blue livery.
Colin Lloyd

awkward/inaccessible place, or had undergone serious damage, the usual course of action was to haul it back to its home garage for repair. At the very least, a towing lorry was just that – a vehicle equipped with a towing bracket and possibly air, vacuum or electrical connections, but some had the addition of crew/workshop areas or canvas tilts. Other facilities common to all were toolboxes, lifting jacks and spare wheels, and the humble towing lorry was the standard response to minor problems like punctured tyres. Unless otherwise indicated, all were in green livery until the change to grey took place.

As mentioned earlier, the first recorded towing lorries were based on the AEC B-type chassis, and later the AEC '506' chassis was used for some of the LPTB's first such types. Nos. 45Z to 54Z and 57Z were described as 'breakdown and towing lorries' and dated from mid-1928. The '506' model was a direct descendant of the First World War 'YC'-type, but built to a lighter specification and still solid-tyred. Some of the batch were classed with the prefix 'EN', and all initially ran on trade plates. 52Z was registered as FXT 328 in October 1939 when transferred on loan to the Tramways Department at Leyton, but reverted to trade plate 007 GH in May 1940 upon its return. All were withdrawn by August 1940, with most passing to the ARP, though some sources suggest they officially remained on the books until 1945.

A haulage function of a quite different kind involved 338H. The former NS 1200 was converted to an unregistered 'towing chassis' in 1936 and used within Chiswick Works as part of the overhaul process. In June 1949 it was scrapped, and replaced by the chassis and cab of ST 314. In this instance however, the new vehicle retained its identity in the ST-class numbering series. Vehicles were also towed within the works using tractors (q.v.).

The introduction of new vehicles to the Green Line services allowed the withdrawal of many early ex-T-class AEC Regal single-deckers and some were converted to service vehicle use between 1939 and 1940. Of these, 399W, 400W and 401W (ex-T 210, T 246 and T 303), 404W and 405W (ex-T 221 and T 241) and 444W (ex-T 164) were assigned for use as 6½-ton towing & stores lorries. The first modifications were in June 1939; the last taking place in August 1940, and they were bodied by Glover, Webb & Liversidge of 561 Old Kent Road, London SE1. Of the six, 399W was destroyed by an air raid in September 1940, but the rest continued in use until the early-1960s (after conversion to diesel engines in 1954), 401W surviving as late as June 1964. These vehicles could be used for delivery work by CDS when not required for towing duties, but one of the less endearing features of the 'W's was that when working hard, the engine and cab got extremely hot. 'Hot enough to fry an egg on the manifold' being the accepted term at the time.

A single AEC Matador diesel-engined haulage model dating from 1933, 457P, was acquired late in 1940 as a 6-ton towing lorry for Charlton Works. Supplied by Mason Kells Motor Repair Works, Brixton, SW2; it looked every bit the typical early-AEC lorry and had started life with haulage contractor C. W. Burch & Sons of Walberton, Sussex. Livery was at first red, the more usual green being applied in September 1947, and it went out of stock in May 1955. Also non-standard among this kind of vehicle was 659B, a Bedford 'OLBD' petrol-engined 5-tonner which commenced use in September 1946. Whilst many other Bedfords were delivered at the time, this dropside was one of only three used for recovery work.

Post-war, the policy of transferring redundant buses to the ancillary fleet continued, with the ST and STL classes now forming donor chassis. STs 6, 523 and 44 had been in use as towing buses using their own stock numbers from 1947, but entered the service fleet in the early months of 1949 after rebuilds as 5½-ton towing lorries. As 719J, 720J and 721J, the trio have been described as the most aesthetically-pleasing bus-to-lorry conversions. The half-cab arrangement was retained, as was the 'rounded' driver's cab. The first two lower-deck bays were also kept and formed a glazed storage/crew area, behind which the side panels curved down gracefully from the roofline to meet the waist-rail. The design echoed the 'Chariot' body style of breakdown truck that was quite common at the time. Although clearly having been reconstructed with some thought, this did not save them from withdrawal in 1955, just seven years later. By this time, the average bus was far more reliable, and these towing lorries were amongst the oldest in the service vehicle fleet. Fleet numbers 743J and 744J were ex-STL former rail carriers displaced by the tramway replacement programme, and are dealt with in the next chapter.

Four STL-class double-deckers reconstructed for towing in the 1950s were 811J (ex-STL 377 in 1950), 1009J (ex-STL 2679 in 1955) and 1016J and 1017J (ex-STLs 2677/2669 – also in 1955). Of the quartet, 811J, 1016J and 1017J had half-tilts, whilst the non-tilt fitted 1009J was uniquely described as a trolleybus towing lorry, replacing 457P in these duties. The distinction was necessary because any trolleybuses requiring overhaul at Charlton works were towed there, whereas those going to Fulwell or West Ham for overhaul could be driven to these depots using the overhead power supplies. The four remained in use until replaced by new deliveries in 1964–65.

AEC Matador 457P started life in 1933 with a Sussex haulier and was bought second-hand in 1940 to serve as towing lorry and general stores vehicle at Charlton Works. This was a very typical AEC lorry of the mid-1930s with its high radiator and heavy-looking cab. This scene is at Wandsworth Depot, to which 457P has just towed D2-class trolleybus 442. Trolleybuses requiring overhaul at Fulwell or West Ham could be driven to site 'under the wires', but those attending Charlton were hauled there by lorry. Arthur Ingram

STL 2679 was rebuilt as towing lorry 1009J in 1955 to replace 457P at Charlton Works. Its typical LT 'goods cab' gave the vehicle a far more modern and standardised appearance than the second-hand 457P. Following the closure of Charlton Works in 1959, it was easily absorbed into the main CDS fleet and continued on general freight duties until withdrawal in April 1965. LT Museum

Bedford 826B was an 'OLBD' model classed as a 5-ton towing lorry from September 1949, but fated to have a far more interesting career with CDS. In September 1953, its body was replaced by the 600-gallon distilled water tank from 1938-built Albion 'KN127' 376A. In this new form it outlasted all other 'O' series until withdrawn in April 1967. Whether as a very belated replacement or not, sister-Bedford 'OLBD' 5-ton open lorry 827B of 1949 was converted to towing use in December 1959, and remained in service until July 1963.

LT's Department of the Chief Mechanical Engineer (Buses) was for many years organised into three divisions, referred to as 'A' (based at Camberwell Garage), 'B' (based at Manor House offices) and 'C' (based at Dollis Hill offices). Engineering Control was based in Chiswick Works between 08.30 – 16.30; outside these hours it transferred to Riverside Garage. Garages were classed as either 'parent' or 'sub' sheds. Each 'parent' would have three or four 'sub-sheds' under its control. The 'parent' shed had a running shift, which included a towing lorry for use on breakdowns within its area. Each parent shed would also operate a stores lorry that did a daily round of the other garages, collecting and delivering parts.

The parent shed was also responsible for major maintenance of the buses, and only these garages had the necessary equipment and stock for this work. However, this system was subject to all kinds of change over time. For one thing, the sheer-reliability of the RT and RM classes made the regular maintenance much more straightforward than had previously been the case. Towards the end of the LBL-era, each garage became fully responsible for all its maintenance work, including preparation for annual 'FFD' (Freedom From Defect) inspection.

The procedure to be adopted in case of breakdown varied between the Central and Country Areas: Rule 30 of the Central Buses' Rule Book stipulated that 'the Driver or Conductor must as quickly as possible communicate with their parent Depot if the defect is serious, but with their home Depot (or sub shed) in all other cases'. Country Buses staff gave separate instructions dependent on what type of vehicle was involved. For coaches it

was stated that 'In the Metropolitan Police Area Green Line Control must be notified. Control will then obtain assistance from the nearest Central Bus garage. Between 23.45 and 06.30 hours (weekdays) or 07.30 hours (Sundays), when Green Line Control is closed, staff must telephone Engineering Control. When necessary in foggy weather Green Line Control remains open throughout the day and night. Outside the Metropolitan Police Area the nearest Country Bus garage must be notified'. The green buses had a far simpler arrangement, whereby 'The nearest Country Bus or Central Bus garage must be notified'. These extracts show how the red and green bus departments assisted each other in emergencies.

With tram and trolleybus crews having access to the LT internal telephone system, staff were advised that 'Telephones are provided for emergency purposes on all routes . . . placed in boxes attached either to the feeder pillars or to the overhead equipment standards.' To unlock the boxes a key was provided on vehicles in either a toolbox or locker. Breakdown reports had to commence with the words 'Control – breakdown', followed by the caller's name, grade and number; the nature of the fault, location; and whether it was on the 'up' or 'down' track. The Control Telephone Rooms, situated at either Hackney Depot (Northern Division) or Oval Station (Southern Division) answered the calls.

As in so many other spheres of traditional service vehicle operation, the 1960s commenced with radical changes, as brand new Ford Thames Traders began to sweep away the old order. Open 5-ton stores lorries 1134F and 1135F were the earliest to appear, but the type started to arrive in towing form from 1962. Nos. 1238F, 1239 and 1240F were 7-ton open lorries and the first to carry the new Cargo Grey livery. Earlier types had made use of small reversible 'towing' plates, but the opportunity was now taken to fit warning boards to cab roofs reading 'L.T. recovery vehicle' in white lettering on red. Two more batches of towing Traders were purchased in the following years, these being 1308F and 1309F (12/63) and 1326F to 1329F (1–2/65). No attempt was now made to provide stores or workshop accommodation and the vehicles outwardly resembled standard dropsides (which they were derived from). One clue however was the 'V' cut into the rear tailboards, which allowed the driver to reverse up to the defective vehicle with the tailboard lowered and tow with the board dropped.

The Traders had vanquished the previous generations of converted ex-buses, but were themselves due for replacement by the mid-1970s. The reliable Ford 'D'-series had been in LT use since 1966, and was the obvious choice for the new vehicles. Between 1976 and 1977, two batches of the 'D1110' variant were introduced and numbered 1930F to 1934F, 1987F and 1991F. The first five were 5-ton towing lorries, the remainder 6¼-ton, and types had a short wheelbase and fixed sides. New legislation on towing placed a restriction on the overall length of the lorry and bus under tow, and the short wheelbase vehicles were introduced to keep within the law. They also had railway sleepers fitted in the body to increase the unladen weight and provide ballast when towing. The warning sign gave way to a shallow headboard on both the front and rear of the cab that displayed the white-on-red legend: 'L.T. recovery vehicle'. Flashing orange lights had been fitted to the Traders, and these were adopted as standard for the new lorries. A slot-in plate below the windscreen could be reversed to show the word 'towing'. Like the Traders, the 'D1110's operated on trade plates,

and towards the end of their lives were 'customised' by garage engineering staff using bus transfers and stickers. It can be seen that there were not nearly enough lorries in existence at any one time to equip every garage, so vehicles were spread around the fleet to provide maximum coverage. In the 1980s, the locations were as follows: Camberwell, Catford, Cricklewood, Gillingham Street (Victoria), Hanwell, Leyton, Merton, Riverside (Hammersmith), Tottenham and Upton Park.

Just one more towing lorry was to form part of the Distribution Services fleet. General Motors had introduced the tilt-cab Bedford 'TL' range in 1980, and seventeen varying versions of this were to enter service with LT in 1980 and 1981. The only one fitted for towing was a 16-ton 'TL1630' numbered 2265B from August 1980. Whether regarded as additional capacity, or the prototype of a new generation, no further examples of the type were to follow for towing use.

Although not provided for LBL, it is worth recording the existence of the two Freight Rover Sherpa '350SL' towing vans 2422L and 2423L. They were used by Distribution Services to assist any car or van-sized vehicle that had broken down. Delivered in 1985, they carried standard grey livery. 2423L went in September 1988, but the other gained white/blue, together with a roof-mounted combined 'London Transport Distribution Services' illuminated sign and orange 'beacon bar'. More recently, in 1999, Mercedes-Benz '408D' 2480M was given a beavertail car-transporter body and the customary orange roof light. A tow-bar has also been fitted, and an unpainted trailer numbered T 41 is available to double the truck's recovery capacity.

BUS CONTROL AND INFORMATION VEHICLES

Whilst not exactly an 'emergency' vehicle, London Transport Buses introduced its own control/information vehicle in August 1996. 4687F is a Ford Transit '190' with high-top bodywork and a nearside sliding window reminiscent of those used on ice cream vans. LTB white livery is carried, but with the addition of removable slip-boards above the side windows. These are able to display the words 'Bus information' or 'Mobile Control Centre' in black New Johnston, plus red/white LTB roundel logos. Between special events, the van is normally kept 'on charge' in Aldgate Bus Station, but regularly attends the West End in the early-hours to dispense night bus information. To this effect, its interior is fitted with a large rack for holding timetables, leaflets and maps. A second example was introduced in 2000. Transit '350' 5040F is similarly equipped to 4687F, but differs in carrying the new red LTB/LBSL livery.

Top: Revised legislation limited the combined length of a lorry and bus under tow, and the 'D'-series had a special short wheelbase to comply with this. One innovation was a very basic form of crane used to lift heavy items onto the flatbed, and this can be seen on the offside rear of 1991F. The slot-in rectangular plate below the windscreen was reversible. Towing lorries tended to be 'adopted' by their individual garages and the final 'D'-series generation were progressively customised with LBL, District and Unit logos towards the end of their lives. Jim Wright

Centre: As in the days of Morden Station Garage, smaller vehicles too can sometimes need rescuing. Freight Rover Sherpa 2422L was one of two employed by Distribution Services to assist their broken-down cars and vans. Delivered in standard grey livery, it was later repainted in the white/blue scheme. The operator is shown as 'London Transport Distribution Services', a title dropped after the department's 1989 transfer to LUL. Colin Lloyd

Right: London Buses' second and current mobile control unit and information unit is this high-top Ford Transit '350' numbered 5040F. Like its predecessor, the vehicle attends major events in the capital liable to disrupt the running of bus services, and is kept in Aldgate bus station when not required. The most obvious and welcome change in appearance from the previous Transit assigned to this role is the reintroduction of red livery. David Rowe

TRAMWAY SERVICE VEHICLES

Most service vehicles used by the Tram & Trolleybus Department formed part of Distribution Services' Group 1, since T&T had many requirements for specialised types. The tram system in particular had long needed a support fleet, part of the reason being the 1870 Tramways Act, which required tram operators to maintain the roadway for 18 inches each side of the tracks. This legislation dated from the horse tram era, but was never rescinded after equestrian power gave way to electricity.

With the earliest trams being horse-drawn and relatively light, dealing with a derailment was just a question of finding additional horsepower to put the car back on the track. However, once the covered top, double-deck, electric tram had established itself, there was a need for something more substantial to render assistance.

The local haulier with his traction engine could be called upon to help in certain cases, but operators really needed their own vehicles.

The LCC Tramways' annual accounts give an insight into the arrangements made in the early years. As an example, in 1911, the following miscellaneous road vehicles were in stock:

Mechanised

Cars (petrol)	…	…	…	…	8
Lorries (petrol)	…	…	…	…	11
Lorries (steam)	…	…	…	…	5

Horse-drawn

Brakes, broughams, traps		…	…	20
Cable-drum carriers		…	…	…	2
Carts	…	…	…	…	…	109
Floats	…	…	…	…	…	3
Lorries	…	…	…	…	…	17
Snow-sweepers		…	…	…	…	11
Tower wagons		…	…	…	…	4
Vans	…	…	…	…	…	90

At least some of these early vehicles originated from the London Tramways Company, when it was acquired by LCC Tramways in 1889. Meanwhile, the smaller council-owned tramways could often make use of the normal council maintenance fleet, obviating the need to operate a dedicated support fleet.

The LCCT operated a number of load-carrying steam wagons designed to carry rails, traction poles and other heavy items. This specimen is a Foden 'Overtype' rail carrier dating from 1914 and was numbered 32PW in the Council's series. These steam wagons retained their LCC numbers following the LPTB takeover, though lost the 'PW' suffix. Despite being a former LCCT vehicle, it was later based at the ex-MET depot at Finchley. Most of the Fodens were withdrawn in the early years of LPTB ownership. Julian Bowden-Green collection

In 1920, the LCCT turned to the firm Clayton & Shuttleworth for six new steam wagons, four of which eventually came under the control of the LPTB. Clayton rail carrier No.39 was based at Deptford Wharf and carried the type of manual crane used on the majority of LT's rail and pole carriers. In this instance, the vehicle displays the letters 'PW' as a prefix; and it appears that over time, the practice varied. To the right, another steam wagon lies sheeted-over and apparently out-of-use. LT Museum

RAIL CARRIERS

The rail carrier effectively preceded the similar-looking pole carrier, in being a vehicle equipped to carry long rails and poles for tramway engineering work. Most of the LPTB's examples were inherited from the LCCT, but others came from the former Underground Group companies, or were post-1933 converted buses. Rail carriers were operated by the Permanent Way Engineer (Trams), who himself came under the Chief Engineer (Trams & Trolleybuses).

Among the elderly service vehicles that joined the LT fleet in 1933, few were more so than the steam-powered Foden 'Overtype' 5-ton capacity rail carriers. These had been new to the LCCT in 1907, and were essentially long-wheelbase, load-carrying traction engines. Heavy metal bolsters supported the poles or rails, whilst basic mechanical cranes were provided to assist with loading. The LCCT operated at least twelve Foden steam wagons (10 to 14 and 30PW to 36PW), the last of which entered service in 1920. Number 11 from 1921 was nominally renumbered as 157D in 1939, though the new number is not thought to have been carried, and in any case, the

various types of support vehicle, and the Albion 'LP' model forward-control six-tonner was the favoured vehicle for use as rail carriers. These also made use of a crane mounted behind the cab to lift rails, could tow trailers, and were divided between Deptford and Poplar permanent way wharves. The crane was mechanically-driven from the gearbox power-take-off, controlled by the driver and fitted with a wire rope rather than chains. Fleet numbers 137A to 139A were 'LP37' variants with an 'EN65A' engine, whilst 140A to 145A were 'LP35's with the smaller 'EN51' engine, and all entered stock between 1931 and 1935 (140A and 141A being the two pre-LT examples).

As with many service vehicles of the time, they had previously been identified in the LCCT numbering series, in this case 55 to 59 and 38 to 41 and then by the LPTB as AN 8 to AN16. The substantial build of this type of Albion was such that some were fitted with stout steel bumpers to push disabled trams. The first of the Albions left the fleet in 1951, the remainder departing over the period 1952–53 once the tram system had closed and LT had lifted such track as it wished to.

Left: This Albion 'LP37' was one of the last vehicles delivered to the LCCT, and entered service as No. 55 just one month before the demise of the organisation in 1933. The crane was worked by a winch cable rather than the chain of the earlier steamers, and like the rest of the Albion rail carriers, it lasted right up until the end of London's trams. The 'trumpet' bulb horn mounted below the driver's windscreen is an archaic touch, whilst the massive front bumper was provided to help it push disabled trams. LT Museum

Below: Four AEC Mercury pole carriers were introduced in 1958 to assist with the removal of trolleybus overhead as the conversion to diesel power gathered pace. Initially, the cabs featured large areas of brightwork, but much of this eventually succumbed to successive layers of green paint. The vehicles were retained for other duties after the last trolleybus ran in May 1962. This one, 1080Q, was not withdrawn until 1967, whilst one of the batch survived until June 1976. The crane is of the traditional manual type and appears almost identical to those fitted to the LCCT Claytons in 1920. Kim Rennie collection

vehicle was withdrawn 1944. Other ex-LCCT Fodens sold or scrapped in the early LPTB-era were 12, 14, 30PW and 32PW to 36PW; the rest having departed prior to July 1933. Published sources state that after the 'official' withdrawal date, some of the Fodens were used to transport trolleybus poles, this being deemed cheaper than hiring alternative vehicles. Under LT, the vehicles had been allocated to either the Electrical or Permanent Way departments. In late-1920, the LCCT ordered six Clayton & Shuttleworth 5-ton steam wagons which were delivered in October and November of that year (37PW to 42PW). The last four of these were acquired by the LPTB upon its creation, but all were scrapped without renumbering in 1937. A small number of other Foden steam wagons were taken over from the LUT and MET concerns. None lasted beyond the late-1930s, nor was it felt necessary to incorporate any of them within a common numbering series. Subsequent development of steam wagons was hit by punitive taxation, and in 1931 Foden belatedly turned to the production of conventionally-engined lorries.

Both the LCCT and the Underground Group purchased fleets of Albions in the early-1930s as a base for

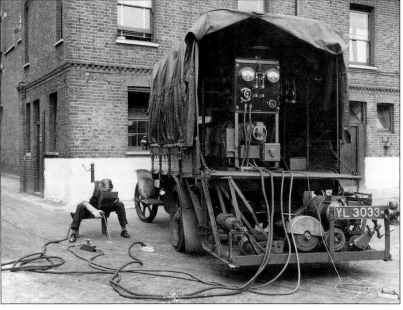

Top: As well as repairs to the track itself, the LCCT, like other tramway operators, was also responsible for the maintenance of the road surface within 18 inches each side. This solid-tyred Karrier 3-ton lorry was engaged on such work and regularly paired with a small 2-wheeled trailer to increase its carrying-capacity. LT Museum

Above: Repairs to the tramway network were always necessary and the LCCT employed a small fleet of welding lorries for this task. This early Karrier 3-ton tilt lorry was fitted with a welding generator powered from the tramway supply and a rail-grinding machine was transported on the low tailboard. LT Museum

Once the decision had been made to convert tram routes to trolleybus, and then later to abandon electric road traction altogether, the need for this type of vehicle naturally declined. However, a final pair of rail carriers was converted from STL-class buses in the immediate post-war period and possibly to assist with the dismantling of the system. Former STLs 297 and 192 were rebuilt and entered stock as 743J and 744J in December 1949 and January 1950. Rather than dispose of them when the trams had finished just two years later, they were given diesel engines and in 1954 converted yet again, this time to towing lorries. As such, they continued to serve LT until 1965 and 1963 when, like so much of the support fleet, new Thames Traders replaced them.

WELDING LORRIES

Welding lorries were used by the Permanent Way Engineer (Trams) to convey staff and equipment to parts of the tram system requiring attention. Work could range from emergency repairs or routine maintenance to full-scale track relaying and even diversions. Electrical power for such activity could be obtained via the conduit or overhead wire, and the lorries boasted tarpaulin covers to protect the equipment and tools. The LPTB divided their new tram network into three areas for maintenance: South Division (containing five districts), North Division (four districts) and West Division (five districts). As the expansion of the trolleybus system began to reduce the

number of trams in use from 1935, the districts and divisions were gradually abolished or combined. By 1940, only the South Division remained, though Permanent Way out-stations were retained north of the Thames to cater for the Kingsway Subway and its routes.

The first batch was inherited from the LCCT in July 1933. Vehicles 115A to 120A were 1931 Albion Model '46' 4-ton normal-control lorries with full-tilt covers dating from August 1931. Previous numbers had been 21 to 26, then AN2 to AN7. Like all subsequent welding lorries, they were painted green. Additional vehicles arrived in July and August 1936 as 192C to 198C. These were Leyland Cub 'SKZ1' 4-ton lorries, part of a larger batch of such types acquired that year for various support roles, and originally numbered 172 to 178. Pre-war allocation was split between Rye Lane and Poplar, but Walthamstow later replaced the latter as the north of Thames location.

Also from the LCCT came 171K and 172K, Karrier Protector 2½–3-ton tilt-fitted lorries used for track repairs that had replaced earlier vehicles and trailers. The Karriers had seats for the permanent way men in the lorry, together with bins for tools and stores. At the rear of the vehicle was a folding table for meals, and behind the cab were two lockers containing eighteen hurricane lamps. Both Karriers towed new trailers built by the Harrow Industrial Company. These carried a small tar boiler and had storage space for short rails, ballast, cement, wood blocks and setts, and their main purpose was to carry out minor track repairs on the LCC tramway system. The lorries each worked with three trailers, so as to give a 24-hour coverage, and were based at Rye Lane and Poplar Wharf. They had dated from August 1932 as Nos. 27 and 28, and in LPTB days still carried LCCT red livery instead of the usually ubiquitous LT service vehicle green. After serving through the war years, they were replaced by more standardised designs in 1947.

Post-war developments saw the withdrawal of the Albions during 1947 and 1948 with replacement by versions of the Bedford OLBD model used as LT's standard large lorry in the 1940s to the mid-1950s. Nos. 660B, 662B and 664B were petrol-engined 5-ton vans delivered in 1946, and differed from previous practice by being of all-enclosed format. Nos. 666B and 667B were metal tilt-fitted and licensed to operate with trailers. A one-off in October 1949 was 813B, a further 5-ton Bedford 'O' series open lorry. With the closure of the tram system on 5th July 1952, most of these relatively-new Bedfords were retained, though transferred to more mundane duties. Bedford 660B had a more drastic change of use however, being converted from van to lorry in April 1954. Not so lucky were the earlier Cubs, which had all been withdrawn by January 1954. The ex-welding Bedfords continued in use until 1960–62, finally displaced by the large intake of Thames Traders delivered in those years.

Above: Slightly more advanced were Karrier Protectors Nos. 27 and 28 (later 171K and 172K) from 1929. They were used by the LCCT's Permanent Way Department and available 24-hours-a-day to carry out emergency repairs on the system. The vehicles normally towed a 'tar pot trailer' to allow for the resurfacing of road surfaces. This is 171K in LT service during the war, complete with white wings and headlamp masks. Both Karriers were replaced in 1947. W.J. Haynes

Left: Replacements for the earliest Karrier welding lorries were built by Albion in 1931 and comprised Nos. 21–26, a batch of six normal-control 4-tonners complete with full-tilt bodies to protect the generator. Albion No. 24 initially became AN 5 under the LPTB, before being renumbered as 118A in 1939. Note the paraffin-powered lamps set out to warn other night-time road users. The batch survived until 1947–48. LT Museum

Left: With the introduction of the Leyland Cub 'SKZ1' to the fleet in 1936, seven were equipped as welding lorries and allocated to the Tram & Trolleybus Department for track repair work. Like the rest of the batch, 197C lasted right up to the end of the trams and was not withdrawn until November 1953. A.B. Cross

Right: With many London local authorities refusing to allow 'unsightly' overhead wires in their streets, the LCCT was forced to use the more expensive conduit system to power its trams. One result of this was the small fleet of water tankers whose duty was to flush dirt and debris from the conduit channel. Two 1925 LCCT conduit cleaners were based on Yorkshire steam wagon chassis and survived long enough to enter the LT fleet in 1933. This is 159D when in a rather run-down condition, including the use of a wooden block to serve as a brake on the offside rear solid tyre. The vehicle had previously been No. 18 in the LCC series. W.J. Haynes

Above: The other ex-LCCT Yorkshire conduit-cleaner was 158D (formerly LCCT No.17). In contrast to 159D, it is seen here in pristine condition on 18th June 1934 following a repaint into LPTB livery, though retains its original fleet number. In time-honoured fashion, coal is stacked behind the cab in bags and additional equipment is stowed on the side hose racks.

Below: The LPTB converted two AEC Regal coaches into a pair of petrol-driven conduit cleaners in 1938, primarily to allow the withdrawal of two Tilling-Stevens petrol-electric flushers numbered P53 and P54. What was to become 113W in 1939 was formerly T 393, and continues to display its old identity for the LT photographer in this official view. The low-built oval tank is

noteworthy, whilst the flushing pump can be seen mounted behind the cab. No.113W operated from Rye Lane Permanent Way Depot, as did sister vehicle 112W. LT Museum

CONDUIT FLUSHERS

As some London local authorities had refused to allow overhead wires to disfigure their streets, the LCCT had to use the conduit system to transmit power to trams. The conduit lay between the running rails, and each tram was equipped with a 'plough' to collect the current. This was detachable, fitted underneath the tramcar, and could be removed or replaced at 'Plough Change Stations', where the trams changed power source from overhead wire to underground conduit – or vice-versa, and at access hatches sited at regular intervals along the track. The conduit system was designed to allow water that penetrated the slot in the road to flow into drains situated at regular intervals. Any dirt or rubbish that entered the slot was pushed by hand, using a long scraper, into one of these.

Two LCCT steam wagons used for conduit cleaning came into the LT fleet in 1933. Both were Yorkshire 7-ton models, featuring space-saving transverse boilers, water storage tanks and pressure flushing equipment. They were first numbered 17 and 18 (later 158D and 159D) and dated from May 1925. These solid-tyred, ancient-looking machines, with chain-driven rear axles must have presented a curious sight to onlookers, but lasted until 1939 and 1948 respectively.

In 1924, two Tilling-Stevens former petrol-electric buses were converted into 6-ton conduit flushers P53 and P54 operating from Rye Lane (reg.nos. XT8785/4). Under LT, these became the responsibility of the Permanent Way Engineer (Trams), but did not survive long enough to gain new numbers, being sold in 1938.

AEC Regal tankers 112W and 113W replaced P53 and P54 in 1938, and were rebuilt from redundant single-deck coaches T 319 and T 393. They were originally private hire coaches with the East Surrey Traction Company and later allocated to Brixton Hill private hire garage. The conversions featured an AEC lorry-style cab and low-profile tanks built by the Steel Barrel Company of Uxbridge. Lockers, fitted on each side of the tanks, were used to store tools. The vehicles normally operated at night and carried a crew of three. Photographs show that 113W (at least) carried a warning sign on the cab roof. Both were withdrawn in 1953.

The final conduit flusher was 742J, another former bus, and this time double-deck STL 332 provided the chassis. This conversion occurred in July 1948 and the vehicle was in stock until May 1953.

TOWER WAGONS

The various municipal and company-owned tram operators which existed in London before 1933 were home to a number of tower wagons whose purpose was to install and maintain the overhead power lines. Given the number of concerns taken over, and the often varying policies of local borough engineers, it is not surprising that the infant LPTB inherited a wide mix of designs dating from many periods. As the process of integration and consolidation progressed, the most non-standard support vehicles fell by the wayside. Many vehicles were not kept long enough to be included in the 1939 renumbering scheme, whilst some that did survive were not given new identities (e.g. a horse-drawn tower wagon that was still on the books as late as 1950).

The Metropolitan Electric Tramways company began using eight horse-drawn tower wagons in north London from 1903. A novel feature of at least some of these was a foot gong which could be rung whilst on the way to emergencies. Between 1920 and 1928, a number of redundant B-type chassis were transferred from the LGOC to the three Underground Group tramway concerns. Those recorded as being re-bodied as tower wagons were as follows:

MET   B 177, 345, 912, 941, 1058, 2501, 2584, 2678,
        4875, 4870, 4959, 5043, 5114;
LUT   B 171, 239, 808;
SMET B 302.

These B-types lasted until 1930, when ten ADC (see also later) tower wagons were delivered. Seven of these went to the MET, whilst the remaining three were for London United Tramways. Indeed the LUT fitted out the vehicles for both operators, and re-used the 1903 towers. In practice, increasing consolidation by the Underground Group meant that overhead wire maintenance was becoming increasing inter-worked.

Most of the pre-LT tram operators required some form of tower wagon from the onset of electrification, but in the LCCT's case these were not necessary until the Council started using the overhead system in 1908 (as opposed to the normal conduit). As has been seen, by 1911 the LCCT had three horse-drawn tower wagons in use. These were described as 'flat wagons', with towers constructed by Messers Watlington, and both horses and drivers were initially hired-in. By 1925, totals had increased to horse-drawn (5), battery (5) and petrol-engined (1). The battery vehicles were obtained between 1920 and 1925 and built by either Electricar/Edison (4) or Electromobile/Edison (1).

The LPTB inherited a number of ex-LCCT tower wagons converted from former buses. They were Tilling-Stevens 'TS3' or 'TS7' petrol-electric models dating from 1919–23, and had been acquired by the Council in the early-1930s. Some had 'CD'-prefixed registrations and originated as buses with the Tilling fleet in Brighton. Written sources differ, but it seems further Tilling-Stevens buses were converted to tower wagons in 1935. As this post-dates the creation of the LPTB, the vehicles concerned may have been among those acquired from the London-area operations of Thomas Tilling Ltd. The 1937 LPTB 'Register of Miscellaneous Vehicles' lists the following such tower wagons in stock:

LPTB no.	Reg. no.	Chassis-type	Built	Sold
1	XP 2390	'TS7'	1924	4/3/37
3	CD 5673	'TS3'	1921	26/6/37
4	XR 729	'TS7'	1924	9/6/37
16	XH 9257	'TS3'	1922	28/6/37
66	CD 5141	'TS3'	1921	20/9/37
116	XP 2372	'TS7'	1923	20/10/37

The common numbering system adopted from 1939, grouping similar makes of vehicle together, led to seven ADC tower wagons being given the numbers 4E to 10E.

Top: The earliest tramway tower wagons were often horse-drawn and one survivor is seen here at Putney in the late-1940s carrying LPTB lettering.

Above: Tower wagons Nos. 117–123 with the Underground Group tramway companies, becoming 4E–10E in 1939. Although built in 1930, two years' after the demise of the joint Associated Daimler Company, the radiator shell of AEC '418' 5E (ex-No. 118) carries the old name, possibly through the use of old components. This vehicle was originally solid-tyred, but gained pneumatics under LPTB control in September 1940. A.B. Cross

Left: Some of the 6-ton AEC '418' tower wagons carried radiators correctly lettered 'Associated Equipment'. No.10E (ex-No. 123) was seen before July 1940, since it is still on solid tyres. D.W.K. Jones

53

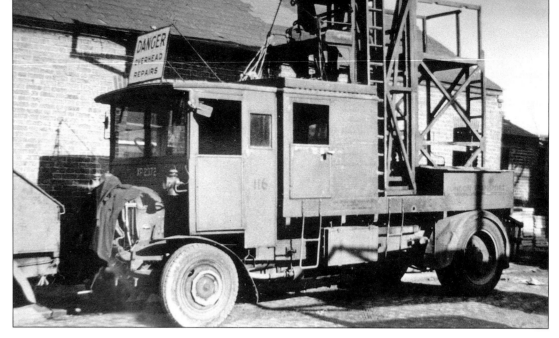

A small number of LPTB tower wagons were derived from Tilling-Stevens petrol-electric buses. The earliest conversions were from solid-tyred, normal-control Tilling-Stevens, but the later batch were semi-forward-control and fitted with pneumatic tyres. The high straight chassis-frame was a disadvantage, requiring a substantial climb to reach the covered workshop area behind the cab. They were among the Board's more unusual support vehicles, although not lasting long. No.116, which was sold in 1937, looked out-of-use when this photo was taken.

Few service vehicles entered the LPTB fleet from municipal operators, but one that did was this Halley tower wagon registered JD 160, which was with West Ham Corporation Tramways as No.103. Retaining its full West Ham livery, complete with gold lining and county borough's coat-of-arms, only the initials 'L.P.T.B.' reveal its new ownership. The red-on-white 'Danger – Overhead Repairs' sign was not unique to LT, but appeared on tower wagons throughout the UK. *Arthur Ingram*

These were ex-LUT or MET solid-tyred 6-ton '418' models from 1930 and previously 117 to 123. The use of the designation 'ADC' is interesting, since the amalgamation of AEC and Daimler only lasted between 1926 and 1928. But this batch of vehicles had been built in 1930, two years after the dissolution of the association. The '418' model was essentially an AEC design, and the vehicles almost certainly had AEC engines. Some radiators definitely had 'Associated Daimler' inscribed on them, but others bore the words 'Associated Equipment' in the same style. The vehicles may have been old stock, built from remaining components or possibly just used older radiators. Certainly, the LPTB record cards described these vehicles as ADCs. All were later modified for towing, and converted from solid to pneumatic tyres in 1940. A curiosity amongst this batch was 6E. The tower and bodywork of this vehicle were new to the LUT in 1924, but its original chassis was replaced by an ADC '418' design in 1930. It ran on solid tyres until fitted with pneumatics in 1940, and as with the other ADC tower wagons, remained in use until 1949.

Amongst the few local council lorries (excluding the LCC) kept by the LPTB were 336V (old No. 105), a 3-ton Vulcan new to Ilford Corporation Tramways in 1931, West Ham Corporation supplied Halley tower wagons numbered 103 (JD 160) and 104 (LM 6516), also JD 394, a tower wagon built by Hallford (i.e. J. E. Hall, Dartford). This company renewed its acquaintance with LT in 1955, when it supplied an escalator to Alperton Station.

Further tower wagons were converted by the LPTB from former NS-class buses in 1936. Vehicles 21H to 28H (ex-Nos. 187 to 194, formerly NS 1839, 853, 1961, 43, 13, 990, 1959 and 1240) had originated as open-top buses, and were fitted with a very basic half-cab when reconstructed for service use. They were more advanced than vehicles 4E to 10E, having the benefit of pneumatic tyres from the start. However, the unfortunate crew had to sit on a rear-facing, uncovered, 'garden seat' mounted above a toolbox that straddled the chassis behind the cab. Somewhat later, a removable canvas tilt was provided for the crews to give some protection from the elements. Both batches lasted until the years 1946–50.

Two further groups of tower wagons joined the fleet in 1935. The older (but higher-numbered) vehicles were 212L to 218L, rebuilt 6-ton Leyland 'LB5's which had previously been buses with independent operators City and Birch Brothers. Although only around ten years old, they would not have fitted well into the predominantly standardised LPTB bus fleet. The bonneted 'LB' had been popular with independent operators, but suffered at the hands of the LPTB from the 'not invented here' syndrome, the implication being that non-AEC vehicles were unwelcome in London. No doubt there was also some wry satisfaction within the ex-LGOC managers in the LPTB, as the pride of the so-called 'pirates' was demoted to mere support duties. In their brief career as buses with the Board, they had been (in order) L 58, 59, 63, 60, 62, 55, 54 and were to see eleven years service in their new form.

The second and third batches were purpose-built vehicles appearing in 1935 and 1937, this time based on new AEC Mercury 4-ton forward-control goods chassis. Delivered as 150 to 157 (1935) and 195 to 202 (1937), they became 75Q to 90Q in 1939. These vehicles had a cab based on the standard AEC design of the time, but enlarged to include spacious internal accommodation, and originally had the refinement of cream or off-white roofs. They were to become a familiar sight and lasted right through to the end of the trolleybus era. In many cases, they were responsible for dismantling the same overhead equipment they had so painstakingly installed a quarter of a century earlier. The wagons were fitted with power hoists to allow the towers to be raised from 15ft to 25ft. They all had a crew compartment and workshop area and a bell system operated between the tower platform and the driver's cab. A readily understood signal system would instruct the driver to raise or lower the tower or to move the vehicle. Eagle of Warwick built the towers and associated equipment and probably constructed the cabs as well. Withdrawal of this batch began in 1960, the last going in October 1962, the final year of the London system. One vehicle, 89Q, has been rebuilt and is now preserved as part of the London's Transport Museum collection.

Though the tower wagon was originally developed to service tramways, it was also used when attending two-wire trolleybus systems (which often replaced the earlier mode of transport). For LT, such types served both forms of electric traction after 1933, and were divided between the Distribution Engineers (Trams & Trolleybuses) North and South. The LPTB was very careful to note that the tower on its wagons weighed between 18cwt and 1ton 1cwt, and that this was not to be included in the stated legal unladen weight. As the tower was considered part of the cargo or load carried, this gave a small, but worthwhile, taxation-saving per vehicle.

In 1938, with the Mercury model out of regular production, two AEC Monarchs were obtained as 4-ton tower wagons. 100N and 101N (ex-EN 26, 27) had bodies by Eagle. They were also long-lived, not retiring until 1961. A year later, in 1939, and possibly with thoughts of forthcoming conflict and the potential damage to overhead power cables, LT purchased a further four AEC 4-ton tower wagons to supplement the existing fleet. Tower wagons 412P to 415P were based on the pre-war Matador haulage model (not the wartime '4x4' Matador); and 413P and 414P were initially unusual in being painted green. They soon gained red livery however, the colour carried by all other LT tower wagons. These Matadors were equipped with 6-cylinder engines and able to haul disabled trolleybuses.

Like their Underground counterparts, the Second World War presented the tower wagon repair crews with their greatest challenge. On many occasions, they arrived at the scene of an explosion before the ARP and Heavy Rescue teams, because the interruption to the current had warned them immediately that something had

Above: Former NS-type bus chassis were used as the basis for a number of ancillary vehicles, including a batch of eight tower wagons. 28H (ex-No.194), was converted from NS 1240 in 1936. It benefited from a canvas shelter behind the cab; on other occasions the crew had to sit on the fixed rear-facing 'garden seat' without any shelter.

Below: The Leyland 'LB' model was popular with several of the independent companies taken over by the LPTB. Some of these chassis were later converted to service vehicles, including tower wagon 216L. This had begun life with 'Genial' in 1923, passing to 'City' in 1927, and became L 62 in the LPTB bus fleet in November 1934. Rebuilt as a tower wagon in 1935, it lasted until 1946. The use of the initials 'L.P.T.B.' on the support fleet did not last long, with gold underlined LT fleetnames of various sizes soon being the preferred option.

occurred. There were 24 tower wagon crews, each consisting of a driver, linesman and mate, and all working an 8-hour shift. Over 24-hours, 216 men were involved in the maintenance of the trolleybus overhead. At times, the LT crews were required to assist in rescuing casualties, such as when mid-way through one job, a second explosion demolished a nearby building. Using the searchlight on their tower, the repair party rescued survivors.

In general, it took an average of four hours to restore services over sections disrupted by bombing. Sometimes temporary supports for the wire were required, though blasts rarely brought down too many poles. Sometimes a crew found the road cratered so deeply that repairs to the overhead would be pointless. On these occasions it was necessary to implement a diversion, and plans would have to be put in hand to dig the 6-foot deep holes needed to take the poles required on the alternative route. As an example of the scale of the work undertaken, in the Northern Division, no fewer than 560 incidents were successfully attended to.

With the ending of the war, the Leyland-based tower wagons were scrapped without direct replacement. By 1948, the earliest tower wagons with AEC/ADC and NS-type chassis were operating well past their normal withdrawal date. At the time, LT was busy withdrawing numbers of AEC Regent STL-class double-deckers since their bodies were in very poor condition. However, the chassis of these were an ideal base for a new generation of tower wagon conversions. These were to employ a combination of new towers, together with some obtained second-hand from the AEC and NS chassis.

What was unusual about these rebuilds is that they retained the original-style bus half-cab, with the fitters being given a workshop area behind it. The retention of the old cab probably had more to do with the severe shortage of raw materials after the war, rather than with any shortcomings or regression within the design office. Kenex built the bodies for these new tower wagons, and judging from photographs, may well have re-used certain components from the old bus bodies, since body parts, like most items, were then in short supply. Vehicles were classed as either 5-ton or 5½-ton, and a number were licensed to tow trailers.

Full conversion details were:

722J	(ex-STL 193)	[tower from 21H]
723J	(ex-STL 184)	[tower from 22H]
724J	(ex-STL 338)	
725J	(ex-STL 186)	
726J	(ex-STL 314)	
727J	(ex-STL 329)	
728J	(ex-STL 401)	
729J	(ex-STL 190)	
730J	(ex-STL 333)	
731J	(ex-STL 294)	[tower from 9E]
732J	(ex-STL 198)	[tower from 8E]
733J	(ex-STL 9)	[tower from 10E]

The first withdrawal was 732J in March 1955, and the rest followed between 1959 and 1960.

The large 'overhead repairs' signs were, like some of the towers, transferred from batch to batch. In spite of LT's justified reputation for corporate design, no attempt was ever made to alter the signs to the Johnston style of lettering. This was one of a number of practices that continued within the trolleybus operation of LT, even after the amalgamation with Central Buses to form 'Central Road Services' on 1st October 1950. White-on-red signs were fixed to the rear of tower wagons during repair work and could read: 'keep right' or 'danger – hanging wire ahead'.

The final batch of tower wagons entered stock in the early months of 1958 and was based on the latest AEC Mercury chassis. This was a lighter-weight vehicle derived from the Monarch and Matador ranges. Instead of the old-fashioned AEC cab with an exposed radiator, these trucks boasted an internal radiator and separate chrome radiator grille and bumper. These new tower wagons, 1073Q to 1077Q, were classed as 7-ton vehicles by LT, and were also bodied by Eagle, just like the original Mercury tower wagons of 1935. They returned to the concept of using a full-fronted design with integral crew compartment/workshop. The vehicles had a high roof, with the innovation of an observation window inserted into a rounded front dome. Cab doors were hinged lorry-style, but the nearside crew-cab door slid to allow access to the workshop area.

The extension of the trolleybus system across large areas of London previously served by trams meant that additional tower wagons were required to install and maintain the new overhead equipment required. The new vehicles were mostly AEC Mercury chassis, along with a pair of AEC Monarchs. The Mercury units had a mix of two- or three-window-length workshop areas, the shorter version making access to the tower easier for the crews. Mercury 88Q (ex-No.200) was of two-bay design, and rests at the Minories some time in the post-war era. *Lens of Sutton*

Apart from the skilled job of erecting the overhead when the trolleybus system was being extended or altered as road layouts changed, the main job of the linesmen and their tower wagons was the maintenance and repair of the overhead. Regular items requiring maintenance were the 'frogs' (points), and the wooden insulators, which could become burnt or worn out. The commonest cause of wire breakage was adjacent to the 'line ears', which gripped the running wires at support spans. Upward pressure of passing trolleybuses tended to bend the wire up each end of the ear, which could lead to fracture as the wire wore down, though of course, worn wire was routinely replaced.

AEC Mercury 82Q (ex-No.157) demonstrates the alternative 3-bay body design, whereby unfettered access to the tower was sacrificed for the advantage of an enlarged workshop and crew accommodation area. Kim Rennie collection

In 1948, a number early STL-class buses were rebuilt as tower wagons, in some cases using towers transferred from the ex-NS-type vehicles. 722J had been STL 193, and the front two bays of the old bus body have been retained and converted to a workshop area, as has the driver's half-cab, probably to save on scarce new materials during this period of austerity. LT Museum

Right: The longer wheelbase of the ex-STL tower wagons is visible in this view of 722J at work in St John Street, Clerkenwell, in front of a wonderful backdrop of period shop fronts. The hand-operated tower was previously carried on 21H (ex-NS 1839). There are minor differences in lettering and numbering when compared with the official view on the previous page. Steve Smith collection

Centre: To help dismantle the world's largest trolleybus system, five new tower wagons were bought in 1958. Based on the short-wheelbase post-war AEC Mercury chassis, their bodies and towers were built by Eagle of Warwick, who had supplied the Mercury tower wagons in 1935. Most only lasted a few years with LT, except 1077Q, seen here in its original glory leaving Fulwell Depot. Julian Bowden Green collection

Bottom: No.1077Q stayed on as a high-level platform for accessing LT premises and structures. Changes included the over-painting of the chrome windscreen surrounds and the alteration of cab door lettering to read 'CDS CHISWICK'. Seen on 26th November 1969, another 10 years elapsed before withdrawal. It was the last ex-trolleybus support vehicle in stock. Jim Blake

Other call-outs involved repairing the overhead where a trolleybus driver had gone too fast through a junction, or the frog had been incorrectly set, leading to the bus going one way, the trolley booms the other. Accidental damage to the span wires was also quite common and broken trolley wires could cause a major hazard to other road users.

By the time the 1958-built Mercury tower wagons had arrived, the system was already doomed. Some of their later duties were the sad task of dismantling what had once been the world's largest trolleybus system. LT reported in May 1962 that more than 28,000 poles were in the process of removal (though some traction poles were retained for lighting use). Valuable items salvaged included a thousand miles of copper overhead wire, hundreds of tons of overhead fittings (many cast in bronze), and similar amounts of subterranean power cabling. Some of the equipment saved was transferred to the Underground, some was sold abroad, whilst the rest was scrapped. Whilst the George Cohen Group was responsible for removing most of the overhead, LT removed some of those poles situated on its own property.

Once the network had been dismantled, most vehicles were disposed of in 1962 or 1964 – one or two continued as trolleybus tower wagons for Walsall Corporation. The exception was 1077Q, which was retained by CDS to provide access to high-level lighting in garages and open air storage yards. Though ultimately residing in Chiswick Works in a semi-derelict state, it remained on the books until sale in May 1979, by which time it was the last trolleybus-orientated vehicle in the service vehicle fleet.

Another long-lasting survivor was 1076Q, sold to Reading Corporation Transport in 1964, and almost unbelievably survived as their vehicle '331' until September 1999, when passed to a demolition contractor for even further use and later into preservation in the care of the Sandtoft Trolleybus Museum. Another local authority to use one of the 1958 Mercurys was Southend-on-Sea Corporation. Former 1074Q was not however used by their public transport section, but rather the 'Pier & Foreshore Department' responsible for the seaside 'illuminations' and parts of the pier itself.

TRAMWAY BREAKDOWN TENDERS

The LCCT introduced four Arrol Johnston 3-ton 12hp petrol-engined lorries for recovery purposes between 1904 and 1905, numbering them 1 to 4. Other means of haulage was by steam lorry, of Foden and later Clayton & Shuttleworth manufacture. One Foden was regularly used to tow cars to and from overhaul.

The first batch of new breakdown tenders (as opposed to modified lorries) were six normal-control Karrier Model 'K6' vehicles ultimately numbered 173K to 178K (old Nos. 89 to 94). They had been new to LCC Tramways between 1929 and 1930 and were of 6–6½-ton capacity. Originally supplied with solid tyres, the vehicles were based on the 'K6' tractor chassis, which featured a deep section frame, a rear drawbar and a massive fender at the front to push disabled trams. A starting handle could pass through the fender, and if the engine should stall, the truck was fitted with a self-starter for immediate re-starting. They were quite versatile and well-stocked for their role, with a 5-ton hand-operated crane fitted to the rear for lifting trams. The tools and equipment carried weighed about 3½ tons, and included oxygen/acetylene cylinders and a special trolley for use in case of a tramcar with a broken axle. The total weight of the tenders was 10 tons and accommodation was provided for a crew of four. The tenders could push a tramcar up a 1-in-20 slope, and the bodies were built by Ramsdens of Liversedge in the West Riding of Yorkshire. A similar vehicle was supplied to the LMS-Northern Counties Committee in Northern Ireland for breakdown purposes.

In a Press Release of 1929, these vehicles were described as 'First Aid Tenders specially designed and equipped to deal speedily with derelicts and other obstructions'. In retrospect, it appears their main role was to attend trams with damaged or broken plough carriers. The ploughs would get stuck or damaged within the conduit, rendering the car immobile. The breakdown truck would be summoned to push the disabled tram to the nearest plough access point to enable repairs to take place or the plough to be removed. The tenders were later fitted with pneumatic tyres and they always ran on trade plates.

The final Karrier 'K6' was 179K from 1934 (originally No. 111). This was similar in appearance to the others in having the usual fender, tool lockers, crane jib and hook; but also had a telescopic tower which sat over the rear part of the cab/crew compartment. It is tempting to speculate as to whether this truly multi-functional vehicle represented the LCCT vision of the future, and was a prototype designed and ordered before the creation of the LPTB. Certainly, Karrier was a regular supplier of vehicles to the LCCT, whereas LT never purchased a vehicle from this source until 1964, by which time the Karrier vehicles were of a distinctly Rootes Group design and specification. Unlike the other Karriers, 179K was fitted with pneumatic tyres from new, and it spent its entire career at West Ham Depot.

All seven Karriers had a very distinctive appearance, which combined a square radiator and bonnet with

The Tram & Trolleybus Department used its own fleet of works cars to move supplies and equipment around. The run-down of the tram system caused these to be progressively withdrawn and more and more of their duties were transferred to the CDS van and lorry fleet. This is works car 011, an ex-LCCT 'L'-type converted to carry wheels. D.A. Thompson

heavily-valanced front cab windows, above which were painted the words 'BREAKDOWN TENDER' in black (later white). They carried a metal red warning pennant to the fore on occasions and operated on trade plates. Sidelights were originally primitive-looking, acetylene or oil lamps, harking back to an earlier era of Hansom cabs, though the headlamps were electric. This was not unusual at the time, since the main lights were powered by a dynamo whilst the engine was running. However, when the vehicle was stationary and working on site with the engine turned off, the battery could not be relied upon to keep sidelights alight, hence the use of an alternative power source.

The Underground Group tram companies used products from within their own orbit. These included five 1930-vintage AEC/ADC '418' model 2½-ton breakdown lorries and a further '418' used for tramway electrical work (later LPTB numbers 7, 9, 70, 81 and 82. The vehicles ran on trade plates and all were withdrawn by 1939. An earlier venture into this field was 041 XY, a solid-tyred British Ensign 6-ton truck dating from 1918. Numbered 'B6' by LT, it was sold in June 1937. 'British Ensign' vehicles were built at Willesden between 1914 and 1923 in a wide variety of forms, and often fitted with Tylor engines.

The creation of the LPTB brought about a number of problems where an operator had interests which ranged beyond the Board's 'Special Operating Area', or outside the new organisation's remit. Examples of this are the tie-up with AEC, the Underground Group's own Union Construction Company and, at the other end of the spectrum, Morden Station (motor car) Garage. The LCC too had a wide range of responsibilities not directly connected with passenger transport, one being the maintenance of the Blackwall and Rotherhithe road tunnels. The LCCT was charged with removing broken-down vehicles from these, and quite naturally used their own tramway breakdown lorries for the task. Initially, this arrangement carried on unchanged after the LT take-over, but in October 1933 was altered to a procedure whereby the LCC gave the LPTB a payment of 18s 3d for each vehicle attended.

Other non-LT vehicles moved by the Board included those obstructing tram tracks through abandonment or breakdown. In these cases, Rule 37 of the Trams & Trolleybuses' 'Rule Book for Drivers and Conductors' advised that: '*employees of the Board may take immediate steps to clear the track, without waiting for the arrival of an Official or the breakdown gang, subject to the reasonable requirements of the Police*'. Although, as stated, the tramway breakdown tenders could assist vehicles belonging to all parts of LT, there was obviously no need for a specific fleet of such types after July 1952.

178K had already departed in December 1949; the rest were paid off between August and October 1952.

TRAMWAY MISCELLANEOUS

In addition to the vehicles dedicated to the Tramways operation by virtue of their special bodywork, a large number of standard-bodied vehicles were allocated to this department. Some of them did not last until the 1939 renumbering scheme, and included fleet number '132', a Trojan van allocated to Acton Tram Depot; and two Thornycroft trucks without fleet numbers which had started life as Metropolitan Railway parcels vans (UU 9710 and YX 5564). There were also four Tilling-Stevens petrol-electric lorries converted from buses: 112 (XN 7332), 113 (XN 7335), 114 (XP 2370) and 115 (XN 7334).

AEC Matadors 103P (ex-E 16) and 109P (ex-E 22) were bought new and allocated to the stores department at Charlton Works. As well as the ex-bus Leyland 'LB' chassis converted to tower wagons, three further 'LB's became stores lorries, one of which, ex-bus L 61, was allocated to the Tramways. It was never renumbered and withdrawn in 1937.

Two 4-ton lorries from Guy Motors, fleet numbers 169G and 170G saw use between the Julys of 1931 and 1946. They ran on trade plates 005 GJ and 006 GJ, and were first numbered as 19 and 20. These Guy model 'T' petrol-engined normal-control 4-ton trucks were fitted with dropside bodies and carried a heavy steel beam forward of the radiator for pushing trams. One of these was featured in a Guy Motors advertising brochure in 1931. Originally supplied to the LCCT, these lorries, like many others in the Council's tramway support fleet, featured 'lifeguards' between the axles to prevent people falling under the wheels. Their job was the distribution of stores and supplies throughout the LCCT network and they were always based at Charlton.

As a postscript, trams returned to the streets of south London in 1999 under the 'Tramlink' project, and passenger services commenced in May 2000. However, as is the norm nowadays, the operation of the system has been contracted to a private company on TfL's behalf. As such, any support vehicles in use are the sole responsibility of First Group subsidiary 'Tramtrack Croydon'.

WORKS CARS

Though felt beyond the scope of this work, the use of various non-passenger-carrying trams absorbed from the LCCT, the municipalities and the Underground Group companies as 'works cars' should be recorded. Though such vehicles could obviously not have continued in use after 1952, LT had already commenced a policy of replacement before then, with certain tasks being transferred to lorries or vans.

TROLLEYBUS SERVICE VEHICLES

The introduction of the trolleybus to the streets of London was a long and drawn-out affair. The very first demonstration of a 'trackless tram' was in 1909, and a number of other trials took place during the next twenty-odd years. Full-scale operation commenced in the south-west corner of London in May 1931 under the auspices of the London United Tramways company, which was part of the Underground Group, when a fleet of brand new AEC 6-wheel, double-deck trolleybuses replaced worn-out trams in the Twickenham area. When the LPTB was formed, it found that the most cost-effective way of replacing time-expired tramcars was to convert routes to trolleybus operation. This followed the experience of the LUT, whose receipts had increased after introducing trolleybuses. Through this policy, the existing electrical power supply equipment installed for the trams could continue to be used, albeit with considerable modification.

The LPTB rapidly set about planning more tram-to-trolleybus conversions, which commenced in 1935 and continued right up to 1940. There were plans to replace trams throughout London with trolleybuses, but the war intervened in the process, resulting in some areas retaining trams up until July 1952.

The regular servicing of the trolleybuses was carried out within depots with unit exchanges being the norm. All the removed units were replaced immediately with overhauled units from the Central Repair Depot (Charlton Works). These included items like front axles, cardan shafts (propeller shafts), differentials, compressors, traction motors and the overhead collection equipment. The trolleybuses were overhauled at two yearly intervals, with overhauls being alternately 'heavy' and 'light'. The heavy overhauling work was carried out at both Charlton and Fulwell, whilst light overhauls could be handled by Fulwell and West Ham. The central stores were situated at Charlton, and there were regular delivery runs carried out by CDS vehicles collecting and returning parts for trolleybuses.

Charlton remained in operation for trolleybus overhaul until 1959, when with the gathering pace of abandonment all major overhauls ceased (for the record, the final trolleybus to pass through the works was AEC / Park Royal N2-class 1669). After this date, any repair work was carried out at individual trolleybus depots, and as trolleybuses suffered failures of major equipment, they would be withdrawn rather than repaired.

POLE CARRIERS

One consequence of the planned replacement of trams by trolleybuses was the need for additional pole carriers. These vehicles were needed to substitute the existing tram traction poles with stronger examples able to carry the additional weight of the overhead. Once the poles had been erected, additional tower wagons were required to install, maintain and repair the wires. Pole carriers were dropside trucks with heavy-duty front and rear bolsters, plus a 'Flowers' loading crane based on the same principles as the much earlier Albion petrol and Foden steam vehicles. The cranes remained very basic, with just a swivelling horizontal jib and steel chain to lift the traction poles. The lifting chain was permanently fixed at the inner end, and relied on the elevation of the jib to lift the traction poles from the lorry platform. The jib elevation was power-operated, but all other functions required the earliest known form of power – the muscle.

The varying requirements of the overhead wire network meant that four standard sizes of traction poles were in use. Individual sizes varied in length between 33ft and 40ft, with the former being the standard size. The erection of the poles involved them being buried in 6ft of concrete. When one considers that some of the overhead equipment at complicated junctions could weigh more than three tons, the need for strong, long poles is apparent. The handling of the poles and fitting of the overhead equipment was a skilled job, and not one for the faint-hearted. To give an idea of the volume of work involved in the setting up of a new trolleybus route, in 1938 LT commented that, for 13 route miles in north London, 1,500 traction poles were supplied. Along with the erection of the new overhead in areas where the trams had previously used the conduit for current collection, the supply of electricity utilised a vast array of electrical equipment. The power was supplied at 11,000 volts to sub-stations situated at 2-mile intervals. The current was then rectified and passed to the overhead lines at 600 volts DC. All of this equipment required regular programmed maintenance, this work being undertaken by the Chief Electrical Engineer's Department. The pole carriers themselves were operated by staff of the Distribution Engineer (Trams & Trolleybuses) North or South.

The first of the new batch of pole carriers arrived in November 1936 and was based on the AEC Mercury 5-ton forward-control chassis. This order consisted of six vehicles latterly numbered 91Q to 96Q (originally 205 to 210). These were joined a year later in September 1937 by 97N to 99N, three similar-looking AEC Monarch 7-tonners (initially identified as EN 23 to EN 25). The first disposal took place in May 1953 (99N), began in earnest in 1959, and the last example (94Q) went out of stock in February 1964. Historians should note that although the original Mercury model was a normal-control vehicle, from 1933 it was also available in forward-control format of 4-ton capacity, which was the version always used by the LPTB. Next in line in size from this date was the AEC Monarch, and then the Matador, of 5- and 6-ton capacities respectively, all normally fitted with 4-cylinder engines.

The AEC chassis was chosen again for the third and final generation of pole carriers. By the early-1950s, the AEC lorry range was beginning to look dated, and in 1953, the new Mercury model was introduced. Able to carry 7-tons, this was the first AEC lorry not to feature an exposed radiator. The cab-style was completely updated at the same time and featured a radiator grille similar in design to that carried later by some Regent III and most Regent V buses, as well as the Mk V lorries. Hampshire Car Bodies built the cabs and bodies of the lorries numbered 1078Q to 1081Q, which arrived in 1958. It is interesting to note in today's era of self-loading vehicles with hydraulic cranes, LT decided to continue purchasing (or possibly transferring) old-style manually-operated cranes found on the original pole carriers. There were hydraulic cranes on the market in the late-1950s, but they were heavy, and in LT's eyes, somewhat unproven.

AEC pole carriers 96Q and 97N look almost identical, but the former is a Mercury from 1936, whilst the latter is a Monarch dating from the following year. The rail/pole carrier could also carry sand and ballast in containers to work sites, but naturally the need for these materials decreased once the rubber-tyred trolleybus began replacing the tram.
Kim Rennie collection

Therefore, the Board resorted to the equipment they knew best. Overall, the purchase of these quality vehicles speaks volumes for LT's attitudes at the time, in that they bought the best vehicle for the job, rather than a vehicle that might just about be able to cope with the work. They were used in the progressive dismantling of the trolleybus overhead equipment, until the system closed completely in May 1962. They were then re-deployed to general freight duties. Vehicles 1078Q and 1080Q departed from the fleet in 1967, leaving 1079Q and 1081Q which lasted until 1975 and 1976 respectively.

TROLLEYBUS TOWER WAGONS
(see tramway tower wagons)

TROLLEYBUS RESCUE TENDERS

The trolleybus rescue tenders or trucks were another of the instantly recognisable vehicle types operated by LT over the years. Although provided by two different manufacturers (or three, if the final design had been proceeded with), all followed the same basic design. The first third of the body featured a steel tilt and was used as a workshop, then followed a short open area with large tool lockers on each side accessible from the lorry floor or from the road side. At the rear was storage space for two spare wheels, one each for either an AEC or Leyland trolleybus, (though there was no mechanical means of lifting these on and off the lorry bodies, just sheer brute force). Tenders were allocated to most depots, with the exception of small

Trolleybus rescue tenders were a familiar sight in London throughout virtually the whole life the system. This was the prototype, Leyland Cub 'SKZ1' No.169 (later 189C) dating from 1936. The body differed from subsequent vehicles by having a flat roof on the fixed metal tilt. Each tender carried two spare wheels, one each for an AEC and Leyland trolleybus. They might also be called out to replace fuses or, at a last resort, tow disabled vehicles back to depot. Phil Moth

An official view of AN 57 (later 363A) at Chiswick shows how the tenders operated. Twin ramps allowed spare tyres to be loaded or unloaded, hinged dropside panels provided access to equipment lockers on either side, whilst further items could be carried in the rack contained within the tilt-cover. When new, AN 57 had an off-white cab roof and red wheel centres, but both were later repainted in more practical colours. LT Museum

sheds like Lea Bridge and Isleworth, which relied on a larger depot for help, and most lasted right through to the end of trolleybus services in 1962. Despite their diminutive size, they were capable of towing broken-down trolleybuses, albeit very slowly. It is not clear what arrangements were made before 1936, though the AEC/ADC '418' lorries were definitely listed as 'Breakdown Lorries'. Many of the tower wagons were also listed as being 'Equipped for Towing' and undoubtedly could tow broken-down trolleybuses. As well as responding to failures, tenders were also used to tow night route trolleybuses past sections of wire being worked on by engineers.

The first purpose-built tender for the trolleybus fleet was No. 169 (later 189C) dating from 1936. This was a Leyland Cub model 'SKZ1' 4-ton rescue truck built at the Leyland factory at Kingston-upon-Thames. Six more Cubs arrived in August 1936 as 218 to 223 (becoming 203C to 208C). As 189C's chassis number was considerably lower than the rest, it may well have served as a prototype or trial vehicle.

A year later, LT switched to the Albion 'KN127' model as a base for eight more 4-ton trucks. These had similar-looking bodies to the Leylands. Nos. 224 to 227 became AN 18 to AN 21, but were re-numbered again as 121A to

124A in 1939. The remaining four arrived as AN 30 to AN 33, later known as 133A–136A. All were in red livery, and carried the LT 'TROLLEYBUS' bullseye motif on their body sides. Aside from Albion 122A, which went in 1958, the rest continued to serve the trolleybus fleet until its demise.

Although both the Albions and Leylands lasted until the very end of trolleybus operation, consideration was given to the replacement of such types. In April 1957, a pair of Morris (badged 'Austin') 'LD' 1½-ton, half-tilt trucks numbered 990AS and 991AS arrived as prototypes for a new generation of breakdown tenders. (A pocket of operation from Isleworth and Fulwell depots was to be retained for a few years after the end of the rest of the system). However, when operators in Spain made a reasonable offer for the comparatively new Q1-class trolleybuses, the electric-to-diesel conversion programme was brought forward, and it was obvious no further development in this field was required. Numbers 990AS and 991AS were therefore re-designated as stores vehicles in 1958–59, a task they continued to perform until withdrawal in 1965–66. Given their ultimate fate, it was appropriate they had been delivered in green livery, the only rescue trucks so-finished.

The premature wearing-out of the trolleybus wires resulted in NS 760 being converted to 'overhead wire lubricator' No. 203 (later 41H) in 1936. Livery was red, relieved by a black-edged cream stripe and obviously derived from that carried on the trolleybuses themselves (no Chiswick Green here!). Unfortunately, the vehicle had a short life, being destroyed by enemy action in October 1940.
D.W.K. Jones

OVERHEAD WIRE LUBRICATORS

Some of the more obscure vehicles operated on behalf of the trolleybus fleet were the 'overhead wire lubricators'. Whilst the title is self-explanatory, it might be wondered just why the wires required lubricating. The reason was simply that, before the introduction of carbon collector shoes on trolleybus booms, the wires had to be graphite-coated to prevent premature wear. The lubricators ran mainly at night and were fitted with twin booms, looking at first glance like hybrid petrol-engined trolleybuses.

When the management noticed how quickly the overhead wires were wearing out, a solid-tyred NS double-deck bus formed the base for the first lubricator. What had been NS 760 was re-built in 1936. Re-numbered first as 203, later as 41H, it received a red livery with a black-edged cream relief band around the lower deck in a similar fashion to the trolleybuses themselves (as did most lubricators). Modifications included full re-panelling, plus the fitting of pneumatic tyres. The upper deck was open to the sky, with transverse bracing at the front supporting the two trolley arms. The arms appeared to be standard, but had the addition of lubricant canisters and spotlights. The lower deck had a pair of hinged doors at the rear, above which was a standard Trams & Trolleybuses 'CAUTION – OVERHEAD REPAIRS' sign. To help the driver follow the overhead wires an additional window was fitted above the main windscreen. It also functioned as a part-time tree lopper. The Second World War cut short the career of this unusual vehicle, as it fell victim to a bombing raid in October 1940.

As the system's route mileage increased, 41H was

To cater for the increase in trolleybus mileage, a second overhead wire lubricator was introduced in 1938. Rebuilt from T 320, its body was superficially similar to that on 41H, albeit with a more modern AEC radiator. Although assigned the number 114W in the 1939 service vehicle series, it continues to display its previous identity in this early view. Visible on the mock trolley booms are spotlights and the graphite lubricators. The other vehicle is also of note, being 336V, a Vulcan 3-ton tower wagon new to Ilford Corporation Tramways in 1931.
LT Museum

The overhead wire lubricators were also used for activities such as trolleybus overhead repair and tree lopping. On this occasion an engineer climbs a ladder from the upper deck of 114W to reach a traction pole on the Holborn Loop at Chancery Lane Station. When compared with the earlier photo, it is clear that a certain amount of re-panelling has been applied at some stage as, amongst other changes, the vehicle has gained a second relief band. F.G. Reynolds

joined by a second 6-ton vehicle, 114W. This was rebuilt at Charlton Works from AEC Regal T 320 in March 1938. The overall appearance of 114W resembled the earlier 41H, but with a modern upright AEC radiator. It left LT stock in May 1959 having been out of use for some time, passing to Lammas Motors. A third lubricator, 442W, was formed from AEC Regal T 306 in September 1939, actually entering stock in March 1940 (the gap between conversion and entry into service being a common occurrence). It departed to dealer Lammas before 114W in August 1952. In May 1941, the lubricator fleet had a part-time addition, when ADC/AEC '418' tower wagon 7E was converted to carry lubricating arms. The main telescopic tower apparatus was removed, whilst that part of the assembly over the rear axle was adapted to form a fixed-height inspection / working platform.

An STL bus became the fifth and final example of the type to be constructed. 734J was previously STL 12 from the first batch of this class, and had originally entered service at Clay Hall Garage in March 1933. It was used from October 1948 until March 1955, when the carbon inserts fitted to boom heads rendered the lubricating vehicles redundant. An interesting point about the conversion of ex-T-class Regals into lubricators (and conduit cleaners) is that this is the first example of LT rebuilding 'modern' buses for support roles. Previous conversions had involved types that had entered service on solid tyres.

TROLLEYBUS TOWING LORRIES
(*see bus towing lorries*)

What may have been a replacement for the bomb-damaged 41H was ADC/AEC '418' tower wagon 7E, which was fitted with a pair of lubricating arms in May 1941. To assist the driver in following the overhead wires, a small window was fitted in the cab roof. The surviving overhead wire lubricators became redundant in 1955 following the introduction of carbon inserts on trolley heads. D.W.K. Jones

In pre-LPTB days, a number of B-type chassis were fitted with both open and closed lorry bodies to provide support services for the LGOC. B 753 demonstrates the basic nature of the open-cabbed and solid-tyred design, and was among ten such vehicles retained for use at Walthamstow after AEC was formed as a separate entity from the LGOC in 1912.
Arthur Ingram collection

The new LPTB inherited a wide variety of vehicle designs and makes from its constituent organisations. It is clear however that some form of standardisation already existed within the Underground Group of companies. Similar types had been allocated to both road and rail use and many were numbered in common series. At the other end of the scale, one-off types inherited from independent bus operators and the municipal tramways were usually disposed of quickly and often before being given LPTB fleet numbers.

Some of the earliest/original petrol-engined vehicles used by the LGOC were the B-type lorries and vans, sixty of which were in stock by 1914. Built by AEC and based on the famous bus, they retained the steel-flitched (reinforced) wooden chassis of the bus, as opposed to the complete steel chassis of the later 'YC'-type lorry purchased in great numbers by the military. Ten of the B-type vans passed from LGOC to AEC ownership in 1912 following the latter's establishment as a separate entity. The LER was allocated B 4880, B 4881 and B 4882 for railway support duties, and of this batch, B 4880 and B 4882 lasted long enough to enter the LPTB fleet prior to withdrawal in October 1934. Two B-type lorries were sourced from the experimental X-type buses, with X 39 and X 58 becoming B 5133 and B 5134 upon conversion.

Although the B-type lorries and vans rendered sterling service ferrying parts to and from operational garages and AEC's Walthamstow Works, there was soon a need for additional heavy-duty trucks. This was met with the purchase of AEC 'YC'-type lorries fitted with

Tylor engines and classed as 5-ton stores lorries (though the Army classed them as 3-tonners). From the inception of the B-type bus and right through to 1923, AEC had used Hammersmith-built 'Tylor' engines in its bus and lorry chassis. The B-type lorries had been fitted with Tylor 28hp engines, whereas the 'YC'-types could boast a similar make of engine, but this time producing 45hp.

The earliest of the 'YC'-types in LPTB service dated from 1919. Most came second-hand as 'war surplus' vehicles and were referred to by the LPTB as the 'AEC YC-Tylor' model. Vehicles 58Z to 74Z came into this category and were supplied between 1919 and 1921 as Chiswick-based stores lorries. Previous identities had mainly been within an EN-prefixed series, with re-numbering carried out in groups, depending on the operating department concerned. The vehicles were solid-tyred, and several were converted from charabancs or so-called 'lorry-buses'. Although all were initially used as 5-ton stores lorries, 69Z was converted to a 5-ton tipping lorry in December 1928 to cart cinders away from the Chiswick boiler house. 65Z was fully-enclosed and assigned to stationery distribution duties, whilst either 62Z or 63Z (the records are unclear) carried a tank for distilled water. All operated on trade plates one time or other, and most lasted until around 1946, some having been used by the ARP during the war. 69Z and 74Z were the very last in stock, forming part of the Rolling Stock Engineer's 'Miscellaneous Vehicle Pool' at Chiswick until autumn 1948.

In 1928, a batch of solid-tyred AEC '506' models, later numbered as 45Z to 54Z, was purchased for use as stores and towing lorries at LGOC garages. Despite their 'heavy-duty' image and being fitted with an AEC 45hp engine, few of these '506' trucks lasted as long as their 'YC'-type predecessors. This particular model had been introduced during a bad period in the history of the company, and were considered old-fashioned and over-weight even as they entered service, hence their early demise. The guaranteed market of the Underground Group might have partially insulated AEC from the needs of the real world, but they had the sense to realise their potential predicament. This resulted in the recruitment of the talented John Rackham in 1928 as Chief Engineer to update all of their models, both passenger and goods.

latter were used to power some ST- and T-class buses during the war years, though 183C did not run on gas itself. One of the less-recorded jobs undertaken by CDS during the war was the delivery of anthracite to various bus garages and termini for use in the 'producer-gas' project. Other service vehicles known to have been involved in this scheme were ADC '418' tipper 3E, Bedford 'WLB' 149B and Morris Commercials 284M and 327M.

Also quite standardised were the Albion 'KN127' and 'LP35' 4-, 5- and 6-ton chassis dating from 1937–39. These were bodied in a variety of forms, including 6-ton railway breakdown and recovery tenders, rail carriers, half-tilt

Left. D 1017 was used by the LGOC's Advertising Department and carried a heavily-ribbed body combining a fixed forward section with a removable rear canvas tilt.

Below: Many of the LGOC's AEC 'YC'-type lorries lasted long enough to appear in the LPTB fleet. This unknown example ran on trade plates and was allocated to Chiswick Works for stores duties. Though still on solid tyres, the driver had the benefit of a more substantial cab, albeit with unglazed canvas doors, and the lights have now been converted to electric. Livery appears to be Chiswick Green with a cream roof. The model was derived from the 'Y'-type lorries built for the military during the First World War. David Rowe collection

Most of the normal-control Leyland 'LB' ex-buses in the service fleet were converted to tower wagons, but three were re-bodied as 5-ton stores lorries. 210L (ex-L 57) was previously owned by 'Miller' and new in March 1927. After joining the LPTB fleet in August 1934, it re-emerged as a pneumatic-tyred lorry in February 1936 and ran on trade plates 076 XM from Camberwell Garage. The second vehicle, 211L (ex-L 64) had a more interesting origin, being built by bus operator 'City' using spare parts some time before its registration in August 1929. It passed to LPTB in November 1934 and gained a lorry body and pneumatic tyres in July 1935. It was based at Chalk Farm and carried trade plates 011 YH. Both of these 'LB's ran until spring 1946. A third, L 61, dating from 1924, ran on trade plates 071 XY, but was sold in February 1938.

The Leyland Cub 'SKZ1' was the first new quality commercial vehicle type to be ordered by the LPTB in some quantity, with 29 entering service in 1936. Some were dedicated to specialised uses like trolleybus rescue, tramway track welding or catering; but 180C to 188C and 190C and 191C were 4-ton open, half-tilt or full-tilt lorries. Fully-enclosed versions were catering or ticket vans 199C to 202C. Lorries 180C to 186C were first listed in the Leyland Cub bus number series as C99L to C105L, whilst 190C and 191C were licensed to tow trailers. 183C was licensed to tow 'producer-gas' trailers in July 1943. The

Above: These three 4-ton Leyland Cub 'SKZ1's were clearly all destined for LPTB use, with the outer vehicles numbered C100L (181C) and C101L (182C) carrying Chiswick Green livery plus 'Building Department' cab door lettering. The centre lorry is painted red and exhibits a 'Bexley Depot' allocation. Though no fleet number is visible, it must be either 167 (187C) or 168 (188C); which were the only Leyland Cub open lorries delivered in this colour.

and full-tilt lorries, ticket vans, trolleybus rescue trucks and tippers. Three separate numbering schemes were applied: A plain ex-LCCT numerical series, an 'AN' prefix, and finally a number plus the suffix-letter 'A'. The whole class was eventually grouped in the 121A to 145A and 360A to 384A number range (excluding a Morris – 371M). The Albions were forward-control models with many bodies provided by the exotically-named Cunard Carriage Company of Ealing. Lorry-bodied KN127s lasted until the beginning of the 1950s, but those vehicles employed on specialised tasks survived much longer, with the rescue trucks remaining as late as 1962.

One of the definitive LT service vehicles is an ex-AEC bus chassis with dropside body and deep panelled sides extending down from the lorry platform. Quite exceptionally, the first vehicles with this style of body were two Thornycroft 'Cygnet' bus chassis ordered by small independent companies, but delivered to the LPTB and used as lorries from 1935. 334T (first numbered NY 11) had been destined for 'St Albans & District', whilst sister 335T (NY 12) should have gone to 'Peoples of Ware', and both were bodied by Chalmers of Reigate after delivery to LT in chassis form. They remained in use until 1950, but no further vehicles were to come from this manufacturer (itself taken over by AEC in 1960).

The characteristic body style of the duo, with deep side valances extending below body platform level, was to set the standard body design for heavier service vehicles until the post-war era. These lower panels were removed from many of the CDS vehicles in the 1950s, due to the difficulty in keeping them damage-free in the working environment of a lorry. To enable the load platform to be flat throughout its length on the converted bus chassis, most bodies were placed on additional spacers to raise them above the rear wheel-arches.

Above left: The SKZ1 was chosen as the LPTB's first standard lorry, with 29 examples bodied in various forms entering service in 1936. This is 180C, a 4-ton open lorry with full-tilt which began life numbered as C99L in the joint series which included the C-class Leyland Cub buses. Allocated to Works & Building at Parsons Green, it was in use until 1949. A.B. Cross

Left: 'SKZ1' No.170 was used by Trams & Trolleybuses at Rye Lane Permanent Way Depot. The official view shows the vehicle before registration and bearing its original identity in full-size gold transfers. The vehicle was reclassified as 190C in 1939, gaining the more familiar smaller white fleet numbers in the process. The cream or off-white cab roof was a common feature on pre-war service vehicles.

The next stores vehicles were among a batch of petrol-engined AEC Matador '346'-models entering service in 1936–37. Those that came bodied as lorries followed the design example set by the two Thornycroft vehicles of 1935 with deep valances. These AECs were the last new lorries of this make to enter the fleet for some twenty years. The Matadors were numbered E 15 to E 22 (later 102P to 109P) and operated as 7½-ton forward-control open/stores lorries. Their standard AEC-style full-fronted goods cab design was to be reflected in the later bus-to-lorry conversions, and became synonymous with the service fleet in the 1940s/1950s. The 1939 allocation of the batch was as follows:

Fleet number	Reg. number	Trade Plate	Usage	Location
102P (ex-E 15)	CLX 400	—	Railways	Acton Works
103P (ex-E 16)	NLP 611*	029 XY	Tramways	Charlton Works
104P (ex-E 17)	KYY 972*	071 XY	Central Buses millwrights	Chiswick Works
105P (ex-E 18)	—	024 GH	Central Buses stores	Chiswick Works
106P (ex-E 19)	—	006 GH	Central Buses stores	Chiswick Works
107P (ex-E 20)	—	012 GH	Central Buses stores	Chiswick Works
108P (ex-E 21)	—	019 XE	Central Buses stores	Chiswick Works
109P (ex-E 22)	—	075 GC	Tramways	Charlton Works

* Registered later

No. 105P was fitted with a 'tailboard loader' in March 1951 (removed 1958), 106P gained a similar facility in September 1950, whilst 105P to 107P were regularly used on the Chiswick–Aldenham component ferry service. 108P was re-bodied as a gully emptier in 1949 (q.v.). This vehicle had originally replaced a 'Provincial S-type' chassis, one of a pair inherited from East Surrey. Withdrawal of most occurred in the late-1950s. The last one to go was 109P in November 1958, which had formerly operated the waste-oil barrel collection service.

The small container seen on the nearside front panel of many AEC service vehicles was part of the 'Autovac' fuel system. Vacuum from the petrol engine manifold was utilised to lift petrol from the chassis-mounted fuel tank into the cab mounted container from where it flowed by gravity into the carburettor. On conversion to diesel engines this system was removed.

Of the 198 Dennis buses inherited from independent bus companies by the LGOC and LPTB, five were rebuilt as normal-control 5-ton lorries to serve the support fleet.

Top: Setting a style familiar for three decades were the two Thornycroft Cygnet chassis ordered by Hertfordshire independents but sent straight to the LPTB. The goods bodies fitted to the pair in 1935 were designed to conceal the bus-style chassis, with lower side panels reminiscent of the STL-class vehicles being bodied at the time. The fixed quarter-tilt was also to become a regular feature of the LT service vehicle. This is 335T, originally destined for People's of Ware and first numbered as NY 12. D.W.K. Jones

Centre: Despite its 1950s registration, 104P was actually one of the 1937 batch of AEC Matador stores lorries. Though allowed to run on trade plates whilst solely concerned with bus engineering, a conventional registration was required following its transfer to the general CDS fleet. Another change that had occurred by 1952 was the removal of the lower valances, giving the vehicle a much less dated look, though the quaint cab door handles remained. John Gillham

Right: Of the eight AEC Matador open lorries delivered in 1937, E20(107P) was one of four allocated to Chiswick Works for general duties. A legal loophole of the time allowed LT to operate such types on permanently-affixed trade plates. D.W.K. Jones

Right: AEC Matador 109P was fitted with an Anthony Hoists tail-lift in 1951 to facilitate the conveyance of oil drums. Less radical, but just as important to the operation, were the side guardrails added to contain the cargo. The wearing of a peaked cap with civilian clothing is unusual to today's eyes, although a long common practice amongst London's taxi drivers. *LT Museum*

Below: A number of non-standard buses were rebuilt as lorries. Dennis 5-ton No.156D started life in 1928 with Twickenham-based independent A.G. Summerskill. Upon becoming a railway stores vehicle, it initially retained its bus stock number of D 183, as shown in this wartime view. *D.W.K. Jones*

The more modern cab, complete with winding windows, of Morris Commercial Equiload 332M looks much neater than the earlier 30-cwt design. But the 6-stud wheel discs give away its heritage. No.332M was allocated to the Distribution Engineer at Acton, a title that referred to electricity rather than goods, and powered trams and trolleybuses as opposed to Underground trains. *Lens of Sutton*

152D was new in September 1924 to 'Gordon', converted to lorry (with pneumatic tyres) in June 1932 as D 194, then renumbered to D 189 in January 1934. 153D started life with 'Sphere' in October 1926, passed to the LPTB in August 1934, and converted to lorry (with tyre change) in March 1935 as D 198. 155D originated with 'Premier' in October 1926 and entered LT stock as D 188 (D 195 from January 1934). It was rebuilt as a lorry in August 1934, though in this case pneumatic tyres were already fitted. 156D had been new to 'Summerskill' in June 1928, and was acquired in November 1933, becoming D 183. Conversion to lorry took place in June 1934, and again, pneumatic tyres were already in place. 'Missing' number 154D was a sludge lorry (q.v.).

The Morris Commercial 'C'-type was the main choice for a medium-sized vehicle in the 1930s. Between 1933 and 1937 a large number were introduced in various numbering series, eventually becoming 261M to 323M. The LPTB described these vehicles as the 'EA' range since these two letters were the prefix for the engine number. This model range had been introduced in 1933 and featured parts common to different weight ranges. The vehicles could have either 4- or 6-cylinder engines and came with a factory-built cab. Almost all those in LPTB use were 25hp 30-cwt trucks in various guises including box-vans, dropside, half-tilts and full-tilts; but 263M and 264M and 267M to 270M were 14hp 1-ton lorries.

The 'C'-type remained in production until 1937, when the 'CV' model was introduced. This new range went under the odd name 'Equiload', denoting the fact that the load and braking stresses were equally distributed between axles. The LPTB moved to this more modern Morris Commercial Equiload range in 1938, and 324M to 333M were in use from then as 25hp 30-cwt dropside or half-tilt trucks. There was also a later post-war Equiload chassis that featured semi-forward control, but none of these entered LT service.

The introduction of a fleet of brand new Green Line coaches from 1937 to 1939 based on AEC Regal (T-class) and Leyland FEC (TF-class) coaches led to the withdrawal of all the early-1930s AEC Regal single-deckers. Many of the better vehicles came to have their bodies removed and the overhauled chassis converted into towing lorries, open trucks and stores lorries numbered between 387W and 453W. Aside from the towing lorries (detailed earlier), vehicles involved in 'open' and stores use were as follows, along with their 1940 departmental allocations:

Right: Former T 165 became 439W and was given a normal-height floor, but with the addition of low hinged dropsides. Seen here at Putney Bridge, the vehicle's official allocation was to the CME (Road Services) Miscellaneous Vehicles Control Pool at Chiswick. *Bill Aldridge collection*

Centre: The dropside body on 420W (ex-T 159) was lower than normal on such conversions. The difference in floor height can be discerned by the amount of rear wheel-arch cutting into the body in comparison with similar-looking ex-T-class vehicles. Allocated to Works & Building, on this occasion it appears to have been in use on yet another of LT's extensive Derby Day operations. *Bill Aldridge collection*

**Acton Works based
for Chief Mechanical Engineer (Railways)**
407W (ex-T 245), 408W (ex-T 256),

**Central and Country Bus garage based
stores or towing lorries**
397W (ex-T 257), 398W (ex-T 294), 399W (ex-T 210), 400W (ex-T 246), 401W (ex-T 303), 402W (ex-T 227), 403W (ex-T 242), 404W (ex-T 221), 405W (ex-T 241), 406W (ex-T 269), 444W (ex-T 164), 445W (ex-T 163), 446W (ex-T 181), 447W (ex-T 171), 448W (ex-T 169), 449W (ex-T 174)

Spare vehicles not allocated at the time:
450W (ex-T 199), 451W (ex-T 160), 452W (ex-T 176), 453W (ex-T 172)

**Chiswick Works based
stores lorries for the Chief Stores Superintendent**
387W (ex-T 278), 388W (ex-T 284), 389W (ex-T 238), 390W (ex-T 299), 391W (ex-T 259), 392W (ex-T 243), 393W (ex-T 282), 394W (ex-T 304), 395W (ex-T 260), 396W [battery-carrying lorry] (ex-T 279)

**Chiswick Works based
Miscellaneous Vehicle Control Pool for Chief
Mechanical Engineer (Road Services)**
439W (ex-T 165)

Permanent Way Engineer (Railways)
440W (ex-T 167) [replacing AEC 45Z]

All were provided with a new full-width lorry-style cab, and in most cases, open dropside bodies, both provided by the Transport Engineering Company. A few vehicles had the addition of full or half-tilts, and their overall appearance followed that of the bus-chassised Thornycroft stores lorries (334T and 335T) from 1935. The Regals were seen regularly throughout the LT operating area and in many cases had long lives, lasting through into the 1960s; indeed, most had longer lives as lorries than coaches.

For the first few years after the war, probably all of the fleet was petrol-powered. As the pressures on the older bus fleet eased with the arrival of new buses, a number of good-quality diesel engines became available from scrapped buses. These engines were thoroughly over-hauled and then used to replace petrol engines in all the AEC service vehicles destined to last for a few more years. Replacement of the survivors was eventually effected by the first generation of Thames Traders.

These conversions dated from 1939–40, and were the last service vehicles rebuilt using the AEC Regal I single-deck chassis. Henceforward, all bus-to-lorry conversions were to be based on double-deck chassis. By 1945, the earlier single-deckers were too old for rebuilding, but the much larger double-decker fleet was able to supply a considerable number of good-quality chassis whose bodies were well past redemption. The ex-bus service vehicle

Above: Fixed-sided AEC Regal stores lorry 447W (ex-T 171) was one of the vehicles whose lower side valances were removed after the war due to the damage they received in day-to-day use. It seems to be being loaded with coal or coke on this occasion, but if so, since the body did not tip, the process will have to be reversed by hand upon reaching the lorry's destination. *Bill Aldridge collection*

AEC Regal 408W had been converted from T 256 in 1939 and was used to carry railway wheel-sets between Underground depots and Acton Works. The combination of a long wheelbase and short rear overhang could overload the front axle and was one of the reasons leading to the demise of the ex-PSV lorries. In the early-1960s however it was still hard at work and was found circling Shepherds Bush Green. Phil Moth

fleet was, in a roundabout way, responsible for the first private preservation of a London bus. One of the original AEC Regal single-deck buses, T 31, was retained at Chiswick Works into the 1950s to train CDS drivers in the use of the crash gearboxes found on service vehicles. T 31 entered preservation in 1955, and is now in the care of Cobham Bus Museum.

Wartime strictures saw the appearance of 29 American-built, Ford V8-engined '01W' model 3-ton Detroit-type lorries between 1940 and 1943. All were purchased via W. H. Perry Ltd, the main Ford dealers, and were registered in a block of FXT-prefixed numbers. They were distinctively-American COE's (cab over engine) with their left-hand drive and upright oval radiator grilles. The majority were in fixed or dropside configuration, but 470F and 471F differed in being 'hand tippers', whilst 488F was described as 'covered'. Being so unconventional to the LPTB's usual standards, it is not surprising that most were disposed of around 1949–50 (if not before). This particular model had the distinction of being the first Ford to feature an open propeller shaft instead of the torque-tube enclosed propeller shaft used on their earlier trucks. They occupied the entire 468F to 495F numbering block, all were in green, and had 'CAUTION LEFT HAND DRIVE' exhortations painted on their tailboards.

After the war, the LPTB was able to re-commence the process of standardisation interrupted by hostilities. Between 1946 and 1947, the first batch of fifteen normal-control petrol-engined Bedford 'OLBD' 5-ton lorries were delivered. Numbers 653B to 667B appeared as either open trucks (sometimes with half- and quarter-tilt covers) or box-vans (with some of the latter assigned to track welding use for the Trams & Trolleybuses Department). A second general-usage batch of twenty entered the fleet from 1948 to 1953. Nos. 807B to 810B, 812B to 820B and 822B to 828B also came in a variety of forms; with open, semi-open, bolster, towing and even tipper truck bodies. One oddity was 826B, a 600-gallon distilled water tanker carrying the tank transferred from Albion 376A. It was to be one of the last Bedford 'O's on the books by the time of withdrawal in 1967.

Replacement of the Morris Commercial 'C'-type 30-cwt trucks was carried out between 1948 and 1951 using the 30-cwt Bedford 'KZ' and 'KD' models. The 'KZ's were box-vans with standard-design Bedford bodies built by Spurlings (or built to an identical design) and listed as 834B to 836B and 838B to 844B. The 'KD' models, which were supplied as chassis/cabs, took up numbers 854B to 862B, 864B to 891B and 893B to 896B. Of these, 887B was a box-van, while 857B had a full-length tilt cover.

The majority of KD trucks had half-tilt covers and directly replaced the Morris Commercial 'C' types on bus garage spare parts delivery work. Some of the half-tilt bodies on the Bedford 'KD' trucks had an extra cut-out in the rear of the tilt, enabling a Harvey Frost-engined crane to be safely transferred between garages. These small Bedford 'KD's and 'KZ's were similar looking to the 'O'-series Bedford trucks, and indeed shared the same engine design. However, the 'K' trucks had the engine fully under the bonnet, whilst the heavier models could be described as semi-forward-control, with the engine pro-

In 1941, the LPTB was allocated some US-built V8 petrol-engined Fords. With their upright oval radiator grilles, these left-hand-drive trucks were totally unlike anything else in the fleet. Equipped with a fixed metal tilt, 475F's original function was the repair of air raid damage. Its nearside steering wheel can be clearly seen in this view. The use of left-hand-drive vehicles became quite common during the war, with the presence of the US armed forces and vehicles in UK-ownership acquired via Lend-Lease.

truding into the cab. Withdrawal of the 'K's came around 1960 to 1965, which suggests that the Thames Trader intake was yet again to blame. The new replacements were full-size lorries, and the concept of the smaller open-backed commercial did not re-appear in the fleet again until the 1980s.

From 1948 to 1949, LT also took delivery of seventeen 6-cylinder petrol-engined Austin 'K4' dropside lorries numbered 900AS to 916AS. Primarily used by the Works & Building Department, these 5-ton trucks also had a mix of bolster, half-tilt, full-tilt and covered bodies. Like the similar-looking Bedford 'OLBD's, they averaged around twelve years in service. They were undoubtedly purchased by LT to compare with the Bedfords. In fact the Austin K-series trucks were so similar in appearance to the Bedford range that they were sometimes nicknamed 'Birmingham Bedfords' within commercial vehicle circles, due to their place of birth. Of these, 914AS was fitted with a hand-operated 'EPCO' crane used to install the concrete bus stop posts manufactured by the Works & Building Department at Parsons Green.

With a continuing need for heavy vehicles and a shortage of new types, the ability of LT to convert buses into service vehicles resulted in them rebuilding a further 30 bus chassis. These modifications took place between 1948 and 1950, and six vehicles were designated for 'goods' usage of one form or other:

7-ton half-tilt lorries:	…	821J (ex-STL 372)
7-ton stores lorries:	…	735J (ex-STL 24),
		736J (ex-STL 388),
		745J (ex-STL 317)
6-ton battery lorry:	…	740J (ex-STL 38)
7-ton open bolster lorry:		741J (ex-STL 42)

Vehicles 735J and 736J had bodies by Kenex, whilst 745J received a body transferred from Matador 108P. All eventually had their petrol engines replaced by diesel examples in later years and most survived until the early-1960s.

Battery lorry 740J was equipped with a detachable tail-lift, for which the tailboard was fitted with castor wheels on the underside. This masterpiece of ingenuity enabled the driver to deliver a load of batteries direct to

Top: LT's first standard post-war lorry, the Bedford O-series, appeared in a number of forms. No.807B, an 'OLBD' 5-ton model dropside with bolster, entered stock in November 1948. While H.C. Clark's Aldgate Station building still stands, the adjacent Three Nuns Hotel has long since given way to the ubiquitous city office block. Kim Rennie collection

Above: The Bedford 'OLBD' was fitted with a 27hp 6-cylinder petrol engine, as were most Bedfords delivered before 1951. No.812B, based at Lillie Bridge Depot, was one of a few given three-quarter-length tilt covers, with a hinged flap at the front to allow long loads to be carried. Seen at Putney Bridge Station, the metal staircase in the background gave additional access to the eastbound platform, principally for University Boat Race Day crowds. A.B. Cross

Left: Contemporary with the Bedford O-series were a batch of Austin 'K4' 5-ton lorries, mostly for use by Works & Building. No.908AS, with a mixed load, is guided out to Parsons Green Lane. Behind is sister vehicle 904AS and Albion 369A. LT Museum

Left: Austin 'K4' 912AS had a specially modified full-length tilt designed for the distribution of station stores from Lillie Bridge. The similarity in appearance to the 'O'-series is obvious, and it is little wonder that the K4 trucks were nicknamed 'Birmingham Bedfords'. On the door of the garage behind is painted 'CXX 409', the registration of a 1936 Hillman Hawk first allocated to the Central Buses Superintendent of Rolling Stock. LT Museum

Centre: STL 372 reappeared as 821J in 1950 and was used to carry heavy mechanical items like engines to and from Chiswick Works. To keep the engines in place, ropes were tied around them and then secured to special hooks on the vehicle's fixed sides. The practice of applying a contrasting colour to the cab roof is perpetuated here, though it appears that black has now replaced off-white or cream. Kim Rennie

Bottom: In order to carry batteries around the fleet, 740J (ex-STL 38) was fitted with a low-floor body equipped with a mechanical early form of tail-lift. The latter was operated by a removable crank handle, which can be seen protruding from the rear of the nearside. The low floor height lined-up with the conveyor in the Battery Room at Chiswick but had the disadvantage of causing the rear wheel-arches to protrude into the load space. LT Museum

the garage store. In the days before the universal adoption of fork-lift trucks and pallets, this was an ideal solution to a difficult handling problem. Other former STLs were dedicated to breakdown, towing and specialised Tram & Trolleybus Department use, and as such are detailed elsewhere.

In 1955, the final bus-to-lorry conversions were carried out at the old Nunhead Garage. Of the four ex-STL buses involved, number 1015J (ex-STL 2666) was also used as a quarter-tilt stores lorry, alongside the towing duties it shared with the other three detailed in Chapter 6. Being the last such rebuilds they ended a tradition dating back to the early days of the LGOC. Aside from the red-liveried breakdown tenders, 1015J was one of the last three ex-STLs in use as lorries when withdrawn in June 1965.

Twelve AEC Mercury units were acquired in early-1958, mainlly in connection with the ongoing dismantling of the trolleybus system. Although most were specialised tower wagons or pole carriers, numbers 1070Q to 1072Q appeared as 7-ton open lorries fitted with aluminium bodies by Homalloy and Anthony Hoists tail-lifts. All had the revised rounded Park Royal-style cab with its distinctive radiator grille introduced by AEC in 1953.

The AEC company and other heavy vehicle manufacturers at the time supplied a front-end cab structure, but gave customers the choice of either a 'factory cab' or making arrangements for their own coach-builder to fit one. If the customer required a cab from AEC he could have one, and these were generally built by Park Royal, but fitted at AEC's Southall works. In many cases the customer would order the cab and body from the same bodybuilder and that is why there are a number of detail differences between the cabs on the various Mercury chassis bought by LT. Not until the Leyland takeover and the introduction of the 'Ergomatic' cab did this practice cease.

Livery of these AECs was originally Chiswick Green with unpainted bodies, but later repaints saw vehicles outshopped in all-over grey with a light green cab roof. All three Mercurys averaged around 20 years service, the last not being withdrawn until 1979. In later years, some had their standard enamel commercial vehicle AEC radiator triangles replaced by the green Country Area version, and were the final LT vehicles to carry these.

As explained previously, the vehicle purchasing policy of LT changed considerably in the late-1950s with the decision to buy trucks new rather than rebuilding what were really time-expired buses into lorries. Thus, a significant chapter of service vehicle history began in September 1959, with the arrival of 1134F and 1135F, the first two Ford Thames Traders. These distinctive semi-forward-control lorries were to become LT's standard large vehicle throughout much of the 1960s. LT was to operate numerous examples over the years in a variety of open, semi-open, covered, towing, crew-cab and box-bodied formats; and with payloads of 3, 5 or 7 tons. As with the articulated units (detailed later), the earliest rigid Traders spanned the changeover period from green to grey livery, and individual models initially appeared in both schemes (sometimes even within the same batch of consecutive numbers).

Those not used for more specialised duties (e.g. catering or towing) were as follows: 1127F to 1138F, 1148F to 1151F, 1173F to 1188F, 1201F, 1213F to 1220F, 1229F to 1234F, 1249F to 1260F, 1302F and 1343F to 1357F. Trader 5-ton half-tilt stores lorries 1148F to 1151F from the 1960 intake were transferred to LCBS in January 1970 to assist the new company in setting up its own support services. In early 1973, two 7-ton examples followed suit (1217F and 1251F).

Amongst these Traders, numbers 1250F, 1251F, 1252F, 1254F and 1255F were modified before they were delivered, and had chassis extensions carried out by Baico Ltd. These alterations are carried out where the operator requires a specific chassis/body length that cannot be met by the standard offerings from the manufacture. An example of this would be if a long wheelbase and overall length were needed to carry loads that were bulky but not heavy.

The 'crew-cabs' on the earlier batches of Thames Traders were reputably built by Reliant, and at the insistence of LT's Chief Medical Officer, no side windows were allowed in the rear section. In fact, from the study of photographs it appears that the crew had to use the normal passenger door to obtain access to the cab, then scramble into the rear part. In general terms the Traders were highly thought-of by their drivers, though the brakes were certainly working at their limit when the trucks were fully laden. For a period in the 1960s, LT decided to add a suffix to the fleet numbers on the heavier vehicles to denote the carrying-capacity of the truck or trailer in tons, hence 1137F[5] or 1353F[3].

The Ford Motor Company replaced the Trader with the 'D'-series in 1965, and LT gained its first examples in 1966 with 1384F to 1390F. These were 'D300' 3-ton lorries finished in either half-tilt dropside format, or in the case of 1390F, as a 1000-gallon distilled water tanker. This model was to enjoy an even greater level of success with LT than the Trader, and successive batches of the type entered the fleet throughout the rest of the decade and right on through the 1970s. Indeed 'D'-series were still being delivered as late as 1981.

The 'D'-series was the first volume-produced Ford model to feature a 'tilt-cab', which made it easier for fitters to service and maintain mechanical components. The very earliest 'D'-series trucks had suffered from rear axle and brake problems, but these were eventually overcome. The one fault that did stay with them involved the tilt-cab. If the cab had been tilted and not securely clamped down afterwards, the first time the driver

Top: Very few new lorries entered service in the mid-1950s, and it was not until 1957 that the fleet began to acquire a modern look. Presenting a new image was 1070Q, an AEC Mercury 7-ton open lorry from 1958. As built, it combined a Chiswick Green cab with an unpainted aluminium body by Homalloy. To the rear is 1077Q, the ex-trolleybus tower wagon from the same year. *John Gascoine*

Centre: The first Thames Traders arrived in September 1959 and became the archetypal LT service vehicle of the following decade. This is 1135F, a 5-ton lorry with an expanding tilt, seen rolled back into the folded position. While the cab is in the new Ford Cargo Grey, the body has been finished in the previous Chiswick Green scheme. Also unusual is the cab door lettering, with the LT name underlined, but without the customary large initial and final letters. *John Gillham*

Right: The transfer of engines was among the many vital tasks entrusted to the growing fleet of Thames Traders. Grey-liveried 1251F was a 1962 7-ton fixed-sided open lorry and carried a redesigned radiator grille incorporating the letters 'TRADER'. The chassis had a wheelbase extension by Baico to allow for the fitting of a longer body. It was transferred to London Country in March 1973, as that company gained self-sufficiency from LT with its own engineering support fleet. *A.B. Cross*

applied the brakes, it would tilt forward with the driver inside – a frightening experience. The one saving grace was that the whole cab tilted – seat and floor as well. On the early Leyland Group 'Ergomatic' tilting-cabs, the seat and floor remained in place. This could cause the driver serious injuries if the cab tipped whilst he was still inside.

The 'D'-series models ranged from 'D500's, through 'D550's, 'D600's and 'D800's to 'D1000's. These figures represented the potential payload, but ignored any auxiliary equipment which might reduce this. Later 'D'-series introduced a numbering scheme which gave gross weight and engine size. Examples are 'D0607', 6-ton 4-cylinder 70bhp; 'D0710' 7½-ton 6-cylinder 100bhp; and so on through 'D0910', '1010', '1110', '1210' and '1614'. These new figures were more important as 'Plating and Testing' of goods vehicles was introduced from 1968. Those of the most commonplace box or dropside design were 1384F to 1389F, 1443F, 1514F, 1515F, 1529F, 1577F, 1581F to 1583F, 1588F, 1589F, 1591F, 1592F, 1637F to 1663F, 1722F to 1728F, 1748F to 1754F, 1759F, 1760F, 1780F to 1783F, 1788F, 1876F, 1928F, 1936F to 1941F, 1978F to 1986F, 2031F, 2128F to 2131F, 2215F, 2223F and 2224F.

Top: In the 1970s, the Ford D-series was used for virtually every CDS operation needing full-sized vehicles. This somewhat battered example is 1659F, a larger-engined 'D1000' variant. It was used to carry railway wheel-sets; hence, the curved brackets used to secure these on the flatbed. Kim Rennie

Above left: No.1653F was a 1971-built Ford 'D700' 7-ton lorry fitted with a full-length tarpaulin-covered tilt. Early grey-liveried vehicles had a light-green roof, which was soon dropped as an economy measure. This vehicle is in a slightly darker grey than usual following a repaint. Jim Wright

Above right Ford 'D550' numbered 1728F carried a covered box body. Jim Wright

Right: A more specialised Ford 'D'-series was crew-cabbed 'D1010' cable-drum carrier 1881F. To facilitate the loading of the drums, it was equipped with a sloped 'beaver tail', hinged ramps and an electrically-operated winch. A repaint has led to the disappearance of the white lower cab front panels. Jim Wright

Ford 'D'-series chassis were also used for the final batches of towing lorries acquired before the decision to supersede fixed-tow practice was made (see section on 'towing lorries'). What would have been 'D550' 5-ton lorries 1578F to 1580F were delivered directly to LCBS in April/May 1970. This trio were numbered as 578F to 580F in that operator's short-lived three-figure service vehicle numbering series, whilst LT re-allocated the originally-intended numbers to other types. As well as the full range of dropside, flatbed and enclosed trucks, various custom-bodied vehicles performed such specialised tasks as food distribution, tree-lopping and uniform issue. The vast majority of D-series were in grey, but the railway break-down box-vans continued the tradition of using red livery. HGV-training was carried out in the period November 1971 to April 1983 using 1722F, a 'D700' flatbed with tail-board, which could be loaded with ballast weights to simulate different levels of loading.

There were always a few under-represented types of vehicle within the CDS fleet. For instance, May 1966 had seen an oddity in 1404KG. This 4-ton Karrier Gamecock open lorry was fitted with a very low-height-platform body with Burtonwood tail-lift and dedicated to battery delivery. Despite its non-standard status, it lasted right up until 1981.

Only slightly less rare than the Karrier were 1840Q and 1841Q, both AEC Mercury 10-ton dropside bolster lorries used to ferry bus engines between Chiswick Works and garages. Delivered in 1973 and 1974 respectively, they were fitted with the 'Ergomatic' cab that replaced the very basic Park Royal Vehicles-styled aluminium panelled design in 1964. Both 1840Q and 1841Q were withdrawn in October 1984 and had the honour of being the last-ever AEC service vehicles owned by LT.

Despite LT's numerous earlier post-war purchases, Bedfords had become a distinct rarity by the early-1970s. In March 1974 however, a 6-wheel Bedford 'TK' with low flatbed body and tailboard joined 1722F as an additional HGV-trainer. What now became 1866B was obtained second-hand through the well-known Godfrey Davis firm, who were suppliers of many Ford chassis to LT.

By the late-1970s, the lorry fleet started to lose some of its previously rigid standardisation. A greater range of manufacturers began to be patronised for larger vehicles, with Bedford, Dodge and Leyland finding favour. Following experimental second-hand Leyland 'Terrier' 2091L in February 1978, five more were delivered new that year. 2123L was an open truck, the rest (2124L to 2127L) being 4-ton box-vans. The following year, another five arrived for use by LT Catering as 4-ton refrigerated food vans. 2210L to 2213L remained in this role until disposal in the mid-1980s, but out-of-sequence 2143L was later converted into a curtain-sided lorry, whilst 2213L ended up in dropside configuration. 2143L also had the 'distinction' of carrying the incorrect reversed stock number 'L2143'.

Sharing the same basic cab as the Leyland Terrier range was the larger 'Boxer' truck. Two of these entered service in the first month of 1982 as dropside lorries 2302L and 2305L, and averaged around seven years use. The new purchasing policy saw Bedford become a chassis

supplier again, supplanting the hitherto almost total reliance on Ford for larger vehicles. 1980 saw an intake of thirteen Bedford 'TL lorries. Numbered en-bloc as 2265B to 2277B, they included box-truck and dropside specifications, with the usual varying combinations of tail-lift and crew accommodation. The exception was 2274B, fitted with a 2400-gallon tank and the longest lasting of the batch, not being withdrawn until March 1993. Two further examples were 2308B and 2318B and came a year later, the first being a dropside lorry, the other carrying a box-body.

An unusual purchase in 1966 was 1404KG, a Karrier Gamecock 4-ton open lorry with tail-lift. As on the earlier 740J, the low floor was designed to align with the Battery Room conveyor at Chiswick. The vehicle ran on trade plates until 1970, when revised legislation caused it to be registered with an 'H'-suffix. Jim Wright

Centre: The Mercury name appeared in the fleet for the final time in 1973–74, with the arrival of a pair of 10-ton dropside lorries numbered 1840Q–1841Q. The duo featured the tilting Leyland-type 'Ergomatic' cab and were dedicated to the movement of engines to-and-from Chiswick. They were the last AEC-badged commercial vehicles to be delivered to LT, ending a tradition dating back to the LPTB purchases of 1935. This official portrait of 1840Q when new was taken prior to the formal hand-over, and shows they carried both AEC and British Leyland insignia. The location is unusual, possibly White City greyhound stadium? Distribution Services

Right: A second-hand short-wheelbase Bedford 'TK' numbered 1866B was acquired via Godfrey Davis in 1974 to help CDS drivers pass the HGV test for 'Class 2' 6-wheel vehicles. Such instruction came under the auspices of the Bus Training School Manager, as shown by the lettering on the cab door. The low body was of a type normally used for distributing soft drinks. John Gascoine

Above: Bedford made a return in the form of 13 tilt-cab 'TL's in 1980. One of the most comprehensively equipped was 'TL1260' 2276B, being provided with an orange flashing beacon, crew-cab, quarter-tilt, tail-lift and winch, for use with Lifts & Escalators. Phil Moth

Above right: CDS traditionally over-specifed their standard of vehicle requirements until the early 1980s, when value for money took priority. Dodge Commando 'G10' 2314D of 1981 resulted. Tail-lifts became common features when Health & Safety regulations restricted the weight of items that could be lifted manually. As LT subsidiaries raised their profiles mid- and dark-blue lining has been applied to the cab and 'LONDON TRANSPORT' replaced by 'DISTRIBUTION SERVICES'. David Rowe

A further purchasing policy change was the buying of the lowest-priced vehicles to meet LT's specification. This led to twenty-five Perkins-engined Dodge (formerly Commer) Commando 'G' models entering service between 1981 and 1983, again of varying capacities between 7½ and 16-tonnes. These carried numbers 2303D to 2307D, 2312D to 2317D, 2376D, 2379D, 2383D to 2387D, 2393D, 2400D, 2402D, 2403D, 2405D, 2406D and 2409D. Some had box van bodies, but most were dropsides with additional features such as crew-cabs, tail-lifts, generators, winches or cranes. During the 1970s, ancillary features like hydraulic cranes and tail-lifts were becoming more popular as operators realised how useful they could be, as it meant there was less need for dedicated or specialised vehicles. Many of LT's Commandos could be described as multi-purpose, whereby one modern well-equipped truck could replace two earlier under-utilised vehicles.

May 1982 had seen the delivery of 2378F, a solitary Ford Cargo '1011' dropside with tail-lift. The Cargo model was introduced in 1981 to replace the now venerable

D-series and featured a very plain and square-looking cab. Eleven further Cargo lorries (2380F, 2381F, 2382F, 2388F, 2392F, 2396F, 2398F, 2399F, 2404F, 2407F and 2408F) were delivered in 1983, plus articulated tractor unit 2394F. All were primarily open-bodied, though 2392F and 2408F are recorded as having half- and quarter-tilts. Additional Cargos entered stock in 1986 (2433F, 2434F and 2436F to 2442F), 1988 (2465F to 2468F) and 1990 (2498F and 2499F).

The 1983 Golden Jubilee year of LT saw Leyland providing lorries of their Freighter '13.11', '16.13' and '16.18' designs. This model had already provided a base for bus recovery truck 2372L (16.18) in 1982, but their use expanded to fill general HGV-duties with dropsides 2395L, 2397L (16.13) and 2401L (13.11). Added in 1986 was 2435L, whilst the last of the breed came in 1988 as 2464L. The last two were later repainted in the white/blue LUL-derived livery.

Since 1986 the German firm of Mercedes-Benz had been providing small vans to LRT and in 1987 the first full-sized lorries arrived. 2469M and 2470M were Mercedes-Benz '814' 7.5-tonne dropside vehicles, and were the last large-size vehicles delivered in grey. More '814's arrived in 1990 as 2485M, 2486M, 2487M and 2489M to 2496M and included the final lorries used by LBL. Among the batch, 2485M, 2486M, 2487M and 2489M were dropsides in red livery (Emergency Control Unit 2488M filled the gap in the numbering), whilst 2490M was a box-truck with tail-lift and red-cab/white-body. 2490M later received the white/blue scheme subsequently adopted as standard for virtually the whole service vehicle fleet.

From the mid-1980s, a number of different lettering styles had replaced the usual red 'LONDON TRANSPORT' cab-side transfer and its companion allocation-use black sign-writing. By 1990, this relaxation had gone a stage further and it was becoming common to see vehicles bearing local subsidiary identity, or even no lettering at all. 2485M was allocated to Wood Green Garage and carried the 'Leaside Buses' name complete with swan,

Above left: The Ford 'Cargo' was launched in 1981, replacing the D-series, with LT gaining its first examples in 1982. Leading is 1990 crew-cabbed 2498F, based at Lillie Bridge Depot for Permanent Way gang use, the first such type to be delivered in the new LUL-based white/blue livery. Behind are two Mercedes-Benz demountable trucks, 2509M and 2491M carrying dropside/crew-cab bodies. All three are normally employed during the night hours. Behind is LUL's Ashfield House offices, and now the home of the Railway Training Centre. Kim Rennie

Left: During the mid-1980s, lorries were being sourced from Dodge, Ford and Leyland simultaneously. Crane-fitted Leyland Freighter 2395L, in use from December 1983, is seen at Acton Works in 1990. The leading dropside panel has been lowered, revealing the metal guides for holding rail wheel-sets. The cab door lettering has been crudely applied in red on a white rectangular sticker, a thankfully short-lived practice. To the vehicle's offside is an unidentified white LT bullion van. David Rowe

whilst sister lorry 2486M had small 'London United' coats-of-arms. Both were applied to cab doors in white, and were obviously culled from the LBL 'unit' name transfers introduced in April 1989. These were the last red-liveried large vehicles obtained, all subsequent deliveries appearing in white/blue.

To achieve maximum flexibility, autumn 1990 saw the delivery of new vehicles designed to carry a range of de-mountable bodies, which included dropside, curtain-side, box, breakdown and 'temporary office' formats; and were identified by their own DB-series prefix.

Vehicles 2491M to 2496M were Mercedes-Benz '1114' models for the LUL Emergency Response Unit (already detailed in Chapter 6). The Mercedes-Benz '1114' was the higher capacity version of the '814', with the same engine, but an 11-tonne gross weight. In 1993, six more demount-able-equipped chassis/cabs were delivered for general purpose Underground duties. Numbered 2508M, 2509M, 2534M, 2536M, 2537M and 2540M, they were paired with the DB bodies.

In July 1986, Ford Europe had merged its truck-building operations with the Iveco Company. This company was a wholly-owned subsidiary of Fiat and had taken over the truck building operations of Fiat, OM, Lancia, Unic and Magirus Deutz. A revised 'Super Cargo' lorry was introduced by Iveco in 1993, and CDS gained examples as dropsides 2522F, 2523, 2524F and 2535F the same year. Other Super Cargo chassis were equipped to carry de-mountable bodies (2546F and 2547F), and a further two (2554F and 2555F) arrived in 1995.

With the disposal of the LBL bus business complete by 1995, and much of LT's traditional activities now being carried out by outside contractors, there was no longer a need for large batches of identical vehicles. Consequently, a number of one-off types have joined the fleet in recent years, and seemingly on an ad-hoc basis. 2552M is a 1995 Mercedes-Benz '1820' flatbed fitted with a Palfinger crane, whilst 2571M is a more recent Mercedes, a 1999-vintage '1831 Actros' flatbed also fitted with a Palfinger hydraulic crane. Also new the same year was 2565F, an Iveco 'EuroTech' flat platform lorry.

It was not until August 1941 that the first articulated unit entered the service vehicle fleet. Before this, a number of ordinary lorries operated with small or medium-sized towed or drawbar trailers. For example, in 1937, 18-cwt and 10-cwt trailers numbered 13, 14 and 15 were in use by the Works & Building Department, whilst ex-LCCT Karriers 171K/172K operated in conjunction with 2-axle drawbar trailers for tramway track maintenance.

This first articulated tractor, 603P, was an AEC Matador dating from 1938, and obtained second-hand from Clifford's of Fulham. It was combined with a low-bed machinery-carrying semi-trailer, which had a pair of short axles in line across the rear of the trailer deck. Each axle carried a pair of wheels and both pairs of wheels and axles could be removed (or knocked out) from the trailer and the deck lowered to the ground to enable indivisible items to be propelled onto the load bed. The previous operator

was well known for its large fleet of machinery-carrying lorries. 603P was one of the 'Railway War Damage Plant Vehicles' operated by the Works & Building Engineer from a depot in Hammersmith. Unusually for a vehicle acquired second-hand during the war it was not withdrawn soon after 1945, but instead remained in the fleet until April 1954.

Between 1947 and 1949, ten Bedford-Scammell 'OSS' petrol-engined tractor units entered stock to provide motive power for thirteen new 'MC' mobile staff canteens. In February 1951, a further similar Bedford-Scammell 'OSS' tractor unit was purchased. Numbered 953B, it utilised a Perkins P6 diesel engine instead of the 6-cylinder petrol engine. It normally worked with a single-axle Eagle wooden dropside step-frame trailer fitted with a Scammell automatic coupling. The trailer was unusual in being fitted with a removable tall metal tilt (or canopy) at the front end.

In October 1953, Leyland Beaver 1010L arrived and was ultimately to replace 603P. A Dyson semi-trailer was provided and the new combination classed as a 25-ton articulated machinery carrier. Very unusually the tractor unit was fitted with a power-operated winch and ground anchor which enabled it to move heavy items. One of its most famous tasks was transporting the 1872-built Aveling & Porter 0-4-0T Brill Branch (Wotton Tramway) steam locomotive No. 807 from Neasden Depot to Charlton Works for refurbishment prior to entering the British Transport Commission's museum store. More regular loads included cranes, transformers and escalator parts. Both 953B and 1010L were based at Parsons Green and only ever driven by the senior drivers from that depot. It was always the lot of Parsons Green to get the difficult and complicated transport jobs, even when the request received was to just "move a crane", with absolutely no advice as to the size and weight of the item.

Right: Certain non-articulated trailers were used for the maintenance of the tram and trolleybus systems. This is Eagle 'cable float trailer' No. 65, which was used to move tramway cable drums. Initially based at Acton Tram Depot, by the early-1950s it had been moved to Rye Lane. A.B. Cross

Below: The Board's first proper articulated unit was 603P, which combined a second-hand AEC Matador tractor with a low-loading trailer fitted with twin 'knock out' rear axles. Though described as a '20-ton articulated machinery carrier', it regularly carried far heavier loads than this. Here the vehicle demonstrates the side-loading ramps used to embark small items of plant, plus the wartime additions of headlamp masks and white-edged wings. Equally unique in the LPTB fleet is the vehicle behind, Q188, the 3-axle AEC Q-type double-decker originally designed for Green Line use. LT Museum

Certain ordinary lorries were also licensed to tow trailers. In this case, the Works & Building Department's Albion 'KN127' 4-ton lorry 369A has been paired with a rather primitive-looking step-frame trailer with winch which is apparently numbered '4'.

Although the Bedford-Scammell 'OSS' tractor units used to haul mobile canteens from 1948 are well known, an additional Perkins-engined example was obtained in 1951. As 953B, it operated with an Eagle step-frame trailer and was based at Parsons Green. On this occasion, it was delivering electrical plant to Baker Street sub-station, a site accessed via the disused and now-demolished Leslie Green Bakerloo Line station building. LT Museum

The replacement for Matador 603P was Leyland Beaver 1010L, which entered service in 1953 together with a Dyson step-frame trailer as a '25-ton articulated machinery carrier'. Again, the rear wheels of the trailer could be removed to provide access from the rear. In a change of practice though, the winch was now power-operated and fitted to the tractor. The latter was also equipped with ground anchors, which were used to keep it in position when winching heavy items. LT Museum

An important job came up in 1957 when a large Underground transformer-rectifier burnt out. To quote *London Transport Magazine*: '*An emergency call went to the CDS which was quickly ready with a special articulated truck to take the twenty-ton load. Immediately following the evening peak traffic the bulky apparatus was loaded on to the special vehicle and transported across London to an electrical store. There a new transformer was loaded in its place and hurried back – to be installed and go into service for the peak the following morning. It was speedy work from the lorry men, with no room for a slip-up.*'

For all their usefulness, the above three units were very much in the 'specialised' mode and used sparingly to convey very bulky or heavy items of equipment. However, in December 1959, LT progressed to the general use of the articulated lorry/semi-trailer concept. Six Thames Trader 5416cc tractor units (or 'prime movers' as was the terminology of the day) entered the fleet and were allocated numbers 1139F to 1144F, the last unit having the addition of a 2-ton HIAB crane. By now, LT had presumably decided that the old-fashioned 'Flowers' cranes fitted to the AEC pole carriers were no longer suitable for its needs. Instead, the folding hydraulically-controlled HIAB crane offered greater flexibility and safety when lifting heavy and expensive items like transformers. Delivery coincided with the changeover from green to grey liveries, so although the first three vehicles carried the new scheme, what were numerically the last two appeared in the old colour. Another nine Thames Traders were added in 1961 and numbered in two blocks: 1189F, 1190F, 1191F and 1221F to 1226F. The final Thames Trader prime movers purchased were 1325F and 1358F, and came in December 1964.

All three batches of articulated tractors were fitted with Scammell Automatic coupling gear and operated with fourteen dropside York single-axle semi-trailers dating from 1959–60. Originally referred to by their body numbers, 9862 to 9873 and 9918 to 9920, the trailers were soon reclassified YT 1 to YT 14. Livery was originally Chiswick Green, later becoming grey. An early attempt to match tractors and trailers in sequential order soon proved impracticable, and vehicles were paired indiscriminately from then on. The Traders were later used with the MC canteen semi-trailers, the last of the Bedfords having operated in 1967 (though most of the batch had departed a few years earlier than this). Also new from

Top: The arrival in late-1959 of 1142F, one of six Thames Trader 'prime movers' with Scammell automatic couplings, coincided with the expansion of articulated operation to general freight duties. To work with them, York 'platform semi-trailer' YT 12 was one of 14 new in 1959, originally displaying body numbers on the bolster (in this case 9873). Both tractor and trailer were later painted grey.
LT Museum

Above: The first batch of York trailers survived long enough to be hauled by Ford 'D'-series. Trailer YT 7 rests between duties in front of the Chiswick Research Laboratory.
Julian Bowden-Green

Right: Grey liveried Thames Trader 1189F is seen paired with YT 13, a green York step-frame trailer for carrying light but indivisible loads. Behind is erstwhile Euston Square Station building. J. Murphy

York circa-1961 were step-frame semi-trailers YT 15 and YT 16. Trailer YT 15 was a standard low-loader, whilst YT 16 was a step-frame trailer with wooden dropsides. Both were still operating in the mid-1970s.

The attraction of articulation was that, used properly, it could greatly improve the utilisation of tractor units. For instance, on the Chiswick – Aldenham shuttle, trailers could be left at either site for loading, whilst the tractor unit was travelling with another trailer. The trailers that worked this shuttle were racked-out to hold radiators, axles and other components safely.

Only one Karrier Bantam articulated tractor was operated by LT. This was 1310KB, dating from July 1964 and towing a sloping decked single-axled Carrimore trailer fitted with automatic coupling gear numbered C 21. The crew-cabbed tractor and its dedicated trailer were acquired to move awkward items like bus shelters, and was a further example of LT now ordering purpose-built vehicles for specialised duties rather than converting former buses to the role. As LT was then using a common numbering system for all trailers, there was never a C 1–C 20.

Between 1971 and 1972, five Ford D-series tractor chassis numbered 1664F to 1668F were delivered to replace the Thames Trader units, of which 1664F and 1665F were 'D600' type, the others more powerful

Above: Thames Trader 1223F was specifically allocated to the distribution and collection of bus tyres. Its single-axled full-tilt trailer, YT 19, was equipped with a tail-lift to help loading and unloading. The poster outside the 'Depot Dining Rooms' advertising Billy Fury's now forgotten film 'Play it Cool' suggests the year was 1962, whilst another poster reference to the 'Gaumont Hammersmith' gives a clue to the location. J. Murphy collection

Centre: Ford replaced its Thames Trader with the forward-control D-series in 1965. LT received models from 1966, of which 'D600' 1665F arrived in 1971, with 5th-wheel coupling arrangements instead of the former 'Automatic' type. The very basic crew accommodation is located directly above the trailer's articulation point and must have provided a very uncomfortable ride. The tractor's drab appearance results from a repaint, eliminating the usual factory-finish white-painted areas. Jim Wright

Right: With a wide variety of options available to purchasers of the D-series under Ford's 'Special Vehicle Option', the customer could get almost the exact variant required. Here, CDS has decided on a lengthened-wheelbase Ford 'DA1610' tractor, complete with an extending arm 'HIAB' crane. The step-frame trailer seems to be of the same design as that pictured with Trader 1189F in the early-1960s. If so, it must have been modified to accept the '5th-wheel' coupling equipment. Jim Wright

Left: Between 1976 and 1984, this was LT's largest articulated tractor-trailer combination. Leyland Lynx 1995L is seen with a twin-axle step frame trailer. The cab roof orange flashing lights were fitted after delivery and were later replaced by larger versions. A CO/CP stock train passes in the background on the westbound District Line. Jim Wright

Centre: After two decades of reliance on Ford, Bedford returned to favour in 1979. One of two Bedford 'TL1930' tractors was 2300B, delivered in 1981 and lasting ten years. Lack of investment by General Motors meant the model was the last British-built Bedford lorry. New legislation has brought about two visual changes: the frame on the nearside cab front for holding a 'hazardous goods' sign, and the green plate on the bumper indicating exemption from the 'Greater London Lorry Ban'. The single-axled trailer is one of six built by Crane Fruehauf from 1983–4 and is carrying Underground car wheel-sets. David Rowe

Bottom: Leyland's replacement for the Lynx was the Cruiser, and LT acquired this example as 2389L in 1982. The trailer is YT 29, a York step-frame load carrier. The dropsides enabled loose loads to be carried safely, whilst a hand winch was provided to haul heavy loads over the trailer's beaver tail. At this point, both livery and lettering had remained unchanged for over 20 years. Michael Clark

'DA1610' examples. Of the latter, 1667F and 1668F were additionally fitted with HIAB cranes. Ford 1684F was an extra 1971-vintage 'D600', which together with step-frame trailer K 1 replaced 1310KB and C 21 (the Karrier was sold the following year). 1971 also witnessed a new batch of general-usage York platform trailers. These occupied numbers YT 22 to YT 27 in the common series and were fitted with 'fifth wheel' couplings rather than the Scammell automatic type used earlier. This change in equipment allowed the combinations to work at a higher gross weight, although retaining single axles. Four small 2-wheel trailers were in use from 1967 in conjunction with the ex-BEA '4RF4' uniform issue units, and are described in the chapter on 'specialised vehicles'.

The next development was not until September 1976, with the purchase of Leyland Lynx unit 1995L. The Lynx was the medium weight 26-tonne articulated in the Leyland range and helped form what was then LT's largest articulated unit. It was regularly paired with a York step-frame semi-trailer numbered YT 28 dating from 1977. The early-1980s saw a diversification of types

The British-built Ford Cargo became very popular with CDS in the 1980s. No.2444F was a '1913' variant dating from 1986 and the last Ford tractor unit bought by LT. The trailer is one of the 1983–4 Crane Fruehauf's and has side-guards reminiscent of those fitted to service vehicles in the 1920s. 2444F would appear to have been under-powered, with just 130-bhp available to pull a maximum weight of 19 tonnes, though it is unlikely the unit was ever fully laden.
David Rowe

At least four Cobul 'Tow-a-Van' box-trailers have been operated by LUL. This is CBT 56 in Ruislip Depot on 26th January 1998. The trailer's appearance is factory-finish matt white, with the addition of LUL 'Engineering services' lettering. A miniature wheel-clamp has been attached to prevent theft.
Kim Rennie

entering the fleet and less reliance on such old-established manufacturers as Ford. A DAF 'F2200' tractor was noted as being on loan at Chiswick in March 1979, though did not lead to any orders. Other hired vehicles have included brown-liveried AEC 'Ergomatic' registered WLH 77S, and white-painted Fiat 170 registered CAB 402S.

A later articulated tractor was 2251B, a 1980-built Bedford 'KGA 1930' model that lasted six years. A year later, two tilt-cab Bedford 'TL's were added, and took up numbers 2300B to 2301B. Also non-standard were Leyland Cruisers 2389L and 2410L, which formed part of the 1982–83 intake. The 'Cruiser' was the 'light-heavyweight' 32-tonne articulated tractor derived from the 'T45 Roadtrain' range as a replacement for the Leyland Lynx.

The Ford D-series was replaced by the Cargo model in 1981 and LT received one in crane-fitted tractor unit form in May 1982. Numbered 2373F, this was a '1313' variant and lasted until May 1993. Two more tractors of the '1913' variant (2382F and 2394F) were acquired in 1983. A fourth (2444F) appeared in 1986 and has so far been the last Ford-based prime mover to enter the fleet. 1986 saw another demonstration of the more open procurement policy now in vogue with the appearance of 2455V. This was a second-hand V-registered Volvo 'F717', and the first non-PSV vehicle from this manufacturer to be operated.

Details of trailers used throughout the 1980s and 1990s are sketchy, and little has appeared in published form. DT 31 was a second-hand Darham 3500-gallon distilled water tank semi-trailer acquired in May 1983, whilst SEB-T-42 and SEB-T-43 were heavy-duty single-axle cable-drum carriers from 1985 and 1987 respectively. Four 'Tow-a-Van' box-trailers from Cobul were acquired between 1991 and 1993. Capable of being hauled by cars or small vans, they are classed as CBT 46 and CBT 55 to 57. The year 1993 saw the entry into service of two of the most distinctive trailers ever obtained by LT. CMT 53 and 54 were built by Carrymaster and comprised a pair of very tall-bodied uniform-issue units (described later). A small Scottorn vehicle recovery trailer had entered service in December 1984 as ST 40; by 1996 Distribution Services was using a galvanised steel-framed trailer built by Indespension for the same purpose and numbered T 41. Trailer numbers had traditionally been painted on vehicle headboards in contrasting colours, but from the early-1990s were being displayed black-on-white using reflective registration plate material. Indeed, these plates were often the only clue to Distribution Services' ownership. In some cases, the full maker's classification code is abbreviated to a single letter 'T'.

The year 1985 had seen an event that was to alter the fleet's composition, when the first large Mercedes-Benz lorries were delivered. Special authority had to be obtained from the LRT Board to purchase foreign vehicles. These were later to include articulated units when three tractors of varying sizes arrived. The first was 2471M; a Mercedes-Benz '1625' bought second-hand in 1987 and initially bearing a very non-LT orange/brown livery, relieved by silver stripes. The cab was to carry a roof-mounted wind-deflector for many years (later removed), and the fact that this originally bore the legend '1625' indicates that the vehicle may have been in demonstration use before acquisition. This type must have been adjudged a success, because in October 1989 a second model was added, Mercedes-Benz '1617' 2472M. Delivered in standard grey livery, it was the only Mercedes prime mover to appear in this scheme from new. This was an unusual vehicle, since most '1617' chassis were used as 4-wheel rigid haulage vehicles. This may have been bought to see if this model could be used to replace the older Ford tractor units. Its large full-size cab would have restricted its operation on the railway depot shuttle service and it did not last long in service. The last of the trio was 2474M and entered stock in February 1990. This was the most powerful of the three, a Mercedes-Benz '1726' example and distinguished by a full-width tinted sun visor. It was delivered in a non-standard red livery and is also thought to have been obtained second-hand.

DT 1 (A869 GRU) and DT 2 (B221 PFX) were second-hand DAF articulated tractors dating from 1984. Paired with flatbed trailers, they were used by London Coaches to provide HGV-training from about 1990. Painted red and with gold 'London Coaches' fleetnames, they were not part of the CDS fleet.

A new generation of medium-sized articulated units began in 1993 with the arrival of four Mercedes-Benz '1520's: 2525M to 2528M. A further vehicle, 2552M, was added two years later. All five carried the new white/blue Distribution Services colour scheme. Paired with these were CT 33 to C 38, six Crane Fruehauf platform semi-trailers dating from 1983–84 which had ousted the last of the earlier Yorks. These had at first carried grey livery, but were soon repainted all-over blue to match the new Mercedes. Of similar age was CT 39, a 40ft step-frame Crane Fruehauf trailer used to carry containerised components and parts for repair between rail depots and Acton Works. The reason for it being of step-frame design was to allow the loaded trailer under cable gantries within the depots. A later one-off Mercedes was 2551M, a Mercedes-Benz '2534' of 1995 and the most powerfully-engined model owned yet. It was immediately recognisable by being of 3-axle configuration.

Top: Mercedes-Benz '1617' tractor unit 2472M with 'day cab' paired with Buckingham-built tanker BT 10 at Amersham Station in July 1990 in connection with 'Steam on the Met'. Unusually the tank unit is not self-supporting; suggesting that the older tank may have been re-mounted on a new chassis. As it was carrying water, the tank-side frame to the left of the ladder should have displayed a notice reading 'Non Hazardous' for the information of the fire service, rather than having been left blank. Kim Rennie

Centre: London Coaches, an LRT subsidiary, offered HGV driver-training in the early-1990s using two second-hand DAF tractor units paired with flatbed trailers. Numbered DT 1 and DT 2, the former is seen at Wandsworth Garage in full London Coaches livery and carrying a revised design of 'Lorry Ban' exemption plate. Neither combination formed part of the Distribution Services fleet. M.K. Conway

Left: Following the demise of Aldenham and Chiswick Works articulated operation became concentrated on the Underground. Five medium-sized Mercedes-Benz '1520' tractors entered service between 1993 and 1995 and carried the new white/blue livery from new. On 4th July 2000, tractor 2552M was visiting Neasden to exchange wheel-sets requiring turning on the depot's lathe. The trailer is CT 37, from the 1983–4 Crane Fruehauf batch and now repainted blue. The '1520' model is quite rare in the United Kingdom and combines adequate power with the smaller cab of the Mercedes 814 model. Their small size has ensured their retention, given the restricted access available in certain LUL depots. Kim Rennie

Among the 'one-off' types acquired in recent years is 2551M, a Mercedes-Benz '2534' delivered in 1995. The vehicle is fitted with a 'sleeper cab' to allow extended periods of operation.
The 3-axle flatbed trailer is one of four provided in 1999 by Cartwright's of Altrincham and identified as T 65–T 68. The location is the former Acton Works staff car park which was later taken over by CDS and stands on the alignment of the old South Acton branch. Kim Rennie

Nos. 2559M–2561M are three very large Mercedes-Benz '1835' tractors delivered in 1998. This is the last of the trio, 2561M, which on 17th July 2000 could be found residing in Acton Works. The 'roped & sheeted' trailer is T 67, one of the 1999 Cartwrights. These vehicles are used on runs to the Continent and are thus equipped with 'sleeper cabs'. Kim Rennie

A tiny tanker-trailer is T 70, built by Terrence Baker and used to refuel permanent way tamping machines in LUL depots and sidings. The official operator's name on the orange 'hazard' notice is still listed as 'London Transport'. Kim Rennie

The most recent articulated tractors were delivered in 1998, and represented a further development in the use of such types by LT/LUL. Numbered 2559M, 2560M and 2561M are three Mercedes-Benz '1835 Actros' units. Fitted with sleeper cabs, they allow long-distance haulage operation both at home and abroad. The latter is especially useful given the international nature of today's railway industry, and the need for LUL to source many parts and components from the Continent. More recently, August 1999 saw the delivery of four tri-axle 13-metre platform trailers built by Cartwright's of Altrincham. Numbered T 65 to T 68, some have guide-rails and anchorage points to permit the safe transportation of individual wheel-sets and bogies.

At the other end of the scale, a very small 2-axle trailer with a circular-section fuel tank body had appeared by 2000. Built by Terrence Baker, it is identified as T 70 and has been finished in full LUL livery, complete with 'Support services' fleetnames. This tanker trailer is used to refuel TransPlant railway tamping machines in depots and sidings. Several fuel and water tankers operated with dedicated arctic units on a semi-permanent basis and are described elsewhere.

TIPPER TRUCKS

This Bedford OSBT dates from 1948 and with its comfortable cab, power to spare and brakes to match is in complete contrast to the earlier Fordson 7V type. The body is a standard front-ram design built by or to Bedford specification. 815B was used to transport materials to-and-from the ex-LCC Tramways Permanent Way Depot at Deptford Wharf. LT Museum

One of the LPTB's earliest tippers was this short-wheelbase Albion KS 127, numbered AN 44 (later 365A), seen here when new in 1939 and displaying the twin rams used to raise the body. Though this design allowed the body to be full length, the fact that the rams protruded below chassis level meant that they were liable to damage on rough ground. The vehicle was originally allocated to Chiswick Works but later years saw it absorbed into the main Works & Building Department fleet, where it remained in use until 1952. LT Museum

The LGOC had been responsible for a number of construction projects and B-type bus B 2822 is known to have carried a tipping body on a specially-shortened chassis. From 1933, the LPTB initiated a huge programme of building new garages, depots and lines. Much of the planning and design work was handled by the Board's own staff. Although contractors carried out the actual building work, day-to-day maintenance and repairs remained in the hands of the Board's employees. The latter was co-ordinated from the Works & Building Department's head office and depot in Parsons Green Lane, SW6 (adjacent to the eastbound District Line).

Three ex-MET solid-tyred ADC (AEC-engined) '418' 4-ton hand-tipping lorries dating from 1930 had entered the LPTB fleet. Originally numbered 50, 69 and 84, they had the distinction of being placed at the start of the 1939 renumbering as 1E, 2E and 3E. Middle lorry 2E was fitted with welding plant in September 1936, though retired four years afterwards. The remaining two

survived the war and lasted until 1946. There is a mystery concerning the origins of these ADCs as noted earlier, since the ADC operation had been closed down in 1928.

An older one-off was 55Z (ex-EN 11), an AEC '506' hydraulic tipping lorry which was in use between June 1927 and September 1934. It was then converted to a sludge lorry, a task it performed until withdrawal in December 1939. Particularly long-lasting was 66Z (ex-EN 26), an AEC YC-type with a Tylor engine. This 5-ton hand-tipping lorry was new in 1919 and in use until May 1948. The other pre-war tipper recorded in the 1939-series was 69Z (ex-EN 13, and converted from a 1926 stores lorry). Another 'Tylor' YC-type, it lasted from December 1928 to November 1948 in its revised form.

Two additional vehicles were commissioned in February 1939. These were AN 43 and AN 44, a pair of Albion KS127 hydraulic tippers with a 4-cubic yard capacity (later 364A and 365A). Though both operated from the Parsons Green Works & Building Depot, 365A had first seen use in Chiswick Works. Following post-war deliveries, the duo retired in November 1952.

Before the war, the tipper fleet was not large, but it was assumed (quite rightly) that during any impending hostilities the sheer volume of damage caused to LPTB property through bombing would be immense. By 1940, the Building Department had formed 'demolition and decontamination gangs' which were available at their district sub-offices at Aldwych, Chalk Farm, Chiswick Park, Stockwell, Wembley Park and Whitechapel. The immediate need was for tipper trucks to be able to move away large amounts of rubble from railway tracks, stations and certain roads to enable passenger services to continue. The Board was lucky in being allocated a number of 'Lease-Lend' US-built left-hand-drive Ford V8 'BB' Detroit-type 3-ton models from early-1941 (as mentioned earlier). Six of these were bodied as tippers: 470F, 471F, 472F, 495F, 496F and 497F (472F only from May 1943). Withdrawal came between the years 1944 and 1950.

Left: A number of left-hand-drive American-built Ford Detroit-type hand-tippers were acquired in 1941. The hand-tipping equipment used a handle, gearwheel and screw thread to elevate the body. As built, the body headboard was next to the rear of the cab. However, on 470F, it was moved back by about 4ft to accommodate a tool section. Kim Rennie collection

Centre: The Fordson-Thames 7V with its thirsty V8 petrol engine, poor brakes and cramped cab was hardly the ideal vehicle for the LPTB to purchase. However, during the war, the Government allocated new vehicles and essential users had to be grateful for such types as they could get. This photograph shows 632F sometime between 1945 and 1948, after which it received a new dropside tipper body manufactured by Anthony Hoists. Bill Aldridge collection

Although the LPTB could have been deemed an 'essential user' of commercial vehicles during the war, few new vehicles were allocated to them by the Government, save for two batches of American and British Fords. The LPTB was therefore forced to look for second-hand tippers to supplement the existing small fleet in 1940–41. The purchases were made from a variety of second-hand commercial dealers around London, but the vehicles themselves originated from all parts of the country. They comprised a widely varying mix of types using Austin, Bedford, Commer, Dodge, Ford and Morris designs, and the actual models differed considerably. Most dated from the mid-1930s and only lasted in service for two or three years. The reason for their short service was that they were bought and used specially to facilitate the construction of the 'Government Deep Shelters' between 1940 and 1942. These shelters were aligned and located in such a way as to be capable of being joined up after the war to form the basis of express Central and Northern Line services, though in the event the work was never done. The tippers had capacities of between 2- and 5-tons, with some having hand-powered tipping gear whilst others had the benefit of power take-off-driven hydraulic equipment. There were over 100 of these second-hand vehicles but none remained in service after 1943, by which time the shelters had been completed. Many of the tippers were then transferred to the LCC for rubble removal. Fleet numbering occupied most of the sequence between 498B and 622DG.

January 1942 saw a batch of twelve Fordson Thames (i.e. British Ford) 7V, side-valve V8-engined, 4-cubic yard hydraulic tippers brought into stock. They were numbered 630F to 641F and must have been considered quite successful, since they were re-bodied with new dropside tipping bodies built by Anthony Hoists in 1947 and 1948. Suitably reconstructed, they lasted until the early-1950s. The Board provided an additional two vehicles from its own resources in mid-1944, converting earlier Morris Commercial C-type 30-cwt trucks 272M and 284M to tippers. These had previously been in use since 1935–36 as trucks.

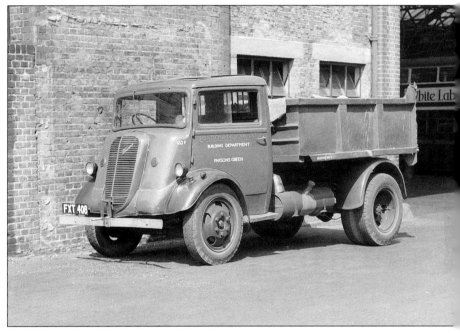

Right: In the autumn of 1950, a batch of seven Leyland Beaver tippers was acquired for general-purpose duties. This included the transport of rubbish and rubble to the various tips then used by LT, as well as the movement of coal and soil. No.950L entered service in December 1950 and saw 11 years' use. Bill Aldridge collection

An unusual purchase was 951L, a Leyland Hippo 6-wheel tipper delivered in 1950. Seemingly destined for railway Permanent Way use at Lillie Bridge, the body was capable of carrying 10 cubic yards of material, but proved too big for LT's operations and 951L was sold after just 5 years' service. Twin rams raised the tipper, and if one were to stick during the operation, the whole body could tip sideways. The spare wheel was mounted in a carrier behind the cab. LT Museum

The final batch of Bedford tippers featured Perkins diesel engines and Anthony Hoists steel tipper bodies. The economical Perkins engine was an optional fitting to Bedford O-series trucks prior to the introduction of Bedford's own diesel later in the 1950s. LT Museum

Post-war, LT tried to return to the high degree of standardisation it preferred. The Leyland Beaver was chosen for large-size tippers and seven arrived as 944L to 950L in 1950. These were quality-built 7-cubic yard tippers with double dropside bodies. Delivered at the same time was 951L, a 19-ton 6-wheel Leyland 0600-engined Hippo capable of carrying 10-cubic yards. Unfortunately, its large capacity could not be fully-utilised and it was replaced after only five years. To provide a smaller-capacity option, the Bedford OSBT or OSBC chassis were used from 1948. 815B to 816B, 917B to 920B and 954B to 960B were delivered with 27hp petrol engines (first two batches) or Perkins P6 30hp diesel-engines (the rest), and were 5-ton 5-cubic yard vehicles (917B to 920B were only

of 4-cubic yards' size). Additional vehicles arrived in late-1957 as 1066AS to 1069AS, four normal-control Austin 503 model 5-ton 5-cubic yard tippers. They were the modernised 'Loadstar' model and had rubber front mudguard edges to reduce the possibility of damage.

One unusual feature of the majority of the LT's tippers was the fitting of a high headboard with protective guard or canopy that projected over the cab. Normally these are only fitted to tippers used in very heavy-duty conditions and it is typical of the attitude of LT then that it tended to over-specify vehicles.

The mid-1950s saw LT praise both CDS and its tipper fleet in London Transport Magazine, when an embankment earth-slip threatened the Metropolitan Line near Uxbridge: '*At short notice a day and night 'bus service' of tipper lorries was set in operation to remove earth from the top of a bank and relieve pressure . . . the record lift of clay was three hundred and sixty tons in a day.*' A similar action was necessary when a Bakerloo Line embankment suffered similar problems: '*A heavy 'dragline' excavator was transported to the spot for the building department. This was soon at work, scraping off the top layer of the sliding mass of earth, whilst CDS lorries stood ready to remove the soil from the site.*' The report concluded with the observation: '*It was a little drama which was played out without an audience and which did not make the headlines*'. Later a recurring land slip at West Acton in 1962 provided soil for an area in Acton Works which later became the Distribution Service Manager's vehicle park.

Further consolidation occurred in the early-1960s, with the Thames Trader being adopted for almost all CDS's medium-weight vehicle needs. Fleet numbers 1192F to 1195F were the pioneer tippers in January 1961, followed by 1208F to 1212F later the same year and 1246F to 1248F in September 1962. The first batch was in green livery, but was later repainted in grey. The rest were delivered new in the latter livery and all were of 6-ton capacity. Together, these new Traders allowed all the earlier types to be replaced.

Right: A picture to make a modern day Health & Safety official blanche! The jolly-looking crew of 1961-vintage Thames Trader 1194F are hitching a ride on the 6-cubic yard body. It certainly makes the case for the crew-cabs fitted to LT service vehicles in later years. The strong headboard was a feature of many LT tippers and protected the cab from the over-enthusiastic loading of rubble by tractor shovel. Kim Rennie collection

Below right: This well-used Ford D800-series tipper 1650F could carry up to 8 cubic yards. In this case, the cab shield fitted to the body appears to have served its purpose well. Like all tippers, the chassis had been strengthened with 'flitch' plates to prevent it buckling when the body tipped. Jim Wright

With the 'D'-series assuming the mantle of the Thames Trader for both the Ford Motor Company and LT, it was natural that the new model was adopted for the next generation of tippers. 1650F and 1651F were D800 8-ton 8-cubic yard tipping lorries in use from early-1971, and effected the end of the Traders. The fact that just two D-series had replaced a much larger number of earlier tippers shows that the need for such types had been reduced and there was an acceptance that vehicles and/or drivers could be hired in as required. A later Ford D800 was 2202F, this time with an unpainted body, arriving in October 1979. The following year, CDS purchased 2264F, a larger D1110 model. Together with 2319F, a D1210 of August 1981, they eventually replaced the inaugural pair of D-series tippers.

The latest development came with 2538M, a 6-wheel Mercedes-Benz 2422 tipper capable of carrying about 14-tonnes, which entered stock in May 1993. Now the only full-size example in the fleet, it has a red-painted Palfinger grab-bucket fitted, this obviating the need to supply a separate hydraulic loading shovel. In Mercedes terms the 2422 refers to carrying capacity and power, in this case of 24 tonnes gross and 220b.h.p. With tractor units the first two figures refer to the gross laden weight of the tractor unit only. With just one large tipper available to Distribution Services, and much of LRT's activity being scaled down in the 1980s and 1990s, it seems appropriate that a return was made to smaller-capacity vehicles. The Mercedes-Benz '410D'-type was used for so-called 'mini-tippers' 2504M and 2542M in November 1992 and June 1993, which were also in white/blue. Similarly-liveried was 2548F, a caged-sided Ford Transit 190 from May 1994. Finally, there had always been other members of the Building Department's fleet such as vans and small dropside trucks. These were normally of the standard design favoured at the time.

No.2542M was a 6-wheel Mercedes-Benz 2422 dating from 1993 and fitted with a Palfinger grab-bucket. Note that the whole body is painted blue instead of just the skirt. This dispensation in the LUL livery guidelines is allowed on vehicles that may become dirty through their regular use. The circular logo applied below the windscreen indicates exemption to certain restrictions placed on lorries operating in Greater London. To facilitate operation of the hydraulic crane and grab, the operator worked from a platform in front of the tipper body – possibly a safer option than working from ground level. Kim Rennie

A number of rigid and articulated tankers have been operated by LT and its predecessors to convey distilled water or fuel. One of the first tankers was B-type bus B 2745, converted to a mobile water tank and tool carrier in 1921, and thereafter used to replenish overheating buses at special events. Withdrawn in 1930, the usual custom was followed, with the body being transferred to a newer chassis. Another early vehicle appears to have been 73Z, an AEC YC-type lorry. This 1919-vintage tank wagon was painted grey and later saw service as a gully emptier.

Thus it may have been designed to carry waste material, rather than uncontaminated water or fuel.

In the earliest days, distilled water for use in batteries was supplied in glass carboys. The water was either distilled or de-mineralised and supplied from Lots Road Generating Station or the laboratories at Chiswick. To reduce the amount of handling the LGOC decided to invest in a dedicated vehicle for the movement of distilled water. The 'Register of Miscellaneous Vehicles' indicates that one of the 1919-vintage AEC YC-type lorries was

Right: The LPTB was a major user of distilled water for topping-up the batteries of buses, coaches and trolleybuses, as well as the electric locomotives used to haul the Underground's engineers' trains. Once the Board had realised the savings of transporting the product in bulk, a new road tanker was commissioned. A brand-new Albion KN127 chassis was used, along with a 600-gallon tank built by Butterfields of the West Riding of Yorkshire. Regarded as an 'ancillary vehicle', it was able to operate on trade plates. First numbered as AN 37, it became 376A in 1939.
LT Museum

Below: This Bedford OLBD started life as towing lorry 826B in 1949, but when 376A was withdrawn in 1953 it gained the tank transferred from the Albion. Again, the specialised role of distilled water tanker allowed LT to operate the vehicle on trade plates, in this case the red-on-white 'general' type. It was the last Bedford O-series left in the fleet upon withdrawal in 1967.
David Rowe collection

used to transport distilled water at one time (either 63Z or 64Z), but it is not clear if the liquid was carried in bulk form, as opposed to individual containers.

Among the large number of Albion KN127s in use from 1937, 376A was unique in carrying a new 600-gallon distilled water tanker body. Before the creation of CDS in 1949, the vehicle formed part of the Chief Stores Superintendent's fleet at Chiswick. When the Albion was withdrawn in November 1953 its water tank was transferred to 826B. This was a standard Bedford OLBD chassis dating from September 1949 which had previously been used for towing.

The normal delivery of distilled water was operated on a regular 'numbered' route, but if CDS were ever short of drivers, this was the first to be cut. The distilled water tankers were whenever possible filled at Lots Road the previous afternoon by a driver whose allocated work had been completed earlier that day. This minimised the problems caused by traffic congestion in the mornings. A major user of distilled water was the Underground, with battery locomotives needing regular topping-up. As the fleet of LT steam locomotives declined, so the number of battery locomotives increased, and thus even more distilled water was required.

With an increasing need for bulk deliveries of distilled water, the purchase of a second distilled water-carrier was authorised. The 'new' tanker was 963J, an AEC Regent II, formerly bus STL 2649, which had a 1000-gallon tank and new cab constructed by Eagle of Warwick. Entering the service vehicle fleet in July 1952, 963J worked alongside 826B. Like most of this type of LT vehicle, it operated on trade plates. Following 963J's withdrawal in March 1961, the Bedford then continued to perform this function until its own demise in April 1967. As was often the case with specialised-bodied types, it had by then outlived the rest of its similarly-chassised compatriots.

Ford D500 1390F was delivered in December 1966 and carried an elliptical 1000-gallon tank. This was the only water tanker in light grey livery, and indeed the last of the line, as the need for distilled water declined as battery technology improved. Nevertheless, the Ford was long-lived and survived until May 1983. Apart from the delivery of water, 1390F had its moment of glory when the air-conditioning for the computers at LT's Newman Street data-processing centre failed. The little D-series was required to pump water up to the computer room to save the equipment from overheating.

The other bulk-liquid product that required conveyance was fuel. This had traditionally been delivered direct to bus garages by the oil companies (and still is), but LT felt it needed the capacity to transfer the product between sites itself. Indeed, an emergency fuel store was provided at Aldenham Works. A further reason for keeping tankers was to cover for any disruption in diesel supply due to a fuel company tanker drivers' strike. Though LT sourced fuel from different suppliers, it wanted the ability to move fuel between garages; and if for any reason the garage fuel dispensing pumps were to fail, a road tanker could be despatched to the shed to fill the buses direct from the tanker.

On 7th November 1934, the LPTB had acquired the City Motor Omnibus Co. Ltd. 'City' was the largest of the independent bus companies taken-over by the Board, operating thirty-nine buses and two lorries. Among these was City's fuel (petrol) tanker, a khaki-coloured Leyland LB-chassised vehicle registered XU 9106. This had originally been A 16 in the City passenger fleet, before being converted to fuel-carrying use. The LPTB re-numbered it L 66 in their common-series for Leyland 'LB'-types, but it does not seem to have survived long with its new owner.

Two Maudslay Mogul MkII fuel tankers acquired from Shell-Mex in January 1954 were 1013MY and 1014MY. The pair carried 1200-gallon tanks and had been new in 1947. The first was disposed of in July 1962, but companion 1014MY did not leave LT use until April 1972. A photo shows 1014MY in Shell livery fuelling RTL

1459 before or after a foreign tour in 1953, so it can be speculated that LT had hired the tanker prior its purchase. Both Maudslays, like many other vehicles from that manufacturer, would have been fitted with AEC engines from new.

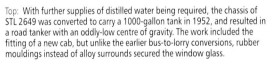

Top: With further supplies of distilled water being required, the chassis of STL 2649 was converted to carry a 1000-gallon tank in 1952, and resulted in a road tanker with an oddly-low centre of gravity. The work included the fitting of a new cab, but unlike the earlier bus-to-lorry conversions, rubber mouldings instead of alloy surrounds secured the window glass.

Centre: Upon the retirement of Bedford 826B in 1967, the duty of distributing distilled water passed to 1390F, a new Ford D-series with an elliptical 1000-gallon tank. By this time, the operating arrangements had altered somewhat and 1390F was fitted with a rear-mounted pump which allowed water to be delivered to relatively remote storage tanks by way of a small hose-reel. In this 1972 view, the vehicle is resting at Chiswick and has gained non-standard black/yellow bumper markings. John Gascoine

Right: The LPTB's first petrol tanker was this Leyland 'LB' inherited from the City Motor Omnibus fleet number A 16. There were many regulations covering the carriage of 'low flash' products such as fuel in bulk, among them the need to have a full-height fire-screen behind the cab (as seen here) and an exhaust exiting in front of this (visible below the cab door). The LPTB subsequently reclassified the tanker as L 66 in a common series that included both bus and lorry Leyland LBs. D.W.K. Jones

LT approached Shell Oil again in February 1971 for the replacements for Maudslay 1014MY. These were 1673Q and 1674Q. The former had been built in 1963 and was a 6-wheel AEC Marshal with 3500-gallon tank. The latter dated from the previous year, and was an articulated AEC Mercury tractor with an oval 3000-gallon capacity trailer. Both were built with the Park Royal-style cab and arrived in a non-standard dark grey livery. Tanker 1674Q was used as much for HGV-training as fuel transportation. The Mercury went first in December 1977, the Marshal lingered on until April 1981.

The only Seddon vehicle owned by LT was 2000S, and re-used the suffix formerly identifying ex-S-class buses. This model 16.4 rigid vehicle was fitted with a 2500-gallon tank and was used from December 1976 to October 1983 (replacing 1674Q). It continued the tradition of using second-hand tankers, first seeing service with Advanced Fuel Oils in 1971. The Motor Panels cabs fitted to these Seddons were renowned for their propensity to rust prematurely, and the vehicle was withdrawn on the day it arrived back at Chiswick and the radiator grille fell off as it drew to a halt. Another non-standard type was

Above: During the war the distribution of fuel for the whole country was taken over by the Pool Board, who rationalised deliveries between nominally competing companies. The Pool Board was allowed to purchase new tankers, including this Maudslay Mogul Mk II. It was later owned by Shell-Mex, but passed to LT in 1954 as 1014MY. The tank itself held a paltry 1,200 gallons but the vehicle remained in use until 1972. *Lens of Sutton*

Right: The AEC Marshal was the lighter 6-wheel chassis built by the Southall concern. The Marshal used the Mercury engine and running gear, and being light but well-built was very popular with fuel companies. The cab is probably of Park Royal origin, but despite its looks was actually quite cramped inside. New to Shell Petroleum in 1963, it came to LT in 1971 as 1673Q and was finished in a non-standard dark grey livery. *Jim Wright*

Fulfilling a similar role to 1673Q was 1674Q, a 1962-built AEC Mercury articulated tanker and also ex-Shell. The tanker was of step-frame elliptical design with a four or five compartment tank, but the individual outlet valves were manifolded to give just one single discharge connection, this being possible only on tankers carrying diesel, kerosene or gas oil. The combination was used as much for HGV-training as for the transportation of fuel, as evidenced by the L-plate being carried in this view at Stockwell Garage. Like 1673Q, the vehicle carried a RT-type Central Bus radiator triangle. *Metropolitan Photographic*

2216B, which paired a Bedford TM1630 model with a 2450-gallon tank. Delivery was in November 1979, but the withdrawal date is unknown.

The next fuel tanker in the fleet was also a Bedford, this time of the TL1630 type. It was one of a batch of Bedford chassis operating at 10-, 12- and 16-tonnes numbered in the 2265B to 2277B range. The vehicle in question, 2274B, was equipped with a 2400-gallon tank and saw service between August 1980 and March 1993. It was longest-lasting of the Bedford TLs, and may have survived even longer had such ancillary activities not been cut short by the privatisation of LBL.

The 'Fuel Crisis' of 2000 and the shortages it caused led to a re-appraisal of Distribution Services policy on the procurement and storage of diesel oil for its fleet. Two Thompson 3-axle 8-compartment tanker trailers, T 71 and T 72, were acquired to facilitate this. In order to move them, a 1996 Scania 113M prime mover constructed to Petroleum Regulation standards was also obtained. All were second-hand, but whilst the tankers remained unpainted, the Scania gained white & blue livery and was numbered without suffix as 2577.

Above: By 1976, LT was still continuing the policy of obtaining its fuel tankers second-hand. A make previously not represented in the ranks was 2000S, a Seddon 16.4 model. The tank was built by Ryland of Birmingham in 1971 to carry domestic fuel oil and had a capacity of 2,500 gallons. Although mechanically sound, the proprietary cab manufactured by Motor Panels on these models was a weak-spot with a propensity to rust. Jim Wright

Left: The Bedford TL enjoyed a brief popularity with LT, and in 1980, the opportunity was taken to body one vehicle as a fuel tanker. No.2274B was a tilt-cab-fitted TL1630 model with a 2,400-gallon tank, and in this case, the nature of the load is correctly identified by orange 'Flammable Liquid' labels. By time of its demise in 1993, it was the last example of the chassis remaining in use with LT. Jim Wright

The 'Fuel Crisis' of 2000 led to two second-hand Thompson tanker-trailers being bought to facilitate the emergency storage and distribution of diesel. In order to move these when required, this second-hand Scania 113M was also acquired. Though numbered as 2577, no suffix letter is carried. Of necessity, the vehicle is constructed to Petroleum Regulation Standards, as evidenced by the exhaust pipe positioned below the front bumper. Kim Rennie

London Transport long-followed the custom of other public bodies in maintaining an internally-serviced and operated network of staff canteens. These were ultimately situated in all parts of the combine, with locations including bus stations and garages (both Central and Country), Underground stations and depots, administrative offices, overhaul works and even power stations. Some premises were open for 24-hours to cater for night-shift workers; these included at times the canteens at Baker Street, Earl's Court and Victoria Garage (the latter for night bus crews). The scale of operations ranged from wooden tea-bars to the huge canteen at Aldenham, capable of serving 800 diners in a single sitting. The canteens were originally under the control of the Welfare Officer, whose section came under the Department of Executive Officer for Staff & Welfare.

For many years, the canteens were able to source food at the major London markets and a small fleet of locally-based vans was used for this purpose. A central provision store was established at Griffith House with regular deliveries of dry goods made to the canteens. After the war, a new Food Production Centre was established in Progress Way, Purley. This was located on the County Borough of Croydon's Purley Way trading estate and occupied a converted 1930s factory unit. The Centre was opened on 23rd October 1950, and gradually absorbed most aspects of the catering operation throughout the organisation. Its creation was the result of a recommendation by Mr E. C. Gezzele, who was recruited from the Army Catering Corps to reorganise LT's canteen service. One intention of the change was the removal of butchery, fishmongery and certain snack production from canteen kitchens and their transfer to a centralised and modern site. Croydon was actually less than satisfactorily placed for LT, as many delivery journeys involved a crossing of the Thames to canteens in the north of the operating area. It was also somewhat restricted from an access point of view, and certain vehicles had to be out-stationed, fuelled and serviced at Thornton Heath Garage during the night. It is believed it was originally intended to open a similar facility north of the river, though in the event this did not occur.

According to *London Transport Magazine*, one of the chief aims of the Production Centre was: '*to ensure a uniformly high standard of goods among London Transport canteens and so raise the standard of catering*'. The Centre was equipped with full butchery and bakery facilities, producing such items as sausages, pies, cakes and even Christmas puddings, and had a loading bay that could accommodate up to eight vans simultaneously.

Another innovation in the immediate post-war years was the opening of the Canteen Training Centre above Baker Street Station in 1949. Again, the intention was to centralise an activity away from individual canteens and, at that time, up to 1200 catering staff passed through the centre each year. This was reputedly the first occasion on which an industrial concern had introduced such a facility for its catering staff.

Prior to the establishment of the Croydon Food Production Centre in 1950, some food supplies were brought to Griffith House for bulk re-distribution to individual canteens. This somewhat artificially-posed picture shows beef suet cartons being loaded into one of the Albion or Leyland delivery vans, whilst a sack of a Spillers' product is being barrowed into the ground floor loading bay. The wicker baskets add a nostalgic touch, as do fruit boxes labelled 'Covent Garden' and metal containers apparently revealing the existence of generic 'London Transport Cake'. The area was accessed from Old Marylebone Road and today plays host to vehicles of the Lifts & Escalators Department. LT Museum

Right: When certain S-type buses were converted to vans by the LGOC in 1928, various items were left unchanged. No windscreen was fitted to catering delivery van 20S (ex-ST 436). The original body frame was used with new panelling and the vehicle continued to display its bus stock number. In the days before centralised food processing had been introduced, 20S first collected fresh produce from the wholesale markets at Billingsgate, Covent Garden and Smithfield and then distributed it directly to garages, depots and works that had canteens. *LT Museum*

Below right: The Leyland SKZ1 model was used as a basis for some catering vans. Two former SKZ1 Tramway Department ticket vans (200C–201C) were converted to the role in 1943, but 202C was delivered new for canteen delivery duties in 1936. For a while, it was numbered C114L in a joint series with the Leyland Cub single-deck buses, but is seen here at Victoria Garage after re-numbering. *Bill Aldridge Collection*

In October 1955, LT had reported that: '*The staff are mostly girls, neatly clad in white overalls and caps, and to help them they have mechanical aids that would make many a housewife gasp with envy – tart cutting and filling machines, cake mixers and automatic rolling pins.*' At that time, 60,000 canteen meals and snacks were being prepared each day for what the organisation was proud to refer to as 'our London Transport family'. In 1956, five thousand bread rolls were being dispatched at 05.30 each weekday morning ready for sale in the big engineering canteens. A total of 185 canteens were then being served by outgoing lorries, whilst incoming vehicles brought in supplies from provisions warehouses and the main vegetable, fruit and meat markets. The same year, no less than a quarter of a million cakes, rolls and pies were produced per week for LT's 87,000 employees. Separate sections of the factory were set aside for groceries, provisions, cigarette/tobacco supplies and catering equipment. Staff could place individual orders for iced cakes made for birthdays, weddings, presentations and other celebrations.

Speaking at a press conference in January 1948, LT Chairman Lord Latham had announced plans for improving staff amenities, including a 5-year programme for better and more numerous canteens, and 1950s witnessed a programme of updating existing premises, as well as providing new facilities. In 1958, canteens were being refurbished or introduced at Bexleyheath, Carshalton, Clapton, Craven Park, Finsbury Park, Golders Green, Hatfield, Hertford, Leyton, Poplar, Reigate and Stevenage. The Golders Green establishment was to be available to the public via a separate counter. To give a contrast to the varying sizes of operations, the Finsbury Park canteen could seat 16 people, whilst the Chiswick operation catered for seven hundred customers. The types of vehicles allocated to catering use reflected the development of the canteen service within LT. Mobile facilities were gradually withdrawn as permanent arrangements were established at garages and terminal points, whilst vans used to transport uncooked supplies gave way to vehicles capable of carrying pre-processed fare.

By December 1968, the *London Transport Magazine* was explaining how preparation for that year's 30,000 LT Christmas puddings had begun in the previous March. Other items produced for the 1968 festive season included 14,000 frozen chickens, turkeys and sausage meat, along with 8,500 tins of shortcake, 5,500 iced Christmas cakes and 6,500 Dundee cakes. In addition, 8,050 special Christmas hampers had been ordered by staff in £8, £6 and £4 sizes. LT was especially proud of the centralisation of the bakery function, believing that it meant 'economic production under ideal conditions' and 'unexcelled value for money for the customer'.

Catering vehicles worked to two separate schedules.

Dry goods such as tea, sugar, bulk products, cutlery, crockery, fats and flour would be delivered weekly. The second schedule involved daily trips to the garages delivering bread, cakes, rolls, sausages and meat, fish, fish cakes, pork pies, vegetables, pre-peeled potatoes and chips. The daily vans had separate compartments within the body for fish, meat and cakes. The Catering Department was quite innovative, and was considering the use of microwave ovens as far back as 1964. As the catering business entered the 1970s, many microwave-prepared meals and other frozen products were transported in freezer-vans. These meals were colour-keyed to ensure the correct timings. For many years, a daily delivery of rolls and cakes was made to the Pullman Car Company at Nine Elms Depot for use on the '*Brighton Belle*' train. Self-service machines were used to provide a service at quiet locations or out-of-hours at the main canteens.

At one time, it was decided on the grounds of cost-saving that some delivery and restocking work should be carried out at night to avoid traffic jams, and a number of trial runs were carried out by management. Unfortunately, they omitted to inform the police about these late night sorties and the inevitable happened. When the vehicles went out and had to wait outside premises to simulate unloading times, the anonymous vans parked outside bus garages soon attracted the attention of the

Albion KN127 4-ton catering van 129A was delivered in 1937 and bodied in a similar style to the Leyland SKZ1s. Pictured at Chiswick when new, with its original fleet number of AN 26 and the cream roof that often complemented service vehicle livery in pre-war days. *LT Museum*

One of four Bedford OLBC was 716B, a 5-ton petrol-engined insulated catering van delivered in 1948 to carry perishables such as fresh fish and meat. A second batch in 1952 was powered by diesel engines. On the leading edge of the body is one of the slot-in plates used to indicate a vehicle's allocation, in this case 'CDS Chiswick'. The location is Wandsworth Garage, which in 1961 was surrounded by terraced housing. *Julian Bowden-Green*

police. Drivers employed on the Catering Service were specially trained in the correct handling of food, and for a time wore white overalls. The drivers carried large rings of keys to gain access during the night to canteens that were closed. The driving staff were supervised by an on-site charge-hand, who in turn reported to the Chiswick Operating Foreman. The Catering Equipment Section were responsible for arranging to provide the canteens with all of the equipment from cutlery to ovens and indeed to remove this equipment as the canteens were refurbished or closed.

In the 1970s, the Government's Prices & Income Policy meant that LT could not increase wages in an attempt to overcome staff shortages. In order to compensate for this, a system of supplying cheap basic foodstuffs and household goods was devised. They were marketed under the 'Home Sales' banner, and some canteens were described as taking on the appearance of an oriental bazaar when the full range of goods was on sale.

Canteens operated under the control of a Catering Controller, a position staffed on a 24-hour basis at Chiltern Court, Baker Street in the 1980s. The Controllers had the responsibility of ensuring canteens were open as advertised, an important job given that bus staff then had an absolute right to catering facilities. The emer-

gency closure of a canteen through staff sickness could lead to every bus crew on meal relief travelling to the nearest alternative premises (often by specially-arranged 'ferry bus'). Although such establishments were then widely spread throughout London, the detrimental effect on bus services can be imagined. A more unusual part of the Catering Controllers' duties was the provision of refreshment supplies during emergency railway incidents. The Incident Officer or Senior Engineering Department Official on site would notify the Headquarters Controller, who would in turn contact the Catering Controller. Details required included the number of persons requiring refreshments, type of provision requested (i.e. meals or tea and sandwiches), estimated time of requirement, exact site and mode of access, name of person to be reported to, not forgetting the account to which the costs should be charged! The provision of emergency food supplies was later entrusted to the Salvation Army (whose organisation performs a similar function for the emergency services), but has now passed to private contractors.

In October 1955, LT had stated that: 'The more that the canteens and the products of the Croydon Centre are used by the staff, the better will be the canteen service provided'. It was a vision that changing circumstances destined to be ultimately unfulfilled. With supplies increasingly being delivered to canteens direct from wholesalers, the catering operation was scaled down in 1980s, and the factory at Croydon finally closed in July 1983. Over a period, the Food Production Centre had become less and less cost-effective, and the growth of 'cash & carry' stores and indeed supermarkets meant that canteens could source food locally and more cheaply. The decision to dispose of 'non-core' activities under the LRT Act probably doomed the department in any case. Other factors included a reduction in users due to the one-person-operation of buses and trains, the closure of garages through route tender losses, and perhaps an inability to adapt to modern eating trends.

DELIVERY VANS

The earliest such vehicles listed are 17S-20S, 5-ton catering vans converted from S-class (AEC model 503) buses S 71, 374, 416 and 436 between 1928 and 1931. The conversion consisted of rebuilding and re-panelling the body and fitting rear doors for the loading of food, but leaving the driver in his single half-cab. Unusually, they retained red livery. Purpose-built vans 127A, 128A and 129A were from the LPTB's large fleet of Albion KN127 4-tonners, but were specifically referred to as catering vans (though 127A and 128A had originally entered service as ticket vans). Other Albion KN127 vans were 378A to 381A and 383A (the latter uniquely titled as a meat van and ex-permanent way breakdown use in June 1942). The title 'meat van' implies that the body was fitted with meat hooks, which slid on roof rails to hang the meat carcases. LT was able to purchase its meat, fish and vegetable requirements direct from the major markets at Smithfield, Billingsgate and Covent Garden. Additional ex-tramways ticket vans transferred to catering use in January 1943 were 1936-vintage Leyland Cub SKZ1s 200C and 201C. Sister vehicle 202C was delivered new to the role, and was first identified as number C114L in the unique joint bus/service vehicle fleet number series. In 1946, the Albions and Cubs were kept at various Central Area bus garages. Two 1940 Ford V8 Detroit-type 3-ton tilt lorries, 468F and 469F, were also being used by the Welfare Officer at this time, and resided in Victoria Garage.

After the war the Bedford OLBC 5-tonner formed the base for insulated catering vans 713B to 716B, dating from 1948. The first Bedfords arrived with petrol engines, but in 1952, the second batch (964B, 965B and 966B), came fitted with Perkins P6 diesels. Members of the 1948–50 series of Austin K4 5-ton lorries (711AS, 712AS

The Austin K4 model was used for three food vans introduced in 1948–49. Marshall-bodied 712AS was described as 'part-insulated', because goods such as bread and cake could be carried in the ambient rear compartment whilst more delicate foods were stored in a separate insulated section entered via a nearside roller shutter.
Julian Bowden-Green

Below left: This official photograph of Austin K4 712AS shows how the rear of such vans were fitted with racks to allow the easy transportation of trays containing non-perishable goods. LT Museum

Below: Fourteen Thames Traders were in use as 5-ton catering vans from 1961. Although the cabs were painted in the new grey livery, the bodies were finished in unpainted aluminium alloy. In this close-up view of 1199F, a driver in period uniform demonstrates the loading of supplies into the insulated compartment. Each food container is labelled with its destination canteen, these being Acton Town, Alperton, Caxton Road, Isleworth, Northfields, Riverside, Shepherd's Bush, Turnham Green and White City. The vehicle's payload indicated at the end of the fleet number, in this case '5', a short-lived CDS practice of the early-1960s. LT Museum

and 922AS) were also assigned to catering as part-insulated food vans (922AS was described simply as a food van). Bodywork was by Marshall of Cambridge who, like Mann-Egerton, had been responsible for rebuilding some passenger-carrying vehicles after the war.

With the Thames Trader providing the standard large vehicle for LT from 1959, vans of this type began to enter the fleet for use by the canteen service. Fourteen Traders were acquired between 1961 and 1963 as 5-ton catering vans. Nos. 1196F to 1199F and 1265F to 1271F had cabs painted in the new grey livery, whilst their bodies were finished in unpainted aluminium. In 1962, catering van 1265F had the distinction of starting a new series of service vehicle body numbers, commencing from M1. However, the allocation of these terminated with body

M103 on Bedford HA box-van 1373B in December 1964. Two of the second batch (1266F and 1269F) were sold to LCBS in February 1971. This was at the time when the fledgling NBC subsidiary was setting up its own canteen service divorced from LT. Additional 5-ton Trader vans delivered from 1963 were 1305F, 1306F and 1307F, though in this case the Homalloy bodies were clad in the same light grey as the cabs.

With the displacement of the Traders from Ford's catalogue, a number of D-series vans joined the Catering fleet. 1584F to 1587F were 1970-built D500 5-ton catering vans and averaged ten years use. In the following year came 1632F to 1636F, D500 5-ton insulated catering vans which returned to the grey cab/aluminium body appearance; plus 1721F, another D500 5-ton van. Smaller D400

99

4-ton vans joined the service in August 1972 (1784F and 1785F). The last D-series was 2060F; a D0710 refrigerated food van in the familiar painted/metal guise, and operated from February 1977 to October 1983. The final vehicles used by LT Catering were delivered in 1979, and were based on the Leyland Terrier chassis. Fleet numbers 2143L and 2210L to 2213L were 4-ton refrigerated food vans whose careers were cut short by the demise of the in-house catering service. Following this, 2143L was later converted to curtain-sided configuration, whilst 2213L found a new use as a dropside-lorry. A number of smaller vehicles have been used by the Catering Department over the years, these would have been of non-specialised design and reflected the standard car or van in use by LT at the time.

MOBILE CANTEENS

Twelve former NS-class buses were converted to mobile canteens in the 1936–37 period and reclassified as 29H to 40H (in sequence, ex-NS 173, 250, 289, 429, 577, 931, 1129, 1698, 1722, 2169, 2295 and 2322). One of the original reasons for the introduction of the 'mobile' concept was the Coronation of King George VI in 1937. Large areas of central London were closed to traffic for the event, and the mobile canteens were to provide refreshment facilities for those staff on bus routes curtailed at the boundaries.

Most LPTB service vehicles were soberly attired in red or green liveries, so all the more odd is this view of 37H (ex-NS 1722) at Chiswick in a strange 'art deco' scheme (presumably red/white). Mobile canteens tended to become relatively down-at-heel when in constant use, but 37H may have been taking part in a display, since a label in the canopy window explains its function. The white-coloured lower-deck windows indicate the position of the kitchen, as does the chimney on the roof. A.B. Cross

A one-off was M 114, later 225M, a Morris 5-cwt van from 1937 equipped as a mobile tea bar. As well as the raised roofline, an extending canopy provided shelter for a counter at the rear. Dwarfed by Loughton's LT 59 on the 38B, and with a uniform jacket resting on its bonnet, M114 awaits custom at the famous Chingford Royal Forest Hotel. Later converted to a box van, it was destroyed by enemy action in October 1940.
D.W.K. Jones

In the event, bus staff went on strike during the Coronation period, leaving tram, trolleybus and Underground services to take up the strain. Some of the ex-NSs retained red livery in their new life, but others received red and white, green or khaki schemes at various stages. They were previously identified as Mobile Staff Canteens 1 to 12, but were not incorporated into the 1939 re-numbering scheme in the same order. Ex-NS 289 was the only single-deck canteen and the first to be commissioned. All lasted until the late-1940s or early-1950s. Each conversion varied slightly, but the double-deckers all featured a kitchen area downstairs and seating upstairs. Locations for the NS canteens included bus termini and the crew changing points at Finsbury Park Station, Vauxhall Cross, Chingford and Hampton Court. The final ex-NS canteen (30H ex-NS 250) remained in service at Hatfield Garage until 1953, where it existed in a semi-static state, with gas and water supplies permanently 'plumbed in'.

A unique vehicle was 225M, originally M 114; a small 5-cwt Morris mobile tea bar, whose tall box-body had a folding canopy fitted to the rear which could be used to shelter the serving counter. Livery was originally green, later red with black wings and roof, and it resided at the famous Chingford (Royal Forest Hotel) bus stand. It regained green livery when converted to a box-van in April 1940, but survived in this form only until October of the same year, when destroyed by enemy action. It was the only powered vehicle to embody the 'tea bar' concept.

The only single-deck ex-NS canteen was 31H, converted from NS 289 in 1937 and seen here in Buckingham Palace Road. The vehicle spent some time in khaki livery, was later based at Chingford and remained in use until November 1948.
Julian Bowden-Green collection

Left: Not quite so mobile were the Westminster-type wooden-bodied canteen trailers. The leading end of the body contained the kitchen and a nearside serving counter. To the rear was a small internal dining area reached via two narrow outward-opening doors. This canteen, complete with LT legal address lettering, was located at Aldgate (Minories) bus and coach terminus, and is believed to have carried a (faded) red livery. *Lens of Sutton*

Lower left: A similar canteen trailer was used at Hayes, Middlesex. In this 1960 view, the dining area can be glimpsed through an open door, whilst on the offside is another door leading to the kitchen. Livery is thought to be red/cream, and mid-way along the body is a gold LT bullseye and the legend 'STAFF CANTEEN'. The partially-visible number plate reads KLB 995, which belonged to 871B, a Bedford 'KD' 30-cwt truck dating from 1950. *Julian Bowden-Green*

LT used some wooden-bodied 2-axle refreshment stalls at certain bus termini but these were hardly mobile in the generally understood meaning of the term. Vehicles licensed to tow these over the years included Morris EA full-tilt trucks 301M/303M, and Bedford KD half-tilt 871B.

Post-war canteen conversions 688J to 693J used ex-Thomas Tilling AEC Regent buses ex-ST 888, 969, 867, 917, 951 and 922 in the period 1946–47. Like most of the ex-NS vehicles, the new batch of canteens wore a red, or red-white livery, and they were eventually withdrawn over the period 1952–55. Locations for the ex-ST canteens included Cricklewood, Kingston, Streatham, Putney (Chelverton Road) and Windsor garages. Regent 693J was later sold to British Road Services for use at their Tufnell Park Goods Depot, eventually being acquired for preservation by the late Prince Marshall and restored to passenger-carrying condition as ST 922. A very short-lived ex-bus canteen was 952J, formerly AEC Regent STL 1812, which served in this capacity only between 1951 and 1953 at Chelsham Garage. As well as providing a service at garages without purpose-built canteens, the 'mobiles' attended such annual events as Derby Day, the Boat Race and the Wimbledon tennis championships.

The Tilling ST was chosen as a replacement for the ex-NS-type mobile canteens, with six buses so-treated between 1946 and 1947. As with the NSs, the kitchen was installed behind the lower-deck front bulkhead. The bodies retained their original open staircase, which must have cooled the meals of those staff ascending to the upper-deck seating accommodation. No.690J had been ST 867 and here looking just a little worse for wear, sits against a backdrop of typical inter-war LCC 'cottage estate' housing. *Kim Rennie collection*

Some of the most famous LT catering vehicles arrived between 1947 and 1949, with the advent of the MC-class mobile canteen trailers and their attendant Bedford-Scammell OSS prime movers. The canteen trailers weighed in at 4½-tons whilst the tractors were a mere 2-tons. Both were finished in Chiswick Green with light green window surrounds. Numbered 700B to 709B, they were originally coupled to trailers MC 1 to MC 10 in that order (with additional trailers MC 11, M 12 and MC 13 not being assigned a regular vehicle). Tractor 700B and trailer MC 1 were the prototypes, and had small variations in transfers and livery. The trailers were built on Scammell chassis, with bodies by Spurlings of Hendon; and the tractors equipped with Scammell automatic couplings. The trailers were fitted with manually-operated stabilisers just behind the coupling gear to ensure they did not 'rock' when customers boarded. Later years saw the tractor/trailer combinations become mixed, and in their final years the trailers were hauled by Thames Trader artics.

Disposal occurred progressively between February 1959 and September 1967. Four combinations were sold to Liverpool Corporation's Transport Department to serve another generation of bus staff. Unit 702B/MC 11 is now in the care of the London Bus Preservation Group; another lasted for years in Ahern's yard west of Romford Station, whilst a third trailer existed as a public tea bar until as late as 1982.

Below: The inside story – the MC-class mobile canteens had the kitchen located at the rear, the seating area was above the coupling, and entry to both was via a door mid-way along the nearside. A small petrol generator was used to power the lighting system; water was carried in insulated underfloor tanks and gas stored in containers located in side lockers. At this point in time, the staffing of LT canteens was still very much a male preserve. BTF

Below right: Former 709B and an unidentified MC trailer was one of four such combinations sold to Liverpool Corporation Transport. Bedecked in LCT's then somewhat dull all-over green livery, it appears to have been given the designation 'CB 12'. J.G.S. Smith

Above: Despite considering it acceptable to convert Tilling STs to mobile canteens, the same period saw purpose-built vehicles built new for the same task, in the form of the Bedford-Scammell OS prime movers and their associated MC-class step-frame trailers. The tractor was connected to the trailer using the famous Scammell Automatic Coupling, whereby the driver did no more than pull a lever to release the trailer from the tractor, the leading wheels of the canteen dropped down automatically and would retract again upon coupling-up. The un-coupling procedure had been executed when this Derby Day photo was taken at Morden, possibly to improve ventilation. Julian Bowden-Green

One of the most distinctive types contained in the service vehicle fleet were the successive batches of tree loppers used to prune overhanging foliage on bus routes. Originally being converted from former buses, a total of five separate batches were operated over the years, prior to such work becoming the responsibility of local authorities and Government agencies.

Modifications to the former buses normally involved the boarding-up of lower-deck windows, the removal of the upper deck from the waistline upward, and the fitting of some form of guard-rail. Seats were obviously removed, as the severed branches were initially placed on the top deck floor, prior to being stored downstairs. Nearside hinged access flaps on the top deck were provided on some batches, and permitted easier access to offending trees, plus a measure of protection to those passing below. The legalisation of covered top buses in 1925 naturally increased the amount of pruning required, and the LGOC employed modified B-type bus B 507 in this role. At first, its existing bus body was merely modified, with windows boarded up and an upper floor trapdoor fitted to allow access to the lower deck. Later, a

larger purpose-built body was fitted and this combination continued in use until B 507 was sold in 1928.

The earliest recorded LPTB tree lopper was based on the chassis of S-type AEC '503' double-deck bus S 384. In this case however, the vehicle was not rebuilt, but received a special Chiswick-built body in 1935. It was numbered 16S in the 1939-series, and as no previous service vehicle number was allocated until then, had retained its original S-class identification before this. Indeed, photographic evidence suggests it continued to display its bus stock number throughout most of its life with LT. Number S 384/16S was in use until November 1945.

As bus passenger journeys increased in the outer areas, there was a gradual move to replace single-deck buses with double-deckers. This action was later particularly prevalent in areas where war-related production was carried out. The conversion of routes to double-deck caused initial clearance problems, as many more branches needed removal, and therefore additional vehicles were commissioned. These were converted from former NS 556 (42H), 1653, 1684 (43H) and 2193 (44H) between 1936 and 1937. Note that NS 1653 was sold in June 1938

The 1920s saw the LGOC convert B 507 into a tree lopper. The outside staircase/rear platform was removed and a certain amount of lower-deck panelling replaced, but other aspects of the body retained clear evidence of its B-type origin. Here, B 507's driver eyes the photographer with some suspicion whilst what appears to be an inspector wields a pair of long-handled cutters from the upper deck. *LT Museum*

The LPTB's first tree lopper was 16S, formerly S 384, and rebuilt in 1934. With a far more thorough modification than given to B 507, the vehicle gained both a windscreen and pneumatic tyres, and had a new body built out over the rear wheels. This is a wartime view; hence the white-tipped front wings and virtually blanked-out sidelight. Bill Aldridge collection

The next type of tree lopper was derived from the NS-type, with four such vehicles being converted in 1936–37. In the case of NS 556, most of the original body was retained, even down to the open rear staircase and lower-saloon windows. The former bus was re-numbered as 42H in 1939, though its new identity was not being carried when this view was taken. Bill Aldridge collection

before being renumbered. Allocated to Country Buses & Coaches, all bar NS 1653 were in service until 1943. There is both written and photographic evidence of the trolley-bus overhead wire lubricators being used on other high-level tasks, such as tree lopping. Among the vehicles concerned was ex-NS 760 lubricator 41H (Tramway-series No. 203), which was also transferred to the service fleet in 1936.

The NSs were replaced by ex-ST-class buses: 646J was formerly ST 40 and ran as such until July 1945 when it was repainted Chiswick Green (body ex-Lewis Omnibus Company ST 1138). Vehicle 647J had been ST 985 and was

fitted with a 90-gallon tank (possibly for week-killer) in October 1945, 648J (body ex-ST 1153) was converted from ST 1001 with a body from ST 1134 (also ex-Lewis). Two more tree loppers were added in September 1945, 650J and 651J (ex-ST 865 and 870). All five eventually carried green livery. No. 646J was classed as a 6-ton vehicle; the others rated at 5¾-tons.

The former STs themselves gave way in 1953 to a fourth generation of tree loppers, with STL-class front-entrance Country Area double-deckers now providing the base for conversion. Nos. 969J to 973J were previously STL 1503, 1039, 1470, 1494 and 1512 respectively and

grey livery, though rather curiously the numerically-newest one (1245F) was later repainted from grey to green, complete with full-sized gold underlined LT fleetnames. Though many vehicles gained the new grey livery upon later overhaul, and there was a certain amount of overlap between the use of the two colours in the 1959–61 period, it is most unusual for a lorry to have regressed to an earlier scheme. All five of the batch carried yellow/black hazard chevrons at the rear. Not surprisingly, vehicles of this type saw most of their use in the Country Area, a fact demonstrated in January 1970 when 1241F to 1244F were transferred to the new LCBS, leaving only 1245F in LT use.

Replacement for 1245F came in April 1976, and was a Ford 'D1010' numbered 1935F, with a nominal 1½-ton carrying capacity. The gross vehicle weight of this lopper was 10 tonnes; it may have been 'down-plated' to a lower gross weight, and therefore reduced taxation rate. Standard grey fleet livery of the time was carried, but with the addition of large 'LONDON TRANSPORT' 'TREE PRUNING EQUIPMENT' sign-writing on either side in red and black. The grey Trader loppers had also carried red fleetnames, these being underlined and of the type used on Underground trains or perhaps leftover from disbanded private hire coach fleet.

LCBS replaced its ex-LT tree loppers in early-1979 by two Ford D0710 chassis numbered 34F and 35F, and which carried bodies salvaged from the Traders. The pair were re-bodied again in November 1984, thus being reminiscent of the proverbial 'old' broom or hammer which has had two new handles and two new heads, yet is still the same object! At least one of the Fords survived long enough to carry maroon/cream 'Kentish Bus' livery. The advent of larger fleets of single-deck buses and withdrawal of rural services means that the need for much tree lopping has been greatly reduced.

In 1946, the tree loppers had been shared between the Operating Manager (Central Buses) [650J], and his counterpart, the Operating Manager (Country Buses & Coaches) [646J, 647J, 648J and 651J]. Later vehicles came under the LT Gardening Section, a department which served both the road and rail sides of the organisation. In the 1950s, separate gangs were in existence to carry out either tree-pruning or tree-felling. The former used the tree lopping vehicles to remove obstructive branches 'with the permission of the owners'. The latter gang carried out the complete removal of trees threatening buses or trains, as well as heavy pruning work. What was described by LT as a 'notable job' in August 1957 was the felling of two 100-ft tall chestnut trees at Uxbridge. The wires of the adjacent trolleybus turning circle terminus were within a foot or so of them, so the offending foliage was removed branch by branch without disrupting services.

A more environmentally-friendly side to the Gardening Section's duties was the maintenance of the flowers, shrubs and lawns on LT premises, of which there was no less than 65 acres in the mid-1950s. Indeed, a common feature of the post-war garage reconstruction programme was the provision of grassed areas around the fronts of buildings which were set back from the road (e.g. Elmers End, Romford [North Street] and Thornton Heath). In order to ensure a regular supply of flowers and shrubs, the department had established a nursery in Acton Works, where up to 100,000 plants were raised each year. Less glamorous but much more important was the seeding of railway embankments to guard against earth-slips. The Gardening Section was renamed the 'Vegetation Control Section' from December 1973, a move which was said to 'indicate more clearly the activities for which this section is responsible'. In 1980, and now as the 'Earthworks & Vegetation Control Section', it moved from Acton to Ruislip Depot, where for a while it operated a nursery whose products were also available for sale to staff.

Top: The only non-Tilling ST to become a tree lopper was 646J, which had combined the chassis of ST 40 with a body ex-ST 1138. A substantial guard-rail was fitted around the upper-deck, as was done on the ex-Tilling STs. It had two more years' use left when pictured here in 1951, and one wonders if the lower-side valance was ever replaced. A.B. Cross

Above: Five additional ex-ST-types were converted to tree loppers between 1943 and 1945. Four of these were Tilling STs, which had been both built and operated by that company prior to its absorption by the LPTB. ST 870 became 651J, and when caught outside Godstone Garage, had started to develop the pronounced waist-rail sag so typical of this class of bus.

were to last ten years in their new guise. Most had the words 'TREE PRUNING EQUIPMENT' in gold below the full-sized fleetnames. These buses were taken from two separate batches of forward-entrance bodied buses, which were very rare in LT double-deck use. The reason for choosing these vehicles was simply that, when new, apart from STL 1039, the bodies had been built by Weymann and were metal-framed, thus more suitable for conversion to open-top configuration than the composite-framed bodies on most other STLs. STL 1039's original body was timber-framed and Chiswick-built, but it had gained a Weymann body upon overhaul after the war. To help remove the branches from the lower deck, the emergency exit in the rear panel was retained.

By the early-1960s, it had been proven beyond doubt that the purchase of new vehicles was far more economical than converting former buses to new roles. The new order was represented at the end of 1962 by 1241F to 1245F, five Thames Trader 5-ton loppers bodied by Marshall's of Cambridge in van form with an upstairs floor. This was the first batch to contain vehicles carrying

The ex-ST tree loppers gave way to five former front entrance Country Area STLs in 1953. Their metal-framed Weymann bodies were better suited to having the roof removed than the more numerous wooden-braced Chiswick designs. An innovation was the hinged nearside platform which, as seen here, could be lowered to allow workers closer access to offending foliage. A.B. Cross

Once CDS had decided to purchase new vehicles rather than rely on converting time-expired buses, the Thames Trader became the standard large design. Five were purpose-built as tree loppers in 1962 and comprised the fifth generation of such types to serve in the LT ancillary fleet. They had crew accommodation within the body and continued to employ hinged upper-deck working platforms. Entering service in November 1962, No.1245F was the only one of the batch not to pass to LCBS in 1970. LT Museum

Looking even more like a removal van than its predecessor, Ford 'D'-series 1935F replaced LT's remaining Thames Trader tree lopper in 1976. Because the cab tilted forward for servicing and repairs, the lower front of the body had an upward-opening flap to allow clearance for this. Julian Bowden-Green

13 CLEANSING AND REFUSE DISPOSAL

Cleansing of vehicles are more often associated with local authorities rather transport undertakings. However, LT was a vast concern with industrial sites as well as the more familiar garages and depots, so the need for such specialised designs is perhaps not surprising.

GULLY EMPTIERS

Amongst the Group 2 vehicles was a small fleet of gully emptiers, and one of their major responsibilities was the removal of floodwater from garages, depots and works. Within bus garages, there had always been a problem with the disposal of contaminated waste water that drained into interceptors. This water came from the washing of buses and that brought in from the streets on vehicle tyres, and could contain petrol and diesel from fuel spills. The LPTB took a very positive attitude to this problem and employed a small fleet of vacuum tankers to empty the interceptors and channel drains that contained contaminated water. The job of an interceptor is to allow clean water to flow into the sewer and retain the contaminants for removal by other means. In the earliest days, the oil collected from the interceptors was simply dumped, but the LPTB very soon arranged for the oil to be recovered and taken to Thames Haven for recycling.

The vehicles employed for this work were not really fully-fledged gully emptiers. In fact, they were single compartment vacuum tankers fitted with a gully arm that could be lowered into the interceptors and drains to remove the contaminated water. A more normal gully

emptier has two separate compartments, one for contaminated water and sludge, and the other for clean water to re-seal the 'U' bend in a gully. (The difference between the two types is that there is only one 'sight glass' on the LT tankers, and no small-bore hose on the front nearside of the tanker for the clean water to enter the gully from the front compartment.) A gully emptier, or indeed any vacuum tanker, works on the principle of creating a vacuum in the tank by means of an engine-driven exhauster. The tank is fitted with a variety of valves that connect to hoses. When the hose is lowered into the water or oil and the valve opened, the water is sucked up the hose into the tanker. The vacuum is retained within the tank by keeping the exhauster running.

The LGOC had been employing gully-emptying tankers for many years. As far back as 1916, B-type buses B 1302, B 1319 B 1514 and B 1523 had been converted to this task, with B 1809 added as an extra vehicle in 1923. One assumes that flooding was more prevalent then, and indeed Sidcup Garage was renowned for its susceptibility to inundation. The first recorded gully-emptying lorries in the LPTB fleet were solid-tyred 56Z and 57Z, and were mounted on AEC '506' chassis. Grey-liveried 57Z arrived in June 1928 and was Chiswick-based, 56Z joined it ten months later in February 1929, and both lasted until July 1940. 73Z was a Tylor-engined AEC YC-type lorry, and began life as a 5-ton tank wagon in March 1919. In March 1921, it was rebuilt as a gully emptier. Although older than both 56Z and 57Z, it lasted until August 1940.

Gully emptier 410P was an AEC Matador with Fowler equipment supplied by Mechanical Services of Herne Hill in 1939. Only 40 of these bodies were ever built and the LPTB had two of the very few fitted to AEC chassis. Even when new, the square configuration looked very old-fashioned, as most operators were by now choosing a circular vacuum tank. The gully arm was raised and lowered by means of a small crane. LT Museum

Also around at this time were a number of solid-tyred 'sludge lorries'. These may have been tipper vehicles with a tank to hold sludge within the tipper body. The lowest numerically of these was also based on the '506' chassis. 54Z (ex-EN 3) had originally been a towing lorry new in 1928. 55Z (ex-EN 11) was also a conversion, this time from a 1928 AEC '506' hydraulic tipper. These vehicles served the fleet in their rebuilt form from October 1934 until withdrawal in December 1939. A third change of use involved 72Z (ex-EN 9). This AEC Tylor also started life as a towing lorry. New in 1919, it was converted in October 1932 and remained in the fleet until July 1940. The last such vehicle so-titled was 154D (ex-EN 12, and before that D 190), a reconstructed Dennis bus formerly owned by independent Martin. Dating from April 1927, it gained both pneumatic tyres and a lorry body in April 1935. Sludge lorries were usually painted grey, but 154D later appeared in green. Like a number of other lorries involved in cleansing work, many of the Z-class were transferred to ARP control in 1940.

The replacements for the AEC '506's and Tylor-engined YC-types were three 7-ton AEC Matadors delivered in April (409P and 410P) and August (411P) 1939. These were of contrasting types for trial purposes. The latter vehicle, 411P, had a circular vacuum tank built by Eagle of the design usually associated with this type of lorry. However, the first two had square tanks built by Fowler of Leeds and provided by Mechanical Cleaning Services of Herne Hill, looking more like army vehicles than street cleaners. These also weighed 1-ton 10-cwt more than the Eagle tanker. Each was of a 1000-gallon capacity, and all three lasted until 1958, 410P and 411P departing in May, 409P lasting one month longer.

An additional gully emptier arrived in April 1949. This was an AEC Matador numbered 108P, and formerly a stores lorry dating from 1937. The vehicle lasted only nine years on cleansing duties and left the fleet in August 1958. The circular tank design was far more suited to this application and that on 411P was retained when the vehicle was withdrawn, subsequently being fitted to new vehicle 1041Q in January 1958. This was an AEC Mercury chassis and was the last of a batch of four such vehicles. The other three, 1038Q, 1039Q and 1040Q had arrived with new tanks from Eagle Engineering of Warwick in 1957. All four were painted green, and three of them saw service until May 1967. The survivor, 1040Q, was withdrawn in January 1969 with the distinction of being the last gully emptier owned by LT. Such work was then passed to either local councils or private contractors.

ROAD-SWEEPERS

Accumulated oil, diesel and grease on garage floors could contribute to potential accidents. To reduce the possibility of buses skidding, the Board, and before that the LGOC, employed a small number of road-sweepers. This group has always been regarded as outside the normal core of the service vehicle fleet, and survived within its own separate numbering systems. They were classed as 'A Assets' and deemed to be part of the plant and equipment, rather than service vehicles.

The earliest sweepers were a batch of solid-tyred, three-wheelers dating from the 1920s and numbered R 1 to R 41. Some were based on the Lacre model 'L', and all were fitted with one contra-revolving full-width brush and water tank used to dampen the dust. The Lacre 'L' made use of a Dorman petrol engine, with the advanced feature of twin overhead camshafts, yet relying on drip-feed lubrication. The drive was through a cone clutch to a 2-speed gearbox, with a roller chain drive to the rear wheel. Later models used Morris Commercial engines, though the overall design altered little. Only Rs 15, 18, 19, 24, 38 and 39 had registration numbers, and none used

trade plates. The unregistered machines were used within garages and had no need to travel on the public highway. R 41 was much larger than the others and had an enclosed cab for the driver. It was always based in Chiswick Works and survived until March 1952 at least, whilst the rest had vanished much earlier. While R 41 differed in being dark green, the other forty were painted red. The Lacre firm was formed in 1902 and originally based in Long Acre, London (their name being a contraction of this address). The sweepers' function was to clean floors, simply moving rubbish into one area, where it would be hand-loaded onto a lorry for disposal. By 1937, ex-LGOC Lacre sweepers R 33, R 36, R 37 and R 41 were still in stock.

Much smaller were the motorised sweepers made by Redshaw and Lister companies. These had their own RL Redshaw Lister Reliance and L (Lister) numbering series, and appeared in both red and green liveries with miniature LT fleetnames. They were small 3-wheel industrial trucks fitted with water tanks, again with contra-revolving roller brushes under the chassis. The vehicles were based on 'Autotruck' principles, with the engine and driven front wheel pivoted from the main chassis. RL 1 was first licensed in 1932 and further machines were delivered from 1933-onwards, the highest stock number known being RL 92 (now at Cobham Bus Museum). During the war, they needed fuel vouchers before being refilled – some used a lot more petrol than others – it doesn't take much imagination to realise where the excess petrol went! One sweeper, which was required to travel between Hertford Garage and bus station, gained Hertfordshire registration number 520 UNK. Those still in LT ownership by the late-1970s were generally in a derelict condition. Around this time, replacement equipment was obtained from the 'Lincoln' company. In a change from previous practice, no attempt was made to adorn the new machines in either CDS or bus fleet livery.

Two mid-1950s full-size road-sweepers served Aldenham and Chiswick Works and were uniquely numbered as BL 1 and BL 2. Again, they were regarded as 'A Assets' outside the CDS fleet, and were based on the Bedford 'A'-series normal-control chassis, coupled with a Lacre 'Road Sweeper Collector' body. BL 1's body was open and surmounted by a half-length square canvas tilt, whilst BL 2 carried a more conventional enclosed design. Both had mechanically-driven brushes and a small rubber conveyor to lift the sweepings into the rear of the body. The body could then tip to dispose of the rubbish. Being confined to the two works, neither carried a registration number. A triangular metal frame projected horizontally from the front of BL 2 just below bumper level. Painted with black/yellow hazard stripes, it provided a base for a removable snowplough blade (a similar paint scheme was applied in chevron form to the rear). Their main livery colour was Chiswick green with black wings, and they were some of the very last vehicles to carry this colour. Both BLs were left-hand drive, the only lorries so fitted since the demise of the US-built wartime acquisitions. Withdrawal dates are not known, but both fell into disuse some time before their respective locations closed.

DUSTCARTS

The dustcart or refuse collector is a typical municipal vehicle, but one which might have been expected to be found in a large ancillary fleet like LT's. Rather oddly though, the species has not appeared until recent times. In the past, LT used standard open trucks and tippers to move refuse from their premises, whilst the Underground ran their own rubbish trains. The latter consisted of flat wagons marshalled between two battery locomotives, which toured the system collecting scrap materials. The 'Croxley Tip' train was mainly used to dispose of civil engineering waste: i.e. rubble, old ballast, drain clearings etc; and was also the last regular steam-hauled working on the Underground. 'Domestic' refuse was cleared from stations by engineers' trains, which carried contractors' bins on standard flat cars and ran after the last passenger workings. More stringent environmental controls and changes in refuse disposal methods led to the end of such rail-based arrangements by the mid-1980s.

During the 1970s, LT was finding that the type of rubbish being collected from premises was changing. Instead of being relatively heavy, refuse was now lighter but far bulkier. This meant that new vehicles had to be purchased to compact the rubbish and ensure fuller payloads could be carried safely.

The aftermath of the King's Cross fire forced LT to re-think the way in which rubbish was collected and disposed of safely. The Fire Brigade could force the closure of any station where combustible material was found stored in an unsafe manner, and this resulted in a far greater control of the collection operation. Whilst originally local authorities would remove the rubbish free of charge (but not to any regular timetable), the need for guaranteed, regular and controlled collections meant that LT was forced to undertake the function internally using additional refuse collection vehicles.

To help keep stations and other premises clear between the regular collections, mini-tippers with caged sides are now employed to act as emergency back-up collection vehicles. These rendezvous with the larger refuse collection vehicles to transfer their loads. The mini-tippers are very useful in modern-day London, offering easy access to restricted areas, and speed and manoeuvrability compared to larger vehicles. A wide range of waste material has to be disposed of, and special arrangements are made to safely dispose of 'clinical waste', toxic materials, acids, fluorescent tubes etc. Indeed, approximately 20,000 tonnes of rubbish is collected yearly.

The first purpose-built dustcarts were 2419D, 2420D and 2421D, three Dodge 'G16' vehicles fitted with Dennis Phoenix refuse bodies. These bodies were built at the Eagle Works in Warwick, thereby reviving an old relationship. Delivered in March 1985 in standard grey livery, they were used to remove rubbish from both road and rail locations, allowing LT to reduce much of its reliance on local authority services. The trio remained unique until September 1990, when two Mercedes-Benz '2421' 3-axle dustcarts fitted with Norba compaction bodies were also acquired. 2482M and 2483M were 24-tonne gross vehicles and delivered in the new white/blue livery. The pair carried large LUL roundels and the legend 'Working for a cleaner Underground' in blue. Although it was rumoured that bodies from the Dodges were to be remounted on new chassis, nothing came of this. In fact re-mounting of refuse collection bodies is very unusual. Due to the wear and tear they receive, a life of seven to nine years is considered average. The new Mercedes effectively acted as replacements for the pioneer vehicles, but 2420D survived as a spare long enough to carry the new colours; uniquely having its compactor body painted all-over blue.

The Mercedes were joined in July–August 1996 by a further full-sized 3-axled pair, this time based on the British-built ERF 'EC8' chassis, complete with 8-litre Cummins engines and Heil compaction bodies. They were allocated numbers 2557E and 2558E in the 'owned' series, but the suffix-letter has never been applied. Their body style is slightly different to that on the Mercedes, though both worked on the principle of compacting the rubbish, and then using an ejector plate to push this out from the rear of the body. As the sides are ribbed, the 'Working for a . . .' etc slogans are applied on metal plates. Both the ERF and Mercedes dustcarts were equipped with illuminated 'Support services' headboards, a feature required on all vehicles whenever possible under the LUL 'road vehicle livery standards' (though not always provided in reality). All four were fitted with a separate compartment for storing 'clinical waste' (Distribution Services being a registered waste disposal organisation). The new ERFs allowed 2483M to be sold in August 1997, sister vehicle 2482M being retained as a spare until August 2000.

Just pre-dating the ERFs in June 1996 was 2556M, a Mercedes-Benz '814' mini-dustcart with Farid bodywork. A 1999 arrival was 2564F, which has a similar body to 2556M, but this time mounted on an Iveco Cargo chassis. Like the rest of LUL's refuse collectors, both are allocated to the Acton Works base. From time-to-time, 1994 Ford Transit cage-sided tipper 2548F is used to deputise for one or other of the mini-dustcarts. The most recent addition to the refuse collection fleet is Mercedes-Benz 'Econic 1823LL' of June 2000. Numbered as 2576M, it had the distinction of being exhibited at the Institute of Wastes Management annual show at Torbay in summer 2000, prior to entering service with LUL.

Most of the work done by all these vehicles is carried out at night and involves visiting Underground stations. For a few years though, there were still a few contracts held with several of the privatised ex-LBL companies, so LUL vehicles could still be seen somewhat unexpectedly at certain garages.

Below left: Bodied by Farid is 2564F, in this case on an Iveco Cargo 'ML75' chassis. This was LUL's second mini-dustcart and arrived in 1999. These vehicles are not able to compact rubbish to the extent of the larger refuse collectors, but have proved to be extremely useful in service. In this view, 2564F is parked-up in a west London street whilst the driver takes a tachograph break. David Rowe

Below: In 1996, two ERF 'EC8' Heil-bodied dustcarts were bought to augment, and ultimately replace, the Mercedes-Benz '2421' machines. Because collected wastes were not as heavy as originally anticipated, the middle axle was fitted with single tyres. This allowed the vehicles to be plated at a lower gross weight, thus substantially reducing their excise costs when compared to the previous Mercedes. 2557E pauses at the new Stratford Jubilee Line station in May 1999 and displays the 'Working for . . .' slogan now applied to the sides of all LUL dustcarts. Kim Rennie

The term 'personnel carrier' is used here in its widest sense, and embraces all the varying forms of non-PSV vehicle utilised to carry employees over the years (excluding saloon and estate cars). These range from today's 'people-movers' (which are really just one step up from an estate car) to the many generations of minibuses; plus certain ex-buses used for staff travel, which although not part of the CDS fleet, can be said to have performed a service vehicle role.

The earliest example of the genre to have been found in the numbered series is 645F, a Ford V8 8-seat 'shooting brake'. New to the fleet in August 1942, number 645F was actually built in March 1939 and had wooden-panelled bodywork constructed by LT. Livery ranged from grey/brown, Chiswick Green (May 1941) and finally khaki (January 1942). Perhaps the precursor to today's small fleet of LT 'people-mover' multi-purpose vehicles, it was based at Chiswick Works in connection with the London Aircraft Production Group's programme and lasted until August 1945.

The next development was in 1949, with the delivery of 929F to 943F, fifteen Ford Thames E83W 10hp 10-cwt Utilecon 'B's. These bore a close resemblance to the standard normal-control E83W van already in LT use, but with the addition of side windows and rear folding seats. Two later deliveries of Utilecon 'A's were 923F in 1949 and 1034F, obtained in 1955. All were in green livery. Replacements for the Utilecons started to arrive in late-1959 with the delivery of the Ford Thames 15-cwt 12-seat Utilabrake. This was a version of Ford's 400E van and looked

much more akin to the minibuses of today. At the time, they must have seemed very modern compared to what they were replacing. Examples joined the fleet as 1145F, 1146F, 1152F, 1163F, 1164F, 1165F and 1322F, and were all in the new grey livery plus light green roof, and with miniature red LONDON TRANSPORT fleetnames. These forward-control vans with the engine between the front seats featured a steering column-controlled gear change for the 3-speed box. The gear change on these Fords was easy to use when new, but as the linkage to the gearbox wore, the driver could find himself getting two gears at once. Identical in mechanical specification was 1317F, a replacement route-survey van, which may also have been used in a personnel-carrying role (as could previous survey vehicles).

A stranger in the camp was 1147B, a green Bedford 'CA' 12-cwt Utilabrake of November 1959, and presumably operated for comparison purposes with the Fords. If so, it does not appear to have been successful, as it was sold exactly four years later. The 'CA', rather like its Ford brother, also featured a column gear change, which was a hangover from the car-derived components used in all these vans.

The world-famous Land Rover had been launched in 1949, and clearly owed much of its design to the wartime US Jeep, but LT did not obtain any examples of the type until the 1963–64 period. During that time, 1287LR, 1288LR, 1291LR, 1316LR and 1369LR were delivered as long-wheelbase 12-seat personnel carriers with diesel or petrol engines. The type has continued to feature in the

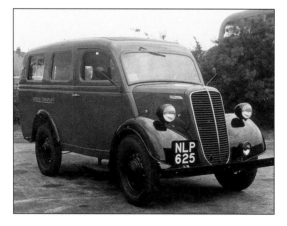

Below: The standard Ford 'E83W' was offered in a personnel-carrying role as the Utilicon 'A' and 'B'. Modifications included two sets of folding seats and passenger windows neatly cut into the sides of the body. This is 1034F, a late model built in 1955 and in use until 1961. The single nearside spotlight was an option commonly specified by CDS at this time. LT Museum

Below right: Sister vehicle 938F dated from 1949 and demonstrates the interior arrangements. As can be seen, the middle and rear seats could be folded down flat to provide a van-type load-space. LT Museum

Bottom: A new concept in personnel-carrying began in late-1959 with the arrival of the Ford 400E Utilabrake. In this early-60s view, 1152F hurries west along Chiswick High Road, whilst in the other direction passes an unmodernised early Green Line RF on the 701. A distinctive feature of the Utilabrakes was the reduced-size LT fleetname in traditional style, but coloured red.
J. Murphy collection

Bottom right: As a new type, 1152F naturally attracted the attention of the official LT photographer. The inward-facing bench layout and, lack of seatbelts would not pass muster today. At the front of the vehicle, the grey hump in the centre is the engine cover, whilst the steering-column mounted gear lever is visible to the left of the driver's seat. LT Museum

fleet on an occasional basis ever since. Some of those that are known to have been in personnel-carrying use were numbered as follows: 1624LR (4/1971 – grey), 1762LR (4/1972 – grey), 4401LR, 4402LR, 4439LR (1994 – white) and 4527LR (1995 – white). Two of the 1994–95 batch were allocated to the Jubilee Line Extension Project for use on building sites during the initial construction stages. Though having LUL cab-side lettering, they did not feature the blue skirt by then standard on most of the rail-based fleet.

With the advent of the Ford Transit, what were now described as 'minibus' versions of the van appeared in 1966 as 1441F and 1442F, both seating fifteen people. The Transit has now been the standard base for LT's minibus-type vehicles for more than thirty years, and numerous variants are in use at time of writing. The need for such types increased drastically when the Underground's rail-based engineering staff personnel carriers (converted from ex-Tube rolling stock) were condemned on 'Health & Safety' grounds. Though the railway side of the organisation has always had the majority of such minibuses, examples have been allocated to LTB for the conveyance of revenue control and route-surveying teams. During the period of LT involvement with the Docklands Light Railway, Transit 3337F served that operator in full DLR red/white/blue livery between 1986–90. Though most LTB/LBSL Transits have been of van design, 15-seat minibus 5017F arrived in mid-1999. This carried the re-introduced red livery (plus the new red/yellow rear door hazard chevrons).

Top left: Land Rovers have never enjoyed widespread use in the fleet, but isolated examples have been operated on-and-off since 1963. A 1970 delivery was 1578LR, with a 'Safari'-style 12-seat body. LT's participation with 'outward bound' training resulted in these rural surroundings. Closer to home, such vehicles were useful to engineers requiring an 'off-the-road' capability. Mike Scott

Top right: Two Land Rover 12-seat Station Wagon Crew-buses were obtained in 1994 for use on Jubilee Line Extension Project sites. This is 4401LR, which was finished in off-white and like other LUL-liveried Land Rovers, did not carry a blue skirt. Behind is Frank Pick House, the building that housed Scientific Services after the closure of the Chiswick Research Laboratory. Kim Rennie

Left: A view not normally associated with LT's usual routines. The early-1980s saw 2203F, a 1979 Ford Transit 12-seat minibus in the depths of Exmoor carrying Railway Operating Apprentices taking part in the Duke of Edinburgh's Award Scheme. This vehicle was of the Mk 2 design (a designation never used by Ford) where there was no frontal difference in appearance between diesel and petrol-engined models. Nick Agnew

Above: The Docklands Light Railway opened in 1987 as an LRT subsidiary and was initially supplied with vans and minibuses numbered in the main service vehicle series. Seen outside Crossharbour Station in November 1988 was 3337F in full DLR fleet livery, assisting with weekend engineering work. David Rowe

By the late-1970s, it was rare for former buses to be re-classified as service vehicles. Two exceptions were FS 13-14, which in 1977 became 2063F–2064F respectively for use at LT's Flagstaff House management training college near Weybridge. Livery for both was dark blue and devoid of any form of identification. The FS-class bodies were based on the parcel van design. *Julian Bowden-Green*

From time-to-time, LT has experimented with alternatives to the ubiquitous Ford Transit. In the 1980s, a number of Bedford 'CF' minibuses were in use by the Underground. 2255B was a 'CF230' seating 12 and carried non-standard dark grey. *Jim Wright*

The Transit had been adopted for LT's PSV bus operations in 1972 as the FS class. These Strachans Pacemaker-bodied 16-seaters were used to pioneer the inaugural minibus routes B1, C11, P4 and W9. Two of the first batch were later transferred to the service vehicle fleet in 1977 and renumbered as 2063F and 2064F. Painted navy blue, former FS 13 and FS 14 were in use at LT's Flagstaff House management training centre to convey delegates until 1979–80.

Transit FS 19 was one of a number of additional minibuses ordered following the success of the new services. By 1985, it was being used to carry staff and equipment for the 'Busco' radio project on the 36 group of routes. Standard livery was retained, but the saloon windows were curtained and the vehicle ran on trade plates. Another use for FS-class buses demoted from passenger work was for conveying teams of inspectors involved in checking tickets on night buses. However, in both these cases, the vehicles continued to be regarded as part of the road service fleet.

General Motors' eventual answer to the Transit in the 1970s had been the Bedford CF, and LT ordered some of the type in various specifications between 1977 and 1980. Numbers 2254B to 2261B were 12-seater minibuses from 1980 and the first five were finished in a non-standard dark grey livery. The final delivery was 2260B, which was painted dark blue and replaced the

ex-FSs on Flagstaff House duties between May 1980 and October 1984 (Flagstaff House was sold by LRT as a 'non-core' activity in 2000, just prior to the establishment of TfL).

Amongst the almost total standardisation on Transits since 1984, a small number of other types have been employed on staff transport duties. 3882B and 3883B were Bedford Midi-Vans to minibus specification and delivered in August and October 1980. The Toyota Spacecruiser design was represented in May 1990 by 3917T and re-introduced the 'T' suffix last used to classify Thornycroft lorries in 1939! The next item from this Japanese firm was 4226T, a Previa people-mover which entered service in September 1992. A further Toyota was 4477T, a Previa 2.4GL 5-door 'people-mover' model from February 1995 in LUL white/blue. A further venture into this concept occurred with 4717F, a Ford Galaxy 2.0GXLi. This 1996 vehicle seated seven and was also finished in Underground colours.

Former PSV-licensed buses were used to transport staff to and from Aldenham Works. This was necessary after the Chiswick body shop had been moved to Aldenham and certain employees compulsorily transferred to the new location. A similar provision had been made when the Reigate (ex-East Surrey) overhaul works were closed circa-1935, and a service between Reigate and Chiswick continued for many years. Vehicles were kept overnight at Central and Country Area garages, prior to their morning run to the works sites. In the afternoon, the reverse procedure occurred, and these arrangements continued long after the 1970 split between LT and LCBS. Types used were usually of the classes in the process of withdrawal, and the buses were not renumbered, repainted or considered part of the service vehicle fleet. The exception to the 'no-repaint' policy involved some of the RMA-class (q.v.). Staff buses also provided an hourly 'employee-only' service between Aldenham and Chiswick during the working day, and between Aldenham and Edgware at lunch times.

When, on 1st April 1985, the operating and engineering parts of London's buses were separated, the new subsidiary 'LRT Bus Engineering Limited' (trading as BEL) assumed responsibility for both Aldenham and Chiswick Works. A number of former BEA RMA-class Routemasters were then in use as staff buses. These initially remained in standard red livery, but later received a dark grey scheme (plus in some cases red window surrounds) which seems to have been influenced by conventional service vehicle practice. Those which carried grey are believed to have been RMAs 6, 8, 9, 16, 19 and 62. RMA 16 (ex-BEA 14) was the first to be repainted in 1985, and destined to be last vehicle of its type withdrawn by BEL on 17th December 1987 after performing an afternoon run to St Albans.

As the staff numbers and activities of the two works declined, the need for such large-capacity vehicles disappeared, and ordinary light-commercial types were substituted instead. Ford Transit 2458F was a 15-seat blue minibus used by BEL from 1987 to 1989. Despite its stock number, it was not in fact owned by CDS. The number 2459 is unaccounted for, but one source suggests it was another non-CDS minibus employed by BEL.

Not in dispute is that vehicles 2460L to 2463L were four 1987-built Leyland Sherpa '300' minibuses delivered for BEL use. These were part of the 'proper' CDS fleet, and the last two at least were finished in a crimson livery. As former parts of LT began to move into the private sector, accurate details become more difficult to obtain, but no identifying markings are believed to have been carried on the BEL-used minibuses. Vehicles 2462L and 2463L are recorded as being withdrawn in October 1992, with the later one being sold to bus operator BTS Travel (the same company had also acquired ex-LT Leyland Freighter recovery truck 2417L and Sherpa 350 van 2456L).

The small vans are perhaps the most unglamorous of the service vehicle fleet, but are also the most numerous, and in many ways perhaps some of the most important of all. In LT's case, several thousand have now seen use over the past seventy-odd years. They have been used to carry such diverse items as bus and train mechanical parts, signal and permanent way spares, lost property, advertising and publicity items, catering supplies, cleaning materials, destination blinds, building materials, ticket supplies and uniforms.

Unlike the larger open and enclosed (i.e. box) lorries, the lightest van types used by LT have always made use of standard 'off the shelf' designs. Though a few 'one-off' types have seen service, the vast majority of vans have been in blocks of identical-looking vehicles, and save for the livery are indistinguishable from others in general commercial use. In view of the large number of such vehicles involved, only a general review of the subject can be given here.

Early vehicles included those operated by the LGOC, which had about forty Model-T Ford light vans in the 1920s. These were allocated to individual garages, Chiswick Works and the Advertising & Publicity Department and survived to about 1926. They were replaced by around fifty 'V-type' vans, a hybrid vehicle assembled in Chiswick Works over one week from components supplied by various manufacturers, and identified in a V-prefixed series. A distinctive feature of the Vs was the radiator shell, which resembled a smaller version of those fitted to NS class buses and bore a cast GENERAL bullseye. Circa 1928, the LGOC purchased four smaller vans of around 5-cwt size from Trojan and numbered these as TV 1 to TV 4. TV 5 to TV 29, possibly 7-cwt versions, followed in 1931, TV 30 came second-hand from independent bus operator 'Renown' in 1934, whilst TV 31 was a 1935 addition, also second-hand, but this time from a dealer. The V-types were withdrawn around 1933 and the Trojans by 1936.

In the immediate period following the formation of the LPTB, vehicles inherited from the constituent companies and organisations remained in operation. The Underground Group had the greatest degree of standardisation, with less so from the LCCT, and very little in the municipal fleets. From the LGOC came a batch of 27 Morris Commercial vans dating from 1929–31 in 12-cwt, 1-ton and 30-cwt categories. These were used mainly as stores vehicles, with twenty-two allocated to individual bus garages, one utilised by the 'Chiswick Progress Chaser',

Top: In 1924, the LGOC built a fleet of small vans at Chiswick to its own design, though using proprietary components. The vehicles could carry a load of up to 15-cwt and were bodied in either enclosed or tilt-fitted format. Vehicle V 1 demonstrates the former option, as well as the asymmetrical windscreen designed to allow the transportation of the long route boards then carried on the sides of buses.
Bill Aldridge collection

Centre: Van No. V 29 carried the open design of body with tarpaulin tilt cover and was allocated to Putney Bridge Garage. The diamond-shaped notice behind the cab door carried the exhortation 'Safety First' and was similar to those applied to the LGOC's buses. Again, the windscreen was cut short on the nearside to facilitate the carriage of lengthy items.
Bill Aldridge collection

Right: Vehicle TV 9 was one of a number of Trojan vans inherited by the LPTB. The design of engine fitted to these vans was unique to Trojan, being a 4-cylinder, 2-stroke design, producing 12-bhp and comprising just seven moving parts. The van was part of a batch of 24 acquired by the LGOC in 1931 and numbered as TV 5–29. Michael Rooum

others by the millwrights at Chiswick and some by the Building Department. Most of this original batch (numbered M 1 to M 27) were de-licensed in 1937, and none survived to become part of the 1939 numbering system. Other Morris vans of various types were numbered M 28 to M 51, and mostly dated from 1933 to 1934, but also included six older ones, some of which, if not all, were inherited from non-LGOC sources.

The first designs bought new in significant quantities by the Board were Morris 10-cwt box-vans in 1936 (M-prefixed, later 228M to 259M). There were also 5-cwt vans based on the contemporary Morris 8 car and numbered 223M to 227M, but 228M to 259M were of a design launched in 1935 as a replacement for an earlier van based on the Morris Cowley. These new vans, known as Series II, had an offset engine to allow the driver sufficient legroom, featured trafficators and a spare wheel hidden behind the rear number plate, yet continued the old tradition of a central accelerator pedal. This model was in turn superseded by the Series III in 1939, but this did not enter serious production for the civilian market until 1945. Both van models featured front 'suicide doors', which were rear-hinged and might throw the driver out of the van if involved in an accident.

The Ford Motor Company had supplied vans from 1930 onwards with the 30-cwt 'AA' model. Known examples are a 1 for Country Bus stores (1930–37), 124 for Tramways breakdown operation (1931–37) and a third, 'F2', for Central Buses Advertising Department (1933–37). The Signal Department used an unidentified fourth Ford, a 5-cwt model-Y. None of these lasted long enough to come under 1939 renumbering, but some others did; including 5-cwt, 1-ton, 30-cwt and 2-ton models of the Ford 'Y', 'A', 'AA' and 'BB'-types. Users included the Signal, Publicity and Building Departments.

Non-standard vans in the in the pre-war years were 147B to 150B, four Bedford WLB 20-seat single-deck buses obtained second-hand from independent operators in 1933–34. The four had Duple bus bodies, but were given new 3-ton van bodies from the same manufacturer by the LPTB. Initially identified using BD-prefixed numbers in the bus numbering series, the origin of the quartet was as follows: 147B (ex-BD 2 from Reliable), 148B (ex-BD 4 from Gravesend & District), 149B (ex-BD 6 from Warwick) and 150B (ex-BD 11 from Harvey). Allocation was to Country Area garages as stores vehicles: North-fleet (147B), Windsor (148B), Hertford (149B) and Watford (150B). Vehicle 149B was used to tow 'producer gas' trailers from July 1943, and may have been converted to run on this fuel itself. All four were withdrawn in the immediate post-war period. There had also been a fifth Bedford registered as KX 7894. This dated from 1932 and was a 2-ton truck used for Country Bus stores, but was withdrawn in 1937 without being numbered.

Top: The 5-cwt Morris Commercial van of the mid-1930s had a striking similarity to the Morris car of the same period. 224M was allocated to the Overhead Electrical Engineer (North) at Leyton Depot, but on this occasion in 1948, seems to have been assisting with LT's Derby Day operations. Such vans had a canvas duck roof and if this began to leak, a temporary solution was as seen here, a sheet of hardboard tied down to the front and rear door hinges. A.B. Cross

Centre: The Ford Motor Company became a major supplier to LT after the Second World War, but had provided a small number of vans from the organisation's early days. This Ford AA 1-ton publicity van started off as F 5 in November 1934. Here it has been renumbered 164F and carries the wartime vehicle accoutrements of white-edged wings and masked lights. A.B. Cross

Left: Few of the non-standard (at least to LPTB eyes) chassis taken over from independent operators remained in passenger service after 1936. Some however became service vehicles, including this Bedford WLB bus from Gravesend & District. Rebuilt as Duple-bodied van BD 4 (later 148B) in 1935, it was based at Windsor Garage as a stores vehicle. J.F Higham

The next small vans from Ford were a pair of 5-cwt YC-types numbered 454F/455F in 1940 and 1941. They were originally built in the mid-1930s, and acquired second-hand by the LPTB for use by Works & Building.

Not until 1946 did the LPTB purchase any new Ford vans, the model chosen being the E83W. These were the antecedents to many more generations of Ford vans. The E83W Fordson 10-cwt van had been introduced in March 1938, and remained in production until September 1957, when it was replaced by the forward-control and higher-capacity 400E model. The E83W vans used the car-derived 10hp 1172cc side-valve engine married to a three-speed gearbox. Like many of the Ford cars of that era, the suspension was by transverse leaf springs with lever-arm shock absorbers. To allow maximum load space within the short wheelbase a semi-forward-control layout was utilised. To give the driver some (restricted) legroom the engine was offset to the nearside, just like on the contemporary Morris vans. This meant that the passenger seat (where fitted) was placed behind the driver's left shoulder. The standard van body was built by Briggs Motor Bodies, but some of those in LT service had larger coachbuilt van bodies. These vans were very basic, and were delivered with just one external mirror, one step (for the driver) and one seat. The radiator grille nearly always had two holes for the starting handle, this was to cope with the offset engine on both left-hand and right-hand-drive versions. Apart from the poor driving position, the other major drawback of this model was the vacuum-operated wipers that were guaranteed to slow down just as the driver was accelerating to overtake another vehicle. Despite these shortcomings, the breed was adopted as the standard small van, and successive batches arrived between 1946 and 1955 (668F being the first in service) and most lasted for between 10 to 12 years.

In 1946, eight Morris Commercial PV 16hp 15-cwt vans (680M to 687M) were delivered for advertising/publicity use, introducing the concept of forward-control on small types. The designation 'PV' stood for parcel van and the vehicles were very square-looking. Unfortunately they contained a lot of green unseasoned timber in their body construction and thus had relatively short lives. They were to be the last Morris vans bought, for although the successor to the PV – the LD, was purchased later, the latter were 'badge-engineered' by the British Motor Corporation as 'Austins'. The LDs began to arrive from 1955, the first batch being 1024AS to 1031AS, 17hp 1-ton general freight vans. Other examples of this type were described as 1-ton box-vans or half-tilt trucks, and continued to be purchased on-and-off until 1964.

Top: The 1935 built Morris 10cwt vans were designed to give maximum carrying capacity within the shortest possible wheelbase. The driving accommodation was certainly cramped, with the engine needing to be offset to even allow room for the driver's legs. Both driver and passenger doors were rear hung since it was a simpler manufacturing process to fit hinges on the vertical 'B' post than on the sloping 'A' post. Originally fitted with rear wheel covers, the vans soon lost these after a few tyre changes. LT Museum

Centre: The Fordson-Thames E83W became LT's standard light van in the immediate post-war years. The steel bodies were built by Briggs with a central roof panel made of canvas. Kingston Garage's 801F entered stock in 1951 and lasted ten years with the organisation. Lens of Sutton

Right: Most of the Fordson E83W vans were fitted with standard steel bodies, but a number carried so-called 'Laundry Bodies' with extra headroom and capacity for larger and lighter loads. These box-van bodies were coachbuilt with wooden frames, aluminium cladding and canvas roofs. 764F was one van so-fitted, here resting in the company of H1-class trolleybus 813. Bill Aldridge collection

Right: Though the Morris PV was not a spectacular success, its successor, the LD, was to become very popular throughout the UK. With the basic design of the PV updated and the sliding doors retained, the Morris LD was in use with most trades in the 1950s and 1960s. In November 1964, green-liveried 1120AS (later deliveries would be in grey) is seen passing Stonebridge Park Garage. The vehicle has been 'badge-engineered' as an Austin, a common British motor industry practice of the time. A.B. Cross

A new model, the 300E, replaced the pre-war 5-cwt Ford van design in 1954. This was based on the Ford Anglia and Popular car of that era, and retained the 3-speed gearbox and 1172cc side-valve engine. To the uninitiated the gearbox could be problematical, since reverse was in the same position as first gear on a 4-speed gearbox. Unwary drivers could be seen shooting backwards at traffic lights! LT purchased vans of this type numbered 1053F, 1054F and 1055F from December 1957, with further batches following. Later car-derived vans of the 1960s-era were the Ford Thames 7-cwt vehicles, with a 997cc overhead-valve engine and 4-speed gearbox known as the '307E' model. These were based on the 105E Anglia saloon and became a popular choice for LT. Ford badged these as 'Thames', linking them to the much larger lorries usually associated with this name. This 'badge-engineering' policy changed when the Escort replaced the Anglia range in 1968. Transits and Escorts fulfilled the requirement for light-commercial vehicles until 1977, when the first of several batches of Bedford HA110 6-cwt and larger CF220 vans arrived. This was at a time when neither Ford nor Leyland had been able to fulfil LT's order book, and many of the new deliveries carried non-standard white or light-blue liveries. (Similarly, in 1969, LT took a number of Escort box-vans in beige.)

The fleet took delivery of its first Ford Thames '400E' 15-cwt vans in 1959. Several more batches were to follow. Some of these had additional seats and windows and were

Centre: The 5-cwt- or 7-cwt-size van was never that popular with LT until the advent of the Ford 300E model in 1957. Although 1054F was one of only three built for LT in that year, this size of vehicle soon began to replace the earlier and larger 10-cwt Fordson E83W vans. These were the first fully-monocoque-constructed vans bought by LT, comprising the front-end panel-work of the Anglia car allied to a van rear of 66-cubic feet capacity. 1054F's location is Wood Green in August 1961 and the 'Whitechapel' slot-in plate suggests railway use. Jason Tilley

Left: Ford's 400E model van was in many ways the first up-to-date 15-cwt van of the late-1950s, with its engine positioned between the seats and easy access for the crew. The large-size van body was ideal for such work as publicity distribution, as evidenced by 1169F (badged 'Thames') with its cheery driver here at Aldgate. In the background, a Green Line inspectors' box can be seen. A.B. Cross

Right: The Austin 'J4'-type enjoyed a brief popularity with LT between the end of 'LD' production and the advent of the Ford Transit. Five examples were delivered in 1964 as 1338AS–1342AS. No.1340AS was used by the Publicity Department, for whom the sliding cab doors proved especially helpful when posting roadside timetable material. As usual, LT had specified a nearside spotlamp. *LT Museum*

Centre: Most of the Ford Transit Mk.1 vans were of conventional appearance, but a few were of this higher-bodied 'parcel van' configuration. As delivered, these vans had their grey livery complemented by a light green roof. The cab door lettering shows that 'diesel engined' 1718F was part of the main CDS delivery fleet. On this day in March 1975, it was paying a visit to Buckhurst Hill Station. *Phil Picken*

Bottom: Ford gave the Transit its first major revamp in 1975, resulting in the loss of external differentiation between the diesel- and petrol-engined models. 2299F represents numerous examples of the type which supported the bus and rail fleets in the 1970s/1980s. This particular vehicle belonged to the Signal Department and lasted four years. *Jim Wright*

described as 12-seat Utilabrakes (i.e. minibuses), but 1166F to 1172F and 1202F to 1207F were 1961-built 1600cc 15-cwt box-vans. In October 1963, a single Bedford CALV 15-cwt box-van entered stock as 1301B for use by the Publicity Department, but did not lead to further orders. Another break from Ford was with the Austin J-type and more LD vans, with LT receiving a number in 12-cwt (J4), 15-cwt (J2) and 1-ton (LD) configuration between 1964 and 1966.

The world-famous Ford Transit was launched in October 1965. LT's first example was 12-cwt capacity van 1410F, delivered in 1966. This particular vehicle had only a short career with the organisation, and was part of a batch of four Transits transferred to the newly-formed LCBS on 1st January 1970. Sisters 1414F and 1415F joined 1410F to 1413F at LCBS in January 1973. One of this batch, 1413F gained some limited fame, being illustrated at St Albans Garage (together with green RT and RF buses) in a Ford Motor Company sales brochure of 1971. The Transit has been a mainstay of the fleet for more than thirty years. Some 750-odd examples in van, minibus and dropside form have been operated, in all four series, and throughout all sections of what has constituted LT. The Transit was offered in both petrol and diesel-powered forms, and the two types could originally be differentiated by the frontal styling (the diesel models had a square radiator grille). A revamp of the range in 1975 removed this distinction, and new versions of the model have since been introduced in 1991 and 2000. The Transit has remained the best-selling van within its designated weight categories throughout the UK, from its inception in 1965 to the 21st Century.

Livery on the Transits was originally grey, but changed to red in the 1980s. Blue van 3751F was in use in 1989 by the Docklands Light Railway as a mobile incident vehicle. London Transport Advertising (later LTA Advertising) was operating plain white vans with LTA logos by the early-1990s, and a similar appearance was maintained after the department's sale to the US-company TDI in August 1994. TDI continued to use the ex-LTA Transit (and Escort) vans until their individual leases expired, after which CDS involvement ceased. (It was renamed again, as 'Viacom Outdoor' on 1st July 2001.) White Transit vans have also been used by the Bus Passenger Infrastructure Unit, LT Buses, and as a one-off, 4780F for the LT Archive Department (later replaced by Transit 5213F with joint LUL/TfL logos). Red-liveried Transits were operated by LBL bus units until the process of privatisation was completed in January 1995. As with TDI, leased vehicles allocated to these subsidiaries tended to operate for a time after the sell-off. In some cases, vehicles were subsequently acquired by individual companies, e.g. Transit vans 4156F and 4219F which remained with Stagecoach East London in 2000 and operated in turn from Stratford (Carpenters Road) and Bow Garage. A Transit dating from 1990 originally supplied to the LT Advertising was seen still in use by TDI in August 2000. New Mk4 (though Ford do not recognise this term) Transits for LUL and LBSL began entering the fleet from July 2000.

With the vast majority of service vehicles allocated to railway use by the late-1980s, red was considered an inappropriate colour for most of the van fleet, and 1989 Transits began to receive an all-blue scheme. This lasted only a short while, since the new white/blue livery was introduced in 1990, which was based on the new corporate livery used on some Underground rolling stock from 1989. As with larger vehicles, additional red and blue frontal chevrons were applied to those types in use in a response role, and have included Transits 3783F (Signal & Electrical Engineers' Dept) and 4852F (Emergency Response Unit). Four Ford Transit vans were based at Wellington Way, E3; and helped supply the confectionery machines installed on Underground station platforms. These vans were in plain white, and apart from black fleet numbers, the only identification was a cab door title reading 'London Transport vending services' in black lower case New Johnston lettering (sometimes with a plain red roundel added). Unusually, LRT took over direct control of the vending operation after private firms pulled out in the mid-1990s. Vending Services was a division of LT Property, but was sold to Cadbury Schweppes in 2001.

Although Fords made up the vast majority of small and medium vans in the 1960s and 1970s, there was always the odd Austin ('AS'-suffix), Bedford ('B'-suffix) and even Land Rover ('LR'-suffix) type added to fleet strength from time-to-time. Land Rovers have been used when an off-road capability is required (e.g. by the Civil Engineering or Permanent Way Departments). 1670LR of December 1970 carried weed-killing equipment, whilst 1972-vintage short-wheelbase Land Rover 1761LR was equipped with a tow-bar and allocated to the Works & Building Department. It was originally grey, but in 1983 was customised by apprentices at Chiswick Works. This involved the fitting of side windows to the body, and a repaint in bus red, complete with red oxide wheels, white roof and plain LT roundels. It passed to Stagecoach upon privatisation and later appeared in a green livery with gold 'Stagecoach East London' fleetnames.

Further fleet variety was added in late-1978 when the first LT-owned Leyland Sherpa vans made their debut. Leyland had introduced the Sherpa in 1976, and LT usage commenced with 15-cwt vans 2144L to 2158L. The design was in reality a modernised version of the Austin-Morris J4 panel-van used by the Board in the 1960s. With leased vehicles being listed in their own series from 1982, what was now referred to as a Freight Rover Sherpa filled second position 3001L. One of this batch, 3011L, was first used by the Public Relations Department. In 1984, it was

Top: After LBL devolved much of its control to local bus 'units' in 1989, a greater diversity became apparent in the service vehicle fleet. Typical of this was Mk3 Ford Transit 3770F, here attending a Leyland Olympian 'non-start' on route 250. Though still numbered in the common series and supplied by Distribution Services, the vehicle carries gold 'South London' fleetnames as well as the legend 'Thornton Heath Engineers'. Also non-standard were the roof-mounted flashing lights and rear-facing lamps to assist with breakdowns. Kim Rennie

Centre: LTB initially continued to use the white livery inherited from the LT Bus Passenger Infrastructure Unit. This combined a white factory-finish together with appropriate LTB logos. In the case of Ford Transit 4545F, no fewer than three aerials can be seen, which indicate the various fleet communication systems fitted. The orange beacon bar was standard on such vehicles and used when required to remain stationary at bus stops. Note that a 'V' fleet number suffix has been applied in error. Kim Rennie

Bottom: The standard appearance of an LUL van for over a decade since 1990. Ford Transit 4484F was one of the 1995-intake and carried 'Engineering services' lettering. To the right, another Transit shows the alternative 'Support services' logo. Also visible in this Acton Works view is Jubilee Line Extension Land Rover 4402LR. Kim Rennie

Right: Land Rovers were not only used in personnel-carrying roles. No.1491LR was a petrol-engined mobile workshop for the Rolling Stock Engineer (Railways) and based at Ealing Common Depot. The livery was non-standard, being Army bronze green, with an off-white roof. The nearside roof-hinged flap could be opened to allow access to an internal workbench. John Gascoine

Centre: With a model still in production in 2003, the basic panel work of the Sherpa van shown here dates back to the Austin/Morris J4 of the 1960s. The type has been variously produced by Austin/Morris, BLMC, Leyland, Freight Rover and now LDV, though all at the same Birmingham factory. This is 2298L, a 1980 Leyland Sherpa '230' single-tyred 2.0-tonne panel van for LT Advertising. Jim Wright

repainted by apprentices at Plumstead Garage, and exchanged grey for a special red/cream/black 'heritage' livery and transferred to the LT Museum a year later. It also lasted much longer than its compatriots, and moved from the leased fleet to become an owned vehicle (though kept its 3xxx number in the leased series). LT Cleaning Services was allocated no less than sixteen Sherpa 230Ds and 250Ds in 1984 as numbers 3153L to 3168L in the batch 3150L to 3169L, and it seems the last of the type was 4216L in 1993. Including minibus versions, at least seventy-five Sherpas have been used. Other products from what has been known as British Leyland, BL, Austin Rover and latterly the Rover Group were 3322L, 3335L, 3531L and 3532L, four Maestro vans dating from between 1985 and 1987. The Sherpas were followed in 1981 by three Dodge S66 vans (D-suffix). This model appears to have been none too popular, as only three more Dodge vans (and one dropside S50 truck) were ever purchased. Of these, 2375D, delivered in 1982, was fitted out as a mobile laboratory (q.v.).

Just as the Transit had replaced the 400E-series of vans, so the small 307E-derived 7-cwt Ford Thames models were themselves supplanted by a new design in 1968 with the arrival of the Ford Escort. Around 800 of these have been in use within almost every part of the undertaking, though their numbers have declined in more recent years, when the Transit has achieved almost universal prominence. Escort vans were in grey until 1972, when red was adopted, then moved to LUL

The LT Museum operated No.3011L, a 1982-built Freight-Rover '230D' van, for ten years; during which time it was a familiar sight at enthusiast events. Delivered in grey, it soon gained this unique red/cream/black 'heritage' livery. Pictured here outside 55 Broadway, the front-end treatment differs markedly from that applied to 2298L two years' earlier. Capital Transport

Left: The Bus Passenger Infrastructure Unit (BPI) was established to control the maintenance of bus stations, bus stops and bus stands. The unit's vehicles carried a neutral all-white livery, and this was perpetuated when operations were merged with the Centrecomm Road Team in 1995. Ford Escort van 4230F, which started life with BPI in September 1992, is seen carrying the new LTB logo and lettering. G. Burgess

Below left: The Bedford HA van was one of the vehicle types sourced from alternative manufacturers on one of the occasions that Ford was unable to fulfil LT's demands. With 2015B nearest the camera, no fewer than 13 Bedford 'HA110' are posed in the dealer's yard in 1977 prior to entering service. Michael Clark

of HA vans were finished in light blue or white when Bedford was unable to comply with LT's wishes. From the same company came the larger Bedford 'CF220', and 18-cwt vans of this type were in use from 1977. A large number were delivered in 1982 as 3082B to 3103B and used for publicity distribution in red livery.

As already mentioned in the section on railway breakdown vehicles, the 'A'-series was one of Ford's less successful designs. LT experimented with A0609 4-ton versions 2062F, 2086F, 2087F and 2088F in 1977 as possible replacements for the higher cubic capacity Transit 'parcel vans'. Number 2062F had originally been on hire before entering the fleet and as described earlier, vehicle 2086F found greater fame when converted to the Underground Communications Unit. In the event, Ford ceased production of the A-series in 1983.

The pick-up truck was a new concept for LT in the mid-1980s, i.e. where a small commercial chassis is provided with a fixed-sided open body and hinged tailboard. Ford had introduced the P100 model, which grafted the front of a Mark IV Cortina to an open body (on later trucks, the front section was replaced by components from the Sierra range). Distribution Services took delivery of at least 23 examples between 1984 and 1990, some of which had a removable cover fitted to the rear (3188F, 3241F, 3295F, 3352F, 3353F, 3354F, 3709F, 3773F, 3777F, 3806F, 3814F, 3815F, 3862F, 3891F, 3892F, 3893F, 4030F, 4112F, 4149F, 4204F, 4268F, 4269F and 4270F). The other provider of this style of vehicle was Peugeot, and twenty-one '504' pick-ups were acquired from 1987 to 1992 (3486P, 3487P, 3488P, 3500P, 3581P, 3643P, 3651P, 3722P to 3727P, 3867P, 3878P, 4205P to 4209P and 4246P). The Peugeots re-used the old code for AEC Matadors, and both batches proved popular with garage engineering staff, soon gaining local identity transfers and roof-mounted orange 'beacon bars'. The last deliveries of both types occurred in 1990, and most had gone by 1993. Almost all were in red (or arrived in that colour), but a white/blue Peugeot 504 was noted in use at Upminster Depot in 1992. Another '504', 4205P, passed to Stagecoach East London upon privatisation, and was still at work for them at Upton Park Garage as late as 1999. The concept

white/blue from 1990. In 1969, a small number of Escort vans arrived in beige owing to the manufacturer being unable to supply the required colour.

A Bedford HA 8-cwt van numbered 1373B had been acquired in 1964, and co-incidentally carried the very last service vehicle body number (M 103) in a new series which had only commenced in November 1962. Though never as numerous as the Escort, the model was delivered in a number of batches up until 1981, when the model ceased production. These too were originally in grey, moving to red in the 1970s, but as with the beige Escorts, a number

Right: As Bedford were unable to supply all of their HA vans in red livery, some were delivered in light blue or white instead. No.2133B is one of the latter and was allocated to the Permanent Way Department. Ironically, what must have then seemed an impractical colour scheme was later adopted as standard for all LUL service vehicles. Jim Wright

Far right: No.2120B was one of the light blue Bedford HA vans. Both types of vehicle had a painted coach-line applied along the waist-rail, indicating that they had come from standard dealer stock as opposed to a special order prepared for LT. Jim Wright

Right: General Motors' answer to the Ford Transit was the Bedford CF, but despite offering independent front suspension and a larger engine, the model was never as popular as its rival. The CF was distinctly American in origin, whereas the Transit had been designed in Europe. Nevertheless, LT bought a number of CF vans in the late-1970s, including this publicity van, 2022B. The yellow notice on the rear door was one of a pair used to warn following motorists that the vehicle was likely to pull up at bus stops.
Jim Wright

Below right: The grey-liveried Bedford CF derivatives all carried this non-standard dark-shaded factory-finish. 2220B was a 'CF220' 1-ton open lorry with full-tilt cover for the Chief Civil Engineer's Department and unlike the similar-looking vans, had the benefit of twin rear wheels.
Jim Wright

made a surprising reappearance from 2000, when three 4x4 Ford Ranger double-cabbed pick-ups, 4985F, 4986F and 4987F, were allocated to the Lifts, Escalators and Pumps Department at Edgware Road, and further examples for other departments have followed. The double-cab was a production option on the Ford Ranger, and enabled additional maintenance staff to be transported safely.

The Ford Fiesta was in use by LBSL as a hatchback car, but at least 54 van-bodied models were operated between 1985 and the mid-1990s. Another much rarer type to commence use in 1985 were vehicles 3333I and 3332I, two Fiat Ducato 1800 vans with the odd suffix of 'I' (code 'I' for Italian?).

General Motors has been represented in recent years by the Bedford/Vauxhall Astra range (first known example 3171B in March 1984); some of which were used alongside or in place of the radio-control estate cars. Including saloon car variants, some 300-odd Astras have served in the fleet, with many continuing to do so at time of writing. With GM beginning to struggle like so much of the British motor manufacturing industry by the mid-1980s, one solution was thought to be the licensed construction of vehicles designed by other firms. The Japanese Suzuki 'Super Carry' was introduced as the Bedford 'Rascal', whilst the Isuzu became the 'Midi-Van'. LT took at least eighteen of the former, and thirteen of the latter, over the 1986 to 1995 period.

Mercedes-Benz began supplying full-sized lorries to LT in 1987, but the first vehicles from the German firm were based on the small 307D model. Numbered 2425M to 2432M, they were 1986-built grey-liveried dropside trucks allocated to the Works & Building Department in the last years of its existence. The same chassis was used for 2445M to 2454M, fitted with curtain-sided bodies for LT Advertising. This range of trucks was used for LUL engineering use from 1990 in white & blue. The 4-tonne gross version of the small Mercedes model entered LT service from 1990; 2475M to 2480M were 408D chassis with de-mountable bodies. Fleet number 2484M was a larger 609D integral van. The year 1992 saw a single 410D de-mountable numbered 2497M. Numbers 2510M and 2511M were two '410D' curtain-sided trucks delivered the

Above right: There was a brief flirtation with the pick-up truck between 1984 and 1990. Some were in use by the Underground, whilst others served the bus fleet as a garage 'runabouts' collecting spares and attending minor breakdowns. Ford P100 pick-up 3241F was allocated to the Plant Engineer (Railways), yet based at Walthamstow Garage, where the Underground made use of spare capacity. The P100 was built in South Africa and featured the front-end panels of a Ford Cortina Mk4. David Rowe

Right: Later Ford P100 pick-ups had their front-end derived from the Sierra car and presented a quite different appearance. 3893F was allocated to Catford Garage, yet saw only three years' use between the Mays of 1990 and 1993. In this case, vehicle identification details were minimal, with little clue as to who the operator was. Colin Lloyd

following year for uniform distribution, and took over from the Carrymaster trailers. Other 410Ds were 2533M (box-van with tail-lift), 2539M and 2545M (dropside). Less-powerful dropsides were 308Ds 2543M and 2544M.

Also popular has been the Volkswagen Transporter, with around fifty of the type (out of 8m built world-wide) having been used by at least three departments of LT since 1991. Pioneer vehicle was 4095VW, with an additional pair added the following year as 4168VW and 4169VW. In 1993, LT's Bus Passenger Infrastructure Unit began a commitment to the German manufacturer for bus-associated use that continues to this day. 4309V to 4317V and 4331V were nine Transporter 1.9's and introduced the revised suffix of 'V' for Volkswagens. This change of letter followed the decision to code Vauxhalls as 'B', rather than the 'V' initially used after General Motors discontinued the use of the Bedford name for commercials. Another seven were received in 1994 to what had now become London Transport Buses, and numbered as 4381V and 4383V to 4388V. Both the BPI and LTB vehicles carried their new plain white livery, plus orange 'beacon bar' on the rear of the roof. The Transporter has continued to arrive in small batches for use by LTB's Area Traffic Controllers, the grade which has now assumed responsibility for emergency and planned route diversions, bus stop closures and the like since the LBL privatisation. Equipment carried inside their vans includes diversion signs, bus stop flag 'hoods', road salt, temporary stops, hazard tape for closing off damaged shelters, and absorbent granules for soaking up oil and diesel spills. Transporter 1.9D's and 2.4i's 4468V, 4469V, 4470V, 4502V, 4506V and 4507V arrived in 1995. An additional van was 4498V for the LT Museum in non-standard dark red and with white stock numbers only.

The Transit then came back in vogue for a few years, with the next Volkswagens not arriving until 1999. Most unusually, the new 4835V and 4836V were in white/blue for direct LUL use, the first known instance of this. LTB returned to the Transporter again in the same year with 4887VW to 4891VW, 4918VW, 4942VW to 4947VW, 4971VW and 5022VW. These saw a reversion to using the two-letter 'VW' suffix, but more interestingly, reintroduced a red livery into the service vehicle fleet. Both short and long-wheelbase models were among these batches, and all subsequently gained red/yellow hazard chevrons on the rear doors, plus the now customary orange 'beacon bar' (now fitted towards the front of the roof).

Another new manufacturer was approached in 1999, and led to a pair of Renault Master 'SM35TD' vans being allocated to LTB as 4919R and 4920R, re-using the old code for mobile cranes. Livery was the now standard red, though earlier vehicles operated by this department were not repainted and remained in white.

Top: Bedford's Midi-Van was based on a Japanese Isuzu design and fitted neatly between the car-derived Astravan and the larger CF model. The overall concept was not unlike the old Ford 400E van, though much more reliable. This is the Central Line's 4288B, seen here at Ruislip Depot at a time when such vehicles were in use as engineers' runabouts. The application of a full-size LUL roundel as carried on railway rolling stock is most unusual.
David Rowe

Centre: BPI soon found that larger vehicles were desirable and adopted the Volkswagen Transporter as a standard design. Equipment carried inside included diversion signs, temporary stops, hazard tape, road salt and absorbent granules. This view of Transporter 4310V was taken on 22nd May 1993 and shows the style of lettering used by BPI during its short life as an independent unit. The first LT Volkswagen Transporters carried a 'VW'-suffix, but some later deliveries have used the letter 'V' formerly used on Vauxhalls.
Colin Lloyd

Left: Some of the most distinctive members of the current fleet are these large US-built Ford Ranger '4x4' pick-up trucks. No.4986F is one of three allocated to Lifts, Escalators & Pumps and can usually be found at Edgware Road (H&C) Station. Their 'chunky' appearance would seem more at home in the American Mid-West. To the right is Cobul 'Tow-a-Van' trailer CBT 55.
Kim Rennie

To give an example of the variety of in-house departments that operated standard vans, in April 1985 the following non-bus garage locations were being used:

Department	Location(s)
Bus Revenue	Hilden House (Vauxhall)
Civil Engineering ...	Lillie Bridge, Pelham Street and Ruislip
Cleaning Services ...	Bow Road, Grosvenor Gardens and White City
Commercial Advertising	Jamestown Road (Camden Town)
Data Processing ...	Newman Street (W1)
Electrical Engineering	Glenthorne Road (W6), Leicester Square and Wood Lane
Leaside Bus District head office	Manor House
Lifts & Escalators ...	Griffith House
Management Training Centre	Flagstaff House (Weybridge)
Permanent Way Engineer	Lillie Bridge and Pelham St
Publicity	Baker Street and Edgware Road
Railway Training Centre	White City
Signal & Electrical Engineering	Baker Street Station, Bollo Lane, Lillie Bridge, South Kensington, Tower Hill, Wembley Park and Whitechapel
Main stores/CDS depots	Chiswick Works and Parsons Green
Ticket Machine Works	Effra Road (Brixton) and Swanley (vehicle kept at LCBS garage)
Wandle Bus District head office	Unifilter House (Mitcham)
Works & Building ...	Bow Road, Chiswick Park, Chiswick Works, Clapham Common South Side, Edgware Road, Grays Inn Road, Junction Road (Holloway), Kennington Park Road, Parsons Green and Willesden Green

(Publicity vans also made use of spare capacity in Stockwell, Stamford Brook and Walthamstow Garages.)

Above left: LTB returned to a red livery in 1999 and this was applied to that year's intake of Transporter vans. Short-wheelbase 4918V exhibits other visual changes, including a horizontal stripe made up from orange squares and the application of red/yellow 'hazard' chevrons to the top-hinged rear door. Early LTB Transporters had their orange beacon bar fitted to the rear of the roof, but later deliveries saw this relocated towards the front. *Kim Rennie*

Above: The Volkswagen Transporter is also operated by LTB in long-wheelbase form, as demonstrated here by 4944VW in leafy Orpington. The rectangular white logos on the sides of all red LTB vehicles were later amended to read 'London Buses' following the transfer to TfL. *G. Burgess*

Together with the Ford Escort, the Vauxhall Astravan was a mainstay of the small vehicle fleet throughout the 1990s. 5033B is allocated to the Metropolitan & Circle Lines and features a redesigned and more stylish front end derived from Vauxhall saloon cars. The vehicle carries the standard white & blue Distribution Services corporate livery introduced in 1990. The building behind was once the Neasden Permanent Way Training School. *Kim Rennie*

Ford gave the Transit its fourth major redesign in 2000 and Distribution Services was soon in receipt of the new model. This example, 5146F, is fitted-out in the standard format for engineering use with dropside body, crew-cab and tail-lift. Seen here 'as-delivered' in Acton Works; it was destined for operation by Lifts, Escalators & Pumps. Alongside is one of the second-hand Thompson 8-compartment fuel tankers bought to combat the 2000 'Fuel Crisis'. *Kim Rennie*

At the time of writing, TfL's London Buses subsidiary continued to rely on Distribution Services for the provision of vehicles. New-style high-top Ford Transit 5301F shows how the red livery of LTB has been retained, but signage subtly changed to remove the word 'Transport' between the 'London' and 'Buses'. Also new is the registration number series, which has replaced the system whose origins could be traced back to 1903. *Kim Rennie*

Right: These are two of the earliest LPTB motor cars. Reg.no.BLH 799 was a 1935 Humber Laundelette originally assigned to a Mr Pitts of the Principal Offices Department, whilst CXX 422 was a Morris 18hp saloon from 1936 allocated to a Mr Shephard. The registration prefixes were both in series used on STL buses. Although originally scheduled for replacement in 1941, the pair still appeared to be in excellent condition when seen here on 24th July 1948. A.B. Cross

Derby Day 1949 saw these two LT cars parked on the Downs. EYK 374 was a 1938-vintage Austin 14/6 (i.e. 14-hp, 6-cylinder) normally used as pool car by the Paymaster's Department. JXN 456 was a post-war delivery, a 1949 Ford Prefect and in stock until 1953. Keeping them company is STL 2325 taking a rest from duties on route 406. A.B. Cross

PRIVATE CARS

A number of unmarked saloons were available for use by senior officials from the earliest motorised days of the LGOC. Like other large organisations, they provided cars to some senior managers, though the private use of these was restricted to Board Members. Other senior managers could only use their cars for business purposes. A fleet of chauffeur-driven cars was operated from a garage in Vandon Street, Westminster, near to 55 Broadway, as well as at Chiswick and Acton. In addition, there was a need to provide vehicles to allow staff to visit some of the less-accessible parts of what was then a 2,000 square mile operating area.

A number of saloon cars came into LPTB stock via certain tram operators. Known model types are: Vauxhall saloon, Vauxhall tourer, Austin 7 tourer, Morris Oxford saloon, Ford 8 saloon, Daimler saloon and even a Bentley sports coupé; though all had been disposed of by 24th May 1934. For the LGOC, private cars during the NS and ST/LT periods were mainly of Morris and Daimler origin.

The legendary Vice-Chairman Frank Pick used a 'Double Six' convertible Daimler registered BXD 500.

The vehicle came into its own on Fridays, when Pick toured various parts of the Board's area. Sites visited could include a bus garage, a stretch of route affected by congestion, or the exact placing of a new bus stop or staff canteen. The day might not end until the early hours, with station rebuilding work being among the last subjects to be scrutinised by Pick's all-seeing eye.

The 1937 fleet list shows the following types of car had been purchased, most having registrations in the BLH, BXD, CXX, CGJ, DLU, DYL, EYK, FJJ and FXT series used on contemporary LT buses. The makes included: Hillman 20.9hp, saloon de-luxe or limousine, Hillman Hawk 20.9hp saloons, Hillman 9.8 and 15.7hp saloons; Humber saloons, limousines, landaulettes and Pullmans; Daimler limousine/landaulette, Morris 18hp, Morris Oxford, Chrysler, Vauxhall, Rover and various Austins. The vast majority of these cars were assigned to 'named' individuals, but the five geographical areas of Country Buses each had a mid-1930s Hillman Minx 'District car' (DYL 926, 928, 925, 940 and 921), whilst others were part of a centralised 'Broadway Pool'. Known users include Humbers BXD 525 (T. E. Thomas – *General Manager, Tramways*), DYL 912 (A. H. Hawkins – *General Manager, Country Buses*) and EYK 368 (W. Graff-Baker – *Chief Mechanical Engineer, Railways*).

Post-war, a varied selection of manufacturers and models were patronised, and again in complete contrast to the usual policies concerning bus and coach procurement. The late-1940s saw vehicle makes range from Austin, Ford, Hillman/Humber and Vauxhall. In the 1950s, LT was using Ford Populars and Prefects, Humber Snipes, and unspecified Austins, Fords and Rovers. Most of these again had registrations in the same series as new buses of the time; and JXC, KGK, KLB, MXX, NLE, NLP and NXP marks were all common. Rare though were NLP 612, NLP 613 and NLP 614, three Daimler Conquest saloons, plus an Armstrong Siddeley Sapphire registered with what would now be classed a 'cherished' plate – PLE 1. Post-1949, both the chauffeurs and the car pool became the responsibility of CDS. Being 'unmarked', there was obviously no need for these vehicles to carry any specific livery, but most if not all were painted black. No such conservatism was to apply in the following decades, when any colour combination became possible.

The 1950s saw a move towards Fords, with Anglias, Prefects, Escorts (side-valve models) and Consuls in stock. There was still room for less-standard types however, with two Austin Princesses, a Rover and a Wolseley entering service. Again, the registration numbers reflected mainstream service vehicle practice, with the SLT and TXV blocks being used. These included SLT 1 to SLT 20 on a batch of Ford Consuls. Other oddities towards the end of this decade were Vauxhall Victors WYL 687 to WYL 700; and Austin A55s WYL 701 to WYL 704.

Just as the parent CDS fleet concentrated on Fords throughout much of the 'Swinging Sixties', so did the car pool, and most of the manufacturer's models produced saw use at one time or other. Known types include the Ford Popular, Anglia, Classic, Corsair, Zephyr and Zodiac. Non-Fords were an Austin A60, Humber Super Snipes, Rover 110s, Triumph 2000s, Vauxhall Crestas and Victors.

This period spanned the change from registration 3-letter prefixes via 3-letter suffixes (briefly), to the year-letter system used until September 2001. AUU, DXY and FJJ (also used as a prefix in the 1930s) suffixes thus gave way to such marks as ALM-B, CUV-C, EYN-C, CJD-D, JLA-D, KLX-D, NHX-E, SMK-F and VLW-G.

Similar arrangements continued into the 1970s, with further Consuls, Cortinas, Escorts, Zephyrs and Zodiacs being delivered. Unusual were Triumph 2000/2500s AML 679H, AML 710H, EGN 496J, GHM 524M, GHM 536M and KJD 612P. Top of the range must have been Jaguar XJ6s EGN 449J, JGF 569K to JGF 586K, MGX 920L, TJJ 1M, TJJ 2M, KJD 612P to KJD 615P, XJ12 MGX 924L and Daimler Sovereigns KJD 661P, OJD 573R to OJD 579R. Lower down the scale were Ford Granada '3000's MGX 921L to MXG 923L, KJD 617P, OJD 585R, OJD 586R. Non-Fords included Leyland Princesses OJD 568R to OJD 571R, OJD 578R and OJD 587R, Opel Rekord KJD 616P, Rovers 3.5 AML 673H, GHM 523M and Vauxhall Viscount JGF 535F. At the bottom were the workhorses of the 1970s staff car fleet, various Ford Escort 1100/1300 saloons and estates (including 1844F and 1846–47F transferred from the 'numbered' fleet) plus a number of Morris Marinas registered with TJJ-M, GHM-N, SMU-N and OJD-R prefixes. As in previous years, registration numbers were all part of blocks used on buses and also the main service vehicle fleet.

By the late-1970s, LT 'private cars' could still be identified by their registration number prefixes. This is a 2-door saloon, whose 'WYU' prefix was also used on around thirty service vehicles. The Popular was a 'budget' version of the Escort distinguished by a lack of chrome-work. *Julian Bowden-Green*

Following the closure of the Licensing Office in Chiswick Works, and the tendency to lease smaller batches, new vehicles were given random registration marks issued via the appropriate dealer. As such, it was no longer possible for the casual observer to identify unmarked saloon and estate cars in LRT service, which were in any case completely indistinguishable from private vehicles.

ROAD SERVICE DEPARTMENT CARS

The earliest car to appear in the 'numbered' service vehicle fleet had been 1200F, a 1961 Ford Thames Escort 1172cc 7-cwt estate in grey. These were based on the old side-valve-engined cars and not the late-1960s Escort. The following year another estate arrived as 1261F. This was a Ford Anglia 1172cc, and was in a non-standard Ascot Grey livery.

The usual conception of what constitutes an LT car began in March 1966, when the trial operation of two Ford Cortina saloons began. This was part of an attempt to increase the effectiveness and efficiency of bus route control, a task that was steadily being undermined by

Increasing traffic congestion led to an experimental pair of Ford Cortina saloon cars being operated by Central Buses. JLA 82D was bought in 1965 as EYN 349C but stored until 1966, when it was converted to a prototype radio-car and re-registered accordingly. In March 1967, it finally entered the CDS fleet 'proper' as 1463F. This official view was taken at the Woodford (Napier Arms) former trolleybus turning circle. The roof-mounted roundel was illuminated and was to become a familiar sight on London's streets for the next twenty years. *LT Museum*

increasing traffic congestion. The two cars had originally been bought in August 1965 and were put into storage without using their booked registration numbers EYN 349C and EYN 350C. In February 1966 they were re-registered as JLA 82D and JLA 83D and converted to prototype radio-control cars.

The livery of the trial cars was red, with the words 'RADIO CONTROL' appearing in white upper case on the front doors. However, the most distinctive items were the illuminated LT roundels fitted to the roofs. These had a red ring and black bar reading 'LONDON TRANSPORT' across it in block white, plus white semi-circular 'infils'. Stock numbers 1463F and 1464F were not assigned until March 1967, the pair having been regarded as 'special vehicles' before then. The cars were 'crew-operated', carrying both a silver and a gold badge bus inspector, and communicated with a control room at the East Divisional Office at Manor House.

At this juncture, it is perhaps worthwhile to explain briefly how the regulation and running of the buses was controlled, and why the radio cars were introduced. Until 1967, with the exception of certain trunk routes that crossed the Central Division, the management of service performance was a parochial affair, with each District

Below: Once the radio-car concept had been proved a success, the lower priced Ford Anglia estate was chosen for the initial production batch. 1480F was the first of eleven similar vehicles, all of which saw service between July 1967 and 1970. 16th March 1968 saw it parked at Hounslow Bus Station.
Jim Blake

Bottom: Liveried cars were also used by other departments of LT. 1675F was a Ford Escort '1100' 2-door saloon in grey and was allocated to the Plant Engineer from June 1971 until November 1976.
Julian Bowden-Green

Superintendent being responsible for route management in his own area. These local superintendents also looked after bus stops and stands, and had to be aware of changes in demand for services on their patch, but only within a clearly defined boundary. A bus route could therefore pass through several 'Districts', whose individual service objectives could be quite different. Supervision on the ground was by senior or 'gold badge' inspectors, and they were general supervisors of the 'point inspectors' who between them acted as route controllers.

The District Superintendents (and the Area Traffic Managers who replaced them) reported to a Divisional Superintendent, of which there had been three all through the LGOC-era. The LPTB had retained the three operating divisions set up by the LGOC, these being (head office in brackets): East (Kingsland Road), South (Nunhead, later Camberwell) and West (Dollis Hill). After the merger with Trams & Trolleybuses in October 1950 to form Central Road Services, these were changed to North East (Manor House), North West (Dollis Hill), South East (Camberwell) and South West (Vauxhall). (These were reduced to three divisions in 1961, but increased to four again in 1964 with the addition of 'Central' at Mansion House Station.

After a re-organisation in 1967, Area Traffic Managers became responsible for a large geographical area, and particular routes were allocated for them to manage over their full length. Supervision for nominated routes became the responsibility of Area Traffic Inspectors, who were generally the senior 'gold badge' Inspectors. The plan was for the new radio control cars to be manned by the ATI and an Inspector, paying particular attention to known trouble spots, and they could easily visit unmanned inspection points as well as outlying locations. Radio had been in use for bus control at major events like Derby Day and Wimbledon from at least the early-1960s, but simply involved placing a large transmitter/receiver in the rear of a standard vehicle.

The experimental radio-car concept was obviously considered a success, as a further eleven vehicles (1480F to 1490F) were introduced the following August. The opportunity was taken to specify an estate car format capable of carrying bulky items like portable 'dolly-stops', step ladders and (in winter) salt. The model chosen was the cheaper and more down-market Anglia model from Ford, and they lasted until 1970. There were also a number of Anglia estates and saloons in grey livery for other use, but the inspectors' cars were immediately identifiable by their roof-mounted roundels. The roundels were later transferred from successive batch to batch, and at least one was still in use in the mid-1990s.

Ford launched the 'Escort' in 1968, and LT began to receive the type from then on in both red and grey liveries. The Anglia radio-cars were supplanted by 1564F to 1576F, thirteen Escort '1300' estates that performed the task between December 1968 and 1971–72. Further batches of radio-control Escort estates were to serve the fleet throughout the 1970s and 1980s: 1729F to 1747F (1971–73), 1797F to 1818F (1973–c.75), 1906F to 1927F (1975–c.77), 2038F to 2059F (1977–c.80), and 2177F to 2198F (1979–c.82). Other departments using Ford estate cars included Catering, plus the Signal and Permanent Way departments of the Underground. The increasing shortage of bus drivers in the 1970s meant that LT began training so-called 'novice' drivers from scratch, and dual-controlled examples were allocated to the Chiswick Training Centre for the purpose.

The LT Design Research Unit redesigned the roundel in the early-1970s into a plain-red style bereft of all lettering. Those fitted to the radio-cars were similarly altered to display the revised symbol in 1977, and many were amended locally from November 1987 by the addition of yellow bars carrying the 'LONDON BUSES' title in red. Another change saw the radio-cars converted to 'OPO',

with the 'silver badge' official being dispensed with. LT was now ordering vehicles clad in the standard manufacturers' colours, and the exact shade of red applied could range from tangerine to maroon or brick red.

The four bus operating divisions were re-organised into eight 'districts', each under its own General Manager, from 1st October 1979. These were initially as follows (head office in brackets): Abbey (Baker Street), Cardinal (Northfields), Forest (Ilford), Leaside (Manor House), Selkent (Camberwell), Tower (Upper Thames Street), Wandle (Mitcham) and Watling (Dollis Hill). All these changes influenced the allocation and deployment of the radio-cars. Each district now had its own District Engineering Manager, bringing the operating and engineering functions together for the first time. From 1st January 1984, the number of districts was reduced to six for economy and the Tower and Watling administrations disappeared. The ATI's were replaced by a smaller number of Chief Inspectors (with much greater responsibility for staff and operations) and Senior Road Inspectors (SRI's), who were in direct control of routes.

Abbey District had been abolished on 15th August 1987, but on 1st January 1988, inspectors attached to a new 'Central Traffic Division' served the five inner-London boroughs and the City. CTD was abolished in early 1990s and its responsibilities split between two new organisations. Central planning functions were undertaken by a newly created Group Traffic Manager's Department located with the 'Bus Passenger Infrastructure Unit' (BPI) at 172 Buckingham Palace Road, the latter overseeing the maintenance of bus stations, stands and stops. The residual central London traffic and control functions were transferred to Network Services at Baker Street, the location of the Bus Controller and Fleet Communications Centre 1979. On 4th April 1992 this section was re-titled 'Centrecomm' and the Bus Controller became the Centrecomm Controller. A 'Centrecomm Road Team' was also formed, to deal with pre-planned and emergency diversions to bus services, and the radio centre is still used to broadcast general messages to vehicles of many London bus operators.

Another round of reorganisation had occurred on 1st April 1989, when the remaining five LBL bus districts were reconstituted to form eleven 'units'. These were as follows: Centrewest, East London, Leaside Buses, London Central, London Forest, London General, London Northern, London United, Metroline, Selkent and South London. The Commercial Operations Unit of LBL had been established as a separate profit centre within that company since January 1986, and adopted the trading name of 'London Coaches' in the following October. Upon the creation of the units, London Coaches was regarded as the twelfth such entity. Again, these changes affected the composition and allocation of the service vehicle fleet. Unit names and symbols could be seen applied to vehicles in the Distribution Services fleet, and there began a move towards the direct procurement of vans by the operators themselves (e.g. London General started its own fleet of support vehicles numbered in a LGF-series).

London Forest was closed down from 22nd November 1991, due to a lengthy industrial dispute associated with the impending sell-off, and the management's proposals to restructure staff wages and conditions prior to privatisation. The other ten units were disposed of between 2nd January 1994 and 8th January 1995. LBL ceased to own vehicles from 4th March 1995, with any remaining under centralised control passing to a new 'London Transport Buses' organisation (q.v.). London Coaches had always been regarded as somewhat different from the rest of LBL, and left LRT after sale on 29th May 1992.

BPI and the Centrecomm Road Team were themselves merged into a new 'London Transport Buses Operating Services' on 2nd January 1995 (trading as London Transport Buses). This was divided into five operating areas: North-west, North-east, South-east, South-west and Central. LTB continued with the BPI-inherited white livery on a fleet of Vauxhall Astras (plus Ford Transit and Volkswagen Transporter vans) listed almost indiscriminately within what was now the main London Underground series.

The neutral colour scheme of BPI had been chosen so as not to clash with the liveries of the now privatised bus companies, and perhaps to demonstrate a definite break from the past. This change did not find favour with the Metropolitan Police, who were used to looking out for red-coloured vehicles to divert buses when road closures took place. In the words of Centrecomm Manager Chris Edney, the sight of a red van approaching "meant that the cavalry was arriving". Thus by 1999, red vehicles were re-appearing in the LTB fleet. Another benefit of abandoning the scheme inherited from BPI was the end of any danger of being regarded as 'white van man', with all the negative connotations associated with that phrase. The seemingly never-ending reorganisation of London's buses saw LTB itself renamed 'London Bus Services Limited' from 1st April 2000 (trading as London Buses), prior to joining the 'Transport for London' authority on the 3rd July of that year.

The decision to widen the range of LT's traditional service vehicle suppliers led to Vauxhall Chevette estate

Top: After Ford ceased production of the Anglia, LT stayed faithful to its replacement, the Escort. Estate 2046F was a 1977 Mk2 version, identifiable by the revised radiator grille, and a member of the sixth generation of radio-cars. By this time, the batch consisted of no fewer than twenty-two vehicles. Though the illuminated roundels had been altered several years earlier to a new all-red design, the frames retained the original dimensions. Jim Wright

Above: What may well have been the replacement for 1675F was this 1976 Ford Popular '1100' 2-door saloon which was also in use by the Plant Engineer. Red livery had been used on the radio-cars since their inception in 1967 but did not spread to ordinary saloons and estates until 1973. Jim Wright

In July 1980, eight Vauxhall Chevette saloon cars were introduced in conjunction with the training of so-called 'novice' drivers. One of the reasons for this was the increase in OPO, and the corresponding decline in the number of conductors' positions. Such cars were usually fitted with a second set of pedals for use by the instructor in emergencies. The 'B' suffix to the fleet number was derived from Vauxhall's Bedford commercial vehicle arm.
Jim Wright

cars being used from 1982. Nos. 3055B to 3076B were the first radio-vehicles to appear in the new 3000+ leased numbering series started that year (though some of the smaller types were already being leased before then). Nos. 3264B to 3283B (1984–86) were the next batch obtained from General Motors and differed by being of van design (and thus may be more accurately described as 'Bedford' Astravan models). The next batch, 3458B to 3478B (1986–90), was split randomly between both vans and estate car Astra 1.3's, and thus contained both 'Bedford' and 'Vauxhall' models. Further radio-vans were 3672B to 3682B (1989–91) and 4010B and 4011B (delivered in 1991, disposal unknown) but not all are specifically identified as such in published sources. Radio-vans 3458B to 3487B remained in operation from 1986 to 1990, 3674B to 3684B operated between 1989 and 1991.

The need for large numbers of radio-cars/vans diminished as the bus fleet began to be fitted with radios capable of being used for route control. However, they continued to be of use for taking LBL officials to incidents around their areas. The last vehicle to carry a roof-mounted red LT roundel (by this time non-illuminating) was K89 HWF, a Vauxhall Astra. It had been inherited by LTB, and started its new life with them as a Centrecomm radio-car. Often kept in Aldgate Bus Station, it was still in use as late as 1997. (An illuminated roundel is carried on the LUL Emergency Control Unit 2488M, utilising roundel frames from one of the radio-cars, but with a new centrepiece bearing the red/white/blue LUL symbol.)

As a possible replacement for the famous Mini, British Leyland introduced the Mini-Metro hatchback, though in the event, the former outlived the latter. LT operated two Metro City saloons as 3113L and 3114L from 1982; but

LT's 'common user' departments also required their own support vehicles. Food was no longer being produced by the Croydon factory in 1987, but LT Catering staff still needed this little Ford Escort '1100' estate, numbered 3292F, to travel between canteens. The 'computer-style' lettering on the registration plate was a short-lived affectation. At this time, the Waterloo bus stand clearly had room to allow for the parking of non-LT PSVs.
Keith Grimes

like the Marinas, they did not precipitate further orders for the type. A large number of Ford Fiesta vans were in use from the mid-1980s. Vehicle 4069F of August 1991 was an exception however in being delivered in saloon form.

Numbers 4877F to 4882F and 4910F to 4912F were a batch of Ford Fiesta 5-door hatchback cars for use by LTB officials. Initially bearing only a stock number in white, they were later given 'London Transport Buses' lettering and roundels contained in white rectangles, plus a body-side stripe made up of orange squares. Illuminated roundels are no longer in vogue, but magnetic flashing orange lights can be applied to vehicle roofs when required. This was an exercise in downsizing, as the original Mk1 Fiesta had been brought in below the Escort as Ford's new small car in 1978. In the light of operating experience, the Fiestas were found to be too small, and the Ford Focus was selected for the next generation of such vehicles.

This un-numbered Vauxhall Astra originated as a Centrecomm radio-car, but transferred to the new London Transport Buses organisation upon its formation in 1995. The roof-mounted roundel no longer lit up, but had become the very last such example used in connection with London's buses. Red livery too was now a rarity, with most LTB service vehicles then in all-over white. Kim Rennie

In 1999, the Ford Fiesta was chosen for use by LTB's Bus Station Controllers. In fact, these hatchback vehicles were found to be a little too small, and future deliveries made use of the larger Ford Focus. By now, traditional red livery and the name 'London Transport' had both been restored. Kim Rennie

Above: The fourth Morris Marina used by the Neasden Breakdown Foreman was 2263M. Livery was again non-standard, this time being tangerine. On 12th April 1981, it had brought staff to Euston Station and was parked in Drummond Street. Kim Rennie

RAILWAY DEPARTMENT CARS

In the rail-orientated part of the fleet, non-Ford oddities were three Morris Marina estates 1894M, 1997M and 2132M from 1975 to 1978. Numbers 1894M and 1997M were operated for comparison with the Land Rovers then in use, 1894M being used by the Chief Signal Inspectors at Acton. They carried non-standard maroon livery (the nearest match available in the British Leyland range) and were specially modified with a strengthened chassis and heavy-duty tyres. The Marinas had been suggested by the operating department as a cheaper alternative to using Land Rovers, but the full extent of their duties was not made clear to those authorising their purchase. At least one Marina lost its sump after being driven over rails in a depot. A fourth Marina joined the fleet in August 1980, 2263M, which was a tangerine-coloured estate allocated to the Rolling Stock Engineer (Railways). BL attempted to revamp the Marina towards the end of its life, and LT's final example was 3019M, an Ital 2.0HLS from 1982. Again, tangerine was the nearest match to red available.

Throughout the years, uniformed Underground 'operating officials' would need to make their way to incidents affecting the railway. These could be anything from signal failures, train breakdowns, staff assaults, to booking office burglaries and the inevitable 'one under' (person trapped under a train). Despite this, no saloon cars were generally supplied to the Railway Operating Department

(very senior officials excepted). Staff were expected to make their way to site by scheduled train, which was often disrupted by the very incident they were attempting to attend! If services were suspended altogether, taxis 'on-account' could be procured by the Headquarters Controller's office at 55 Broadway (later superseded by the Network Control Centre). Another procedure available to 'Car Examiners, Signal Linemen, Handsignalmen and Look-Out Men' enabled them to obtain cash advances for bus or taxi fares at station booking offices. By the mid-1990s, a more enlightened attitude was being taken and certain officials at 'duty manager' level and above had access to 'marked' and 'unmarked' Distribution Services estate cars. Even so, the same period saw a Duty Train Manager commandeer a Distribution Services lorry delivering furniture to Tower Hill, to reach the site of a failure at Mansion House.

Around 1990, the use of saloon-format cars had ceased, and the vast majority of the estates being leased were for Underground use. Deliveries have tended to be split in recent years between Vauxhall Astra and Ford Escort types, with the odd higher-range Ford Sierra or Mondeo model thrown in from time-to-time. An August 1995 one-off was Vauxhall Frontera 2.2 4479B, a 5-door '4x4' off-the-road vehicle leased from Godfrey Davis. Livery was white/blue, but with the unique addition of a horizontal red coach-line separating the two shades. Cab door allocation-use transfers on this read 'London Underground Limited Response unit', and in 2001 it was still in use, being allocated to the Sub-Surface Lines Operations Liaison Manager. In recent years, a number of Ford Focus 5-door estate cars have also seen service with LUL, adding yet further variety to the leased vehicles.

Above: A few LUL departments have been provided with 'top-of-the-range' Ford Mondeo 5-door estate cars in liveried form. White/blue 4913F is used by the Emergency Response Unit's Duty Manager, and in November 1999 attended Neasden Depot in connection with the uncoupling of scrap 1983 Stock cars. Kim Rennie

Below left: The 5-door Ford Focus has been supplied to both LUL and LTB/LBSL. Demonstrating the Underground livery application, a brand-new 5092F sits outside the 'Signal House' building in Acton Works on 19th March 2001. Kim Rennie

Below: No.4479B was a 1995 Vauxhall Frontera '4x4' and the only such vehicle to have been operated. Also unique was the red coach-line along the top of the blue skirt, a feature never applied to any other member of the LUL fleet. Always seemingly elusive, on 19th March 2001, it was captured in the Acton Works staff car park. Kim Rennie

The interior of the 1951 Publicity motorcycle sidecars was carefully designed to hold posters and timetables of varying sizes. Also visible are the tops of two wooden bus timetable frames stowed next to a number of replacement glass panels. LT Museum

ADVERTISING & PUBLICITY

In an organisation that has seen so many differing types, there are some vehicles whose very specialised roles make them difficult to fit into one of the main categories. Not all of these were owned by Distribution Services, and certain examples were operated directly by departments such as the Rolling Stock Engineer (Buses). The Commercial Advertising and Publicity Departments were users of light vans for many years. In 1959, the two were organised separately. The 'commercial' section dealt with the private adverts that appeared on buses, in trains and on station walls. The 'publicity' side dealt with so-called 'traffic advertising' – i.e. timetable notices, full and pocket-sized bus and Underground maps, and even the 'Hop on a Bus' posters then being placed on bus fronts in an attempt to encourage travel. Pre-war, the advertising store had been at Charing Cross Station, re-locating to Shepherd's Bush (Central) Station from November 1951. By 1959, the main stores were located at Griffith House in Old Marylebone Road, and divided between the two types of printed material.

Seventeen vans were then stationed at various points around London, and driven to Griffith House at regular intervals to collect supplies of traffic advertising. The

drivers of these vans were also able to carry out simple repairs to timetable and map frames, being issued with a small tool kit for the task. The commercial adverts were dispatched each morning using five other vans, which serviced garages and rail depots. At this time, the Austin LD 1-ton box-van was the usual type allocated for both commercial and traffic use.

Advertising Department 'hands' were responsible for bill-sticking on stations, escalators and lifts on the commercial side and all road service work. They also did some special work on the traffic side, presumably any notices required on sites facing station platforms and only accessible via the track during non-traffic hours. Certain internal publicity items were posted by uniformed station staff until 19th May 1969, when this become the responsibility of the Distribution & Advertising Manager's Department (local staff were then restricted to exhibiting 'Special Traffic Notices' on easel boards).

Both publicity and commercial advert-fixing in train cars was carried out by staff of the Rolling Stock Engineer (Railways), whilst those of his counterpart, the Rolling Stock Engineer (Buses), performed the same duties on road vehicles. Notices and advert cards on trains were changed during the day, those on buses at night. To keep track of all this, 20 women were employed in the Publicity Office at Griffith House to maintain a card-index system capable of pinpointing any advert on any bus or in any train.

Before the war, station posters were replaced at monthly intervals to a drill that has been described as being almost like a military operation. This was put to the test on the morning of 21st January 1936, when the BBC announced the death of King George V. By mid-day, every poster site at the entrances of the then some 250-odd Underground stations had been stripped of paper, washed clean of paste and left bare. The day before the lying-in-state began at Westminster Abbey, a poster announcing this went up. Then, 24-hours later, a sheet of plain white paper edged in black covered this. The latter remained in situ until after the funeral. It is inconceivable that such a procedure could be carried out in the same manner now, nor that 'blank' posters or sites would remain unsullied for long in today's society.

In LGOC days, special van-bodied B-types were allocated to 'Advertising & Publicity' duties – e.g. B 1017, 1018, 1833, 2036, 2037, 2072, 2480, 2555 and 2678. After 1933, the vehicles used by LT for these tasks were usually of the standard light van type favoured at the time, though interiors were racked-out to allow for the safe storage and easy retrieval of advertisements, timetables and bills.

BATTERY-POWERED VEHICLES

The use of small electric trucks in large industrial works was commonplace, and LT's establishments at Acton, Aldenham and Chiswick were no exception. Owned by the operators of the premises, they used vehicles from such manufacturers as Electricar and Lansing-Bagnall. Being used internally, there was no need for them to be registered, but there are two known examples where this did occur. VLW 676G was a 1968-built Lansing-Bagnall electric truck based at Earl's Court Station. It was used to tow a small trailer conveying signal equipment and stores to and from Lillie Bridge Signal Overhaul Workshop and Earl's Court Signal Maintenance Department (and was owned by the latter). Livery was dark red, and the combination was normally kept at the western end of the high-level passenger walkway that connects the two ends of the station. Before the installation of automatic ticket gates, the truck was able to enter the station via the Warwick Road entrance. By the 1980s, it was unusual to see such a diminutive vehicle threading its way through busy London traffic. When this vehicle was out of service for any reason, it was replaced by a 7-cwt van, but the driver now had to come from CDS. Another small battery-electric truck was an Edison Electric used by the Tramways Rolling Stock division from 1913 to 1938. This originated from Ilford Corporation and became No. 107 in the LPTB Tramway's lorry fleet. Electric vehicles were also in use within the Croydon Food Production Centre. Even in 2002, Neasden Depot employed an ex-LPTB Electricar battery platform truck dating back to 1937.

BOARDS AND BLINDS

From the earliest days of LGOC bus operation in London, the central workshops produced the fare boards, destination boards, and later, destination blinds. By the post-war era, the job of moving blinds and boards was in the hands of a 3-ton or 5-ton half-tilt vehicle kept at Chiswick. Although the Blinds Workshop was to become based at Aldenham, that location had no direct link to individual garages. Instead, Chiswick Works acted as a central distribution hub for new and repaired blinds, with a daily trip to and from Aldenham. The only time that Aldenham got involved in direct deliveries was if major route changes were to affect just one or two garages. The blinds delivery work was not full-time, and often the driver involved would be sent in the afternoon to collect urgent stores from the CAV works at Acton. The CAV Company manufactured and was able to repair early electronic equipment beyond the capability of Chiswick.

BULLION VANS

A little-known facet of LT's operations was its own in-house capacity to move coins and notes. This activity had its origins in the 1960s and followed the theft of fare money being taken between a bus garage and bank. The vans were driven by British Transport Police officers and were deliberately anonymous in appearance. Prior to operations commencing, one CDS employee was given the job of devising a series of alternative routes between garages and banks to ensure that an observer could discern no regular pattern of operation.

The first vehicles were standard plain blue Ford Transit vans with little if any extra protection. In later years, four petrol-engined Mercedes-Benz 310 vans were converted to 'cash in transit' specification by Locomotors of Andover. Registered as A981 HLT, A982 HLT and A983 HLT, they entered service in February 1983, whilst a fourth, C493 WLR, arrived in June 1986. These vehicles were plain white, and like the previous Transits, devoid of numbering, logos and lettering.

Initially operated on behalf of the LT Treasury Department, a 'Bullion Services' subsidiary eventually took on day-to-day control. The latter was another casualty of the outsourcing provisions enshrined in the 1984 LRT Act, and the four Mercedes were withdrawn between 1993 (A981 HLT and A982 HLT) and November 1994 (A983 HLT and C493 WLR). The latter two at least then continued in a similar role, passing to a specialised security vehicle dealer in March 1995.

CABLE-DRUM CARRIERS

Ford D1010 lorry 1881F was in stock from September 1975 to August 1981 as a 5½-ton cable-drum carrier with a crew-cab and winch. It saw exclusive use by the Underground H.T. Mains Engineer. Smaller heavy-duty trailers capable of being towed behind vans and lorries have also been used in this role, the latest being SEB-T-42 and SEB-T-43 (described earlier in section on trailers).

CRANES AND MECHANICAL SHOVELS

Over the years, six mobile cranes have been listed in the service vehicle series. They were used to move stores and materials at places like Chiswick, and the Works & Building Department's base at Parsons Green. The first two were 352R and 353R, supplied by the long-standing crane manufacturer Ransomes & Rapier to the LCCT as their numbers 79 and 80. These were petrol-electric Type 5515 12hp 4-ton solid-tyred models of 1926. The LCCT used cranes at its Deptford and Poplar Wharves, where permanent way materials were unloaded from vessels. Both cranes were up-rated to 24hp between 1940 and 1941. They turned out to be good value for money, lasting until 1964 and 1962 respectively. Maximum speed was reported as being between 5 and 10 mph. 353R was repainted from grey to green in June 1945, and moved to Walthamstow after the abandonment of much of the northern tram system.

Number 460R was a diesel-engined Neal 2-cylinder 2½-ton mobile crane obtained second-hand from Mitchell Brothers in November 1940 (the suffix 'R' now being extended to cover any make) and used at Parsons Green. New in 1937, it subsequently served a third owner in 1949 when sold to British Railways (Eastern Region) at King's Cross. The same maker also provided 961R in 1951. This Type D 1-ton mobile was fated to see only nine years use. More successful was Jones 2-ton crane 968R. This was originally delivered to the George Cohen Group (who

Below: The bullion vans were some of the least-known LT road vehicles. A981 HLT was one of three Mercedes-Benz 310 vans supplied to 'cash in transit' specification by Locomotors in February 1983. In September 1989 it was visiting Northfields Depot, and clearly demonstrates the plain white livery without identification typical of such vehicles in LT use. *David Rowe*

Bottom: This ancient-looking relic is 353R, a 1926 ex-LCCT Ransomes & Rapier 4-ton petrol-electric mobile crane first numbered as 79. Originally based at Deptford Wharf to handle permanent way materials for the LCC tram network, on 6th January 1951 it appeared to have been working on a roadway-patching job. *A.B. Cross*

Top: Before the common use of fork-lift trucks and the palletisation of goods, mobile cranes were very popular within industrial premises for lifting all kinds of machinery and equipment, plus loading and unloading lorries. 968R was 1948 2-ton crane by Jones of Letchworth acquired second-hand from the George Cohen Group in 1952 and based at Chiswick Works. John Gascoine

Centre: No.1292R was effectively an updated version of the earlier Ransomes & Rapier 352R/353R mobile cranes, though now featured pneumatic tyres and a proper cab. This design was not as manoeuvrable as the Jones cranes, which had their superstructure separate from the chassis, but still had many uses within factory premises. 1292R carried a non-standard red livery, which was probably derived from the manufacturer's standard factory-finish. John Gascoine

Bottom: Among the earliest medium-duty tractor loaders were these Chaseside shovels. Forerunners of the ubiquitous JCB, they made use of wire ropes to control the shovel, rather than the hydraulic power of later models. The basis for KLB 876 was a substantially-modified Fordson tractor. This particular example was used to move coal and ash in Chiswick Works, in addition to other general duties. No fleet number was allocated, but the registration number is contemporary with RT-family buses delivered in 1950. John Gillham

owned Jones Cranes) in 1948, and entered LT service in 1952. The final example was NCK Ransomes & Rapier diesel-electric 1292R. Bearing red livery instead of the usual green, it arrived in August 1963.

Unnumbered equipment included two Coles mobile cranes registered SLT 49 (1956) and WYL 724 (1959), Fordson-powered Chaseside mechanical shovel KLB 876 (c.1950) used for moving coal at Chiswick, and Priestman excavator GKH 349, registered by the manufacturer in Hull. In the days before rigorous safety testing was required, items of plant like cranes could last for years before being replaced. Indeed, WYL 724 was still in use at Parsons Green in 1977.

The need for such types declined with the introduction of fork-lift trucks, and when ordinary lorries began to carry their own Epco, HIAB and later Palfinger self-loading equipment. Both 968R and 1292R were in stock as late as the mid-1980s (though possibly in a semi-derelict state) but are unlikely to have survived the demise of Chiswick Works. Nowadays Distribution Services hires such plant from private contractors when required. Several other cranes have been owned by LT, but were not allocated stock numbers. At least one yellow-liveried mobile telescopic-jibbed crane is in use with LUL's TransPlant engineers' trains department. It does not form part of the service vehicle fleet.

EXHIBITION & INFORMATION VEHICLES

Vehicle SMS 753 was originally a standard single-deck rear-engined AEC Swift bus. In November 1978, it was internally refitted as a mobile shop and information centre and reclassified as SPB 753. At first, a red/white livery was carried, but this was subsequently changed to a red/blue scheme. Later used as an engineers' store, the vehicle was disposed of in 1986.

On 8th July 1979, LT celebrated the 150th anniversary of George Shillibeer's first bus service in London. Amongst the plethora of events that took place during that year was the regular operation of a horse-drawn bus service between Baker Street and The Zoo. This departed from the forecourt of the Underground station, where a surplus SMS was in use as an information and souvenir sales point. SMS 730 remained in standard bus livery, but with the addition of white lettering along the roof cove panels stating 'HORSE BUS INFORMATION', plus an LT roundel and the special 'Shillibeer' symbol devised for the celebrations. In addition, several LT posters were stuck to the nearside. When parked at Baker Street, other posters on boards were also hung on the front of the vehicle. When no longer required for this duty, SMS 730 became first, a second recruitment bus, and then later another engineering store. It was withdrawn in May 1985.

The SMD-class were former dual-door SMS buses which had their centre exit doors sealed out of use. This was part of an ill-conceived and ultimately uncompleted scheme aimed at extending the operating life of what were already mechanically-troublesome vehicles. In 1979, SMD 91 was converted to a mobile classroom for use by garage engineering staff. It carried a striking livery of red with white roof, plus large white 'V's that extended down from the roof to behind the entrance door and the offside cab window, then formed a relief band along the waistline. The first two side passenger windows were blanked out and the front destination box carried a white LT roundel in outline plus the legend 'VIDEO-BUS'. Although officially renumbered as STB 91, this did not appear on the vehicle; and despite being supposedly assigned to staff training, it did the rounds of the various LT open days of the time. It was sold into preservation in early-1990s.

A much earlier foray into this sort of activity had been carried out between 1922 and 1925, when re-bodied ex-B-type bus B 2758 operated as the 'Daylight Cinema', exhibiting safety and training films to LGOC staff at garages. In addition, there were occasional public screenings on behalf of the Underground Group. As part of the conversion the vehicle gained pneumatic tyres (which no B-type bus carried in passenger service) and a large box body. The screen was located at the rear, shielded from the sun by hinged panels and films appear to have been back-projected from within.

Former Green Line coach RCL 2221 of 1965 was one of a number of Routemasters re-purchased by LT from LCBS in 1977 for driver training. As part of the Shillibeer celebrations, in April 1979 the lower deck was fitted out as a mobile exhibition room, whilst upstairs a 26in. video monitor was installed. The bus toured garages and other sites where open days were taking place, to show a selection of LT/BTF films. It carried the green & yellow Shillibeer livery also applied to twelve Standard RM's, plus a solitary DMS. During 1981, it was then repainted red with yellow relief, in a style reminiscent of its original Green Line livery. In this new guise, it was ready for further extensive use in 1983, when LT marked its Golden Jubilee with a series of special events. RCL 2221 was later used for the Women's Cancer Counselling programme and had several celebrities on board. It also visited Lille in France to support a British trade fair, and journeyed from John o' Groats to Lands End in support of the charity Barnado's

The creation of LRT in 1984 had put a damper on the sort of large-scale activity witnessed at the Shillibeer and Golden Jubilee celebrations, and the bus generally saw little use until early-1989. It then reappeared in a new livery of white, plus green cantrail band, and adorned

Top: Former SMS 753 reappeared as a mobile 'London Transport Shop and Information centre' in November 1978. Reclassified as SPB 753, it originally carried a red/white livery. A frequent visitor to enthusiast events, here it is attending Cobham Bus Museum during one of the proverbial 'April Showers'. Kim Rennie collection

Centre: The 'Video-Bus' was converted from SMD 91 (ex-SMS 91) and was originally intended as a mobile classroom for bus engineering staff. The red/white livery was unusual to say the least, and perhaps not a little influenced by the car in the contemporary 'Starsky & Hutch' TV series, while the front roundel transfer was of a design first devised for the MB-family. STB 91 was a regular sight at the various garage open-days held in the 1980s and continues to exist in private ownership.
Kim Rennie collection

Bottom: Routemaster RCL 2221, the 'Exhibition Cinema Bus', lost its green & cream Shillibeer livery in 1981 in favour of all-over red together with yellow relief. Note the obscured front upper-deck windows associated with the 26in video screen and that the vehicle has retained its double headlamps.
Kim Rennie collection

with logos championing the virtues of lead-free petrol. In this form, it toured Britain on behalf of a campaign, before being restored to red in December 1989. More recently, it has been used by the London [Transport] Travel Information Service as a mobile enquiry centre. A new red livery has been adopted, which features a light blue cantrail band, plus large 'information' and italic 'i' symbols. The former coach now tours the capital, and can sometimes be seen parked in shopping centres or transport interchange points. At other times, it is present during major engineering works on the Underground or special events. One disadvantage is the vehicle's size, which limits its use in venues like shopping malls, and the Travel Information Service has experimented with portable exhibition stands capable of being erected indoors. It is the only RCL to have retained double headlamps throughout its life and when not in use usually resides in Acton Works.

Another Routemaster, RM 811, was chosen for conversion to a mobile cinema during the absence of RCL 2221 in 1991. After this, it was used as a temporary lost property office reception whilst part of the famous Baker Street establishment was closed for asbestos removal. The former bus retained standard red livery, but was lettered 'Lost Property Office' in white between decks. Parked on the Allsop Place bus stand behind Baker Street Station during office-hours, it was 'wired up' to the Underground's electricity and telephone networks. Although claimants would call at the vehicle, mislaid property was still stored in the bowels of Baker Street, so students were hired as 'runners' to link the two sites when required. In July 1994, when no longer needed, it was repainted into (incorrect) LT Country Area green livery and presented to the David Shepherd Foundation, in exchange for a painting the artist donated to the LT Museum.

May 1982 saw LT purchased a second-hand Leyland National bus registered SCO 422L. The vehicle had started life with Plymouth Corporation Transport ten years earlier and was one of the earlier production Nationals. It was obtained via PSV-dealer Brakell's, and converted by Locomotors of Andover to a mobile shop/information bus for the 1983 Golden Jubilee, taking over the role formerly performed by SPB 753. Rather strangely, it was given the somewhat 'spurious' fleet number 1234L. The 'real' vehicle allocated this number was 1234F, a 1961 Ford Thames Trader dropside lorry retired in 1972. LT then had numerous Leyland Nationals of its own, but these were all of 10.6 metre length. As 1234L had been built to the longer 11.3 metre specification, the additional space was presumably considered desirable. The vehicle was available for non-LT use, e.g. in August 1983 when it was disguised as the 'Hammersmith & Fulham Business Bus'.

Two of LT's own Leyland Nationals also found use in special roles. LS 156 had been new in 1976, but 1994 saw it in employed in the Harrow area to publicise the start of a 'smart card' stored-value ticket experiment. It retained bus livery, but with the addition of yellow and black vinyls. A more drastic conversion involved LS 334. This was used as an exhibition unit in 1995 whilst the LT Museum was closed for a major refurbishment and re-display programme. Repainted red with cream relief around the windows, the bus was usually parked in the Covent Garden piazza, adjacent to the museum's temporary shop in the Old Market Building. Once the museum had re-opened, LS 334 continued in use by them as a mobile shop, a capacity in which it still attends bus rallies and the occasional garage open day.

An exhibition role of a quite different nature was performed by DMS 1515, totally rebuilt in 1991 as the so-called 'Supercar'. This combined the front third of a 'London bus' (i.e. DMS-type) with a mock Underground car and Network SouthEast Class 321 railway carriage. The vehicle was used to promote the '1-day Travelcard' and featured in television advertisements for the product. Colour schemes reflected the then LBL red with grey skirt and white band, LUL unpainted-aluminium, and NSE blue, white and red. DMS 1515 was actually owned by LUL, and normally kept in the disused part of Fulwell Bus Garage between public appearances.

Probably the only LT support vehicle to have starred in a TV advertising campaign, the 'Supercar' was created from DMS 1515 to promote the 1-day Travelcard, and gave the impression of being a combined Tube train, Network SouthEast e.m.u and London bus. The significance of the 'BS' garage code is unclear, since the vehicle was normally kept in the Fulwell Garage store when not required. Kim Rennie collection

FILM UNIT

LT produced its own series of *Ciné Gazette* films in the 1940s, and from 1949, the new British Transport Films Unit made titles connected with transport in London and the Home Counties (and also elsewhere). July 1947 saw the Railway Traffic Circular carry an internal advertisement for a *'Cinema Operator or Projectionist, Office of the Publicity Officer'. The duties of the post included 'the transporting of the Board's films by light van to lecture halls throughout the London Transport area and the display of these films where required'*. The 'light van' concerned was Thames E83W 10hp 10-cwt van 752F, which was in stock between 1948 and 1956 as a 'Mobile Film Unit'. In later years, the Film & Exhibition Service made use of other standard vans, but was sadly discontinued in 1984.

GENERATORS

Portable generators have been used over the years to provide electrical power when no mains supply is available. Often provided in the shape of a small trailer, they have also been fitted to LT's dropside lorries on occasions as an accessory.

The de-mountable body concept of the 1990s allows a change of vehicle use to be effected without employing the drastic re-building of years gone by. One such example was 2478M, a Mercedes-Benz 408D which when new in 1990 carried a red-painted Petbow generator and was in use by LUL's Environmental Improvement Section. By 1999 the plant been replaced by a car transporter platform, and the generating equipment transferred to Mercedes-Benz 410D 2541M for use by the Permanent Way Department. Further examples were delivered in 1999 in the shape of Mercedes-Benz 308D Sprinters 2562M and 2563M. The pair introduced a modernised form of cab styling from this manufacturer and were allocated to LUL's TransPlant engineering section with the generator casings painted white to match fleet livery.

Generators were also carried on or towed by the Tram & Trolleybus Department's welding lorries, whilst the chassis of former a B-type bus, B 2134, was used in this role at Earl's Court as late as 1936.

H. V. MAINS FAULT INVESTIGATION

With the gradual demise of custom-bodied or converted specialised types since the 1980s, a surprise was the appearance of 4404LR in September 1994. This is an all-white Land Rover 110 TDi used for high-voltage mains fault investigation work. The vehicle was initially based at the Signal & Electrical Engineers' depot at 10A Wood Lane, W12, and attends various Underground locations when necessary. In spite of its unique purpose and look, no identifying lettering or logos were displayed, and simple blue fleet numbers (minus the 'R' of the suffixes) were the only clue to LUL use. By early-2000 however, it was noted carrying the lettering 'SeeBoard Powerlink' on cab doors, and passed to this consortium upon its takeover of LT's power generation capability.

INSTRUCTION UNITS

Instruction units were provided to allow garage maintenance staff to gain experience on new vehicle designs. In 1949, a new AEC Regent III chassis was in use matched with an old body from a 'Tilling' ST. The combination toured garages prior to the introduction of post-war RTs. The former bus ran on trade plates and was only identified by its chassis number: 0961079. When no longer required, the chassis was matched to a new Weymann body to produce RT 4761.

One SRT and four RT type buses were renumbered into service vehicle series between 1954 and 1970. SRT 45 was used as mobile instruction unit for engineering staff when STL chassis were being converted into SRTs. The SRT class was an ill-matched temporary mix of new RT class bodies and modified old STL chassis. The reason behind the conversions had been to speed the number of modern-looking vehicles on London's streets when the supply of new AEC RT chassis was forecast to fall behind the supply of new bodies. The instruction unit's chassis had originally been STL 2551. By 1954, SRT 45 had become 1019J and was carrying the body of 'pre-war' RT 19, which had previously been fitted to the chassis of pioneer RT 1. The historic body was transferred to service vehicle 1037J (q.v.) upon 1019J's withdrawal in June 1956. Another part of the jigsaw involved 1020J, being a body-less chassis used for demonstration work. It had been numbered RT 19 in its pre-1954 passenger-carrying days. As already seen, its body had been transferred to ex-SRT 45 1019J. Disposal of the chassis was in October 1965.

The final part of the story was completed by 1037J, created in June 1956 by the marriage of former RT 1420's chassis with the ex-RT 1 body from 1019J. The new combination continued in the same instructional capacity as 1019J, latterly being allocated to West Ham Garage in the 1970s and carrying the long-obsolete red livery with cream cantrail band. The historical significance of the body was not recognised by LT, which allowed sale in December 1978. Fortunately, it was disposed of to preservationist Prince Marshall, who arranged restoration to the visual appearance of the real RT 1 in time for the events commemorating withdrawal of the RT class on 7th April 1979. The vehicle's importance must also have been made known to the DVLC in Swansea, since they allowed the re-use of RT 1's EYK 396 registration number, lost in 1946 when the latter's chassis was dismantled for spares.

To allow mechanics to gain some familiarity with the post-war RT, this odd combination of an RT chassis paired with a Tilling ST body toured garages to demonstrate such advances as air-operated brakes and gearboxes. Below the fleetname can just be glimpsed the words 'MOBILE TRAINING UNIT'. The chassis was later bodied as RT 4761.
Kim Rennie collection

Looking more akin to a prison transport van, Land Rover 4404LR was actually allocated to the Signal & Electrical Engineers' Department as a high-voltage mains fault investigation unit. External identification was minimal to say the least, as evidenced when the vehicle was caught attending Neasden Sub-Station on 21st December 1996. It left LUL control following its transfer to the SeeBoard Powerlink consortium. *Kim Rennie*

Another odd pairing was the chassis of former Craven RT 1420 with the body of prototype RT 1 as 1037J. When first used as a Mobile Instruction Unit, the body was mounted on the chassis of SRT 45 (ex-STL 2551). In June 1956, it was transferred to that of RT 1420, and survived in this form long enough to allow a full rebuild and restoration as 'RT 1' by the time of the final withdrawal of the RT class in 1979. Some of the detailed differences on the 'pre-war' RT body were still apparent when this photo was taken in the forecourt of West Ham Garage in April 1970.
Peter Newman

To cater for the forthcoming decimalisation of Britain's currency on 15th February 1971, ten RT class buses were converted to mobile classrooms for use by bus crews and garage counter staff. RTs 1530, 2322, 2341, 2958, 3556, 3596, 3800, 3823, 4325 and 4601 were equipped with a crude platform door, and a slide screen was fitted to the front of the upper deck, resulting in the front and leading side windows upstairs being blacked out.

RT 3062 served as a classroom at Shepherd's Bush Garage for the training of bus mechanics, and had the distinction of being both the last Saunders-bodied and roofbox-fitted member of the class in LT use. Paddington Technical College ran a special City & Guilds training course exclusively for LT staff. In association with this, a DMS chassis was shortened to fit into a classroom, and itself replaced an earlier RT chassis used for the same task. This was another time-honoured practice, as the LGOC had used the chassis of B 1247 and 1374 for similar purposes.

The final bus conversion was in 1981, when single-decker SMS 300 was adapted as a mobile classroom for the bus department. By April 1985, it was de-licensed and in store at Norbiton Garage. None of these later vehicles were renumbered in the process.

LABORATORY VEHICLES

LT maintained a Research Laboratory within the Chiswick complex in a large purpose-built building adjacent to the North London Railway line. This had its origin in small premises in Fulham used by the LGOC to test petrol and lubricants in the 1920s. December 1960 saw the new £300,000 steel-framed structure opened at Chiswick, which was designed to replace seven scattered buildings at that site, plus laboratories at the Greenwich, Neasden and Lots Road generating stations.

In July 1982, a Dodge 50 S56 with custom body ('custom' refers to the quality of fittings in the cab) was introduced to provide a mobile research facility. Number 2375D was uniquely finished in a livery of blue cab and lower body, with upper part finished in grey. Apart from legal address lettering, no markings were carried, supposedly to prevent the van's purpose being identified (shades of police box-van 710F in 1948 – q.v.). The interior was fitted with a range of storage cupboards and work surfaces and it lasted ten years. The 50-series had replaced the 'Walk-thru' range inherited by Dodge from Commer, and shared a cab design used on the company's American trucks. Other known vehicles used by the laboratory include 2457B, a red Bedford Midi-Van from November 1986 and still in stock in 1999, plus standard Ford Transit high-top van 2507F (1993–99).

Following the closure of Chiswick Works, the original laboratory building was demolished. A new, but much smaller research facility opened in Bollo Lane as Frank Pick House in very distinctive-looking premises next to the eastbound District Line. In 1987, the department was renamed LUL Scientific Services, but closed in 1996.

Mobile laboratory 2375D was based on an American-designed, though British-built, Dodge S56 (5.6 tonnes gross) chassis and featured a van body finished in a non-standard and unusual grey and blue livery. Although LT was clearly happy to draw attention to the vehicle on this occasion, external identification was normally confined to the legal address lettering. Delivered in 1982, it was to see ten years' use.
Kim Rennie

MOTORCYCLES

The use of motorcycles is an aspect of LT about which little appears to have been published. However, details of the fleet make-up in 1938 show the following: fifteen BSA 350cc motorcycles were used by Central Buses or Country Buses (Operating), and registered DLU 173 to DLU 186 and EYK 395. They dated from 1937 (EYK 395 from 1938) and DLU 182, 184 and 186 had sidecars fitted in 1940. A further nine Triumph motor-cycles were allo-cated to Country Buses (Operating), registered EYK 394 and FJJ 621 to FJJ 628 in 1938–39. Also dating from 1939 were twelve BSA 350cc machines for Central and Country Buses registered FXT 156 to FXT 167. Machines sidecar-fitted and allocated to Chiswick in 1940 were a mixed batch of AJS 350cc models registered FXT 176/5, LHX 595, EYV 122, DYF 504 and FLN 256. Most of these appear to have been de-licensed between 1942 and 1944. Around 1948, further BSA machines were acquired: Solo machines were JXC 370 to JXC 377, whilst JXC 378 to JXC 392 were sidecar-fitted combinations. During the war, motorcycles were allocated to LT despatch riders in order to maintain communications throughout the organi-sation. Early machines were delivered in plain black, though others appear to have been painted Chiswick Green.

Many solo machines were used to allow ticket inspec-tors to intercept buses operating in the remoter parts of the system. A bus could be flagged down and checked at any safe location, allowing the tentacles of 55 Broadway to

Above: During the Second World War, BSA 350cc motorcycle combinations with box sidecars were used to distribute mail and messages throughout LT. The masked headlights and white-painted wings carried by this pair at Camberwell indicate the difficulties of night-time travel during the Blackout, though clearly crash helmets were deemed unnecessary under normal circumstances. LT Museum

Below: Between 1951 and 1957, two motorcycle combinations were used by the Publicity Department to distribute printed material. The sidecars differed from the earlier mail version by having a slot to accommodate a small ladder, and in that the lid hinged on the nearside to allow the rider access whilst seated. Although the style of the drivers' headgear had now altered, it still offered little protection, whilst the overall appearance was reminiscent of the former German Wehrmacht. LT Museum

spread to even the most infrequent and rural services on the very edges of the Board's area. The inspectors initially wore a standard uniform cap, but were later given cork peaked crash helmets fitted with a silver supervisory badge. On Derby Day, some motorcycle combinations were loaned to Morden Depot for use by the fitters, who would help the AA Patrols in keeping the roads leading to Epsom clear of broken-down vehicles. The timed internal mail service also used motorcycle combinations, and motorcycles were still in use in the Country Area until at least 1960.

The Publicity Department also used motorcycles for the fixing of bus stop panel timetables. Two combinations registered VMM 762 and VMM 763 dated from 1951 and carried a box-locker sidecar with an extendable ladder stowed in a slot at the front. No fleet numbers of any kind have been discernible on any of the machines recorded on film, but livery was Chiswick Green. They were replaced in 1957 by standard Austin 1-ton box vans 1051AS and 1052AS. A further venture into this field were SLT 52 to SLT 55 and SLT 60 to SLT 67 from 1956–57, and known only to have been of BSA manufacture.

One vehicle which certainly did carry a stock number, and which belongs under this heading in legal terms at least, is 337V. In use from June 1935 (as No.158 in the Tramways series), it was a Raleigh 2-cylinder 3in-bore 7hp box-tricycle. It had a low box-body supported by two wheels at the front, with a motorcycle rear frame, saddle and engine mounted behind. This was one of two similar machines used for tramway electrical repairs. An earlier 1932 model carried the number '5', but was sold in 1937. 337V itself was sold in June 1940.

In spring 2001, LBSL commenced an experiment in south-west London using three Honda Pan European ST1100A solo motorcycles registered Y161 NLO, Y162 NLO and Y163 NLO. Ridden by specially-trained Area Traffic Controllers, they reportedly allowed a 17 per cent quicker response to incidents. Livery was all-over white, with red/white reflective diced banding. Twin orange flashing lights were fitted to the fore, with a third adjacent to the rear pannier and capable of being raised upward on a telescopic stalk. Further machines have subsequently followed, though again no fleet numbers are allocated.

RECRUITMENT VEHICLES

During the 1980s, several redundant AEC Swift SMD/SMS-class single-deck buses were converted to new uses. SMD 441 became a mobile recruiting office in March 1981 and was repainted into a white livery with red skirt and roof. The cove panels were lettered 'LONDON TRANSPORT RECRUITMENT', and the last word could be

covered by a paper sticker if the bus were used for other purposes. Examples of this included promoting the Havering area experimental 'Multi-Ride' pre-paid ticket experiment and the ill-fated GLC 'Fares Fare' scheme. It was unofficially re-coded '441R', though the number was never actually carried. SMD 441 was withdrawn from use in 1986 and sold in March 1987. Sister-vehicle SMS 730 was converted to the same role at Peckham Garage, and stationed there for a while.

With Britain entering a recession in the mid-1980s, the number of staff leaving the service reduced drastically. LT's satellite recruitment centres at Chiswick Works, Manor House and Peckham had already closed, leaving just the famous long-standing establishment at Griffith House, NW1. A new purpose-built recruitment centre for both bus and rail staff was opened in the ground floor façade of Baker Street Station in the latter years of the same decade and in premises which had once been the 'Chiltern' bar. This was to prove very short-lived, and soon severed all connection with the employment of bus staff as the units prepared for privatisation. The Baker Street office later closed completely, and in 2000 the area was re-converted back into a pub named The Metropolitan Bar. Preliminary assessment of potential LUL staff is now carried out by external agencies.

ROAD-ROLLERS

Vehicle 962R was a solitary Y type D 30-cwt road-roller built by Green, and the only machine of its type ever to be given a number. This very small vehicle was in stock

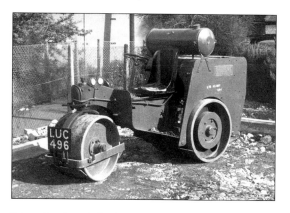

This was the only road-roller given a number in the service vehicle series. It was 962R, a Type 'D' 30-cwt model from Green, dating from 1951. Initially used to resurface former tram tracks, in 1962 it was consolidating the base for a new public car park at Acton Town Station. *John Gillham*

between 1951 and 1969 and was first used to resurface redundant tram tracks. Smaller still was unnumbered Stothert & Pitt vibrating road-roller 525 FJJ from 1961, a single-wheel machine guided by the operator from behind. The registration plate was affixed to the nearside, and the letters 'LTE' crudely stencilled on the front identified the owner.

ROUTE-SURVEY VEHICLES

In the very earliest days of route planning the LGOC simply used a pedestrian-pushed wheel to measure distance accurately to give a basic parameter for measuring and costing new bus and coach routes for fares and schedules purposes. This method sufficed until March 1929, when the journal Motor Transport had reported that the LGOC was using a 30-cwt Chevrolet vehicle to check on distances and to test clearances, gradients, cambers and headroom on existing and new routes. It had a spoked bicycle-type fifth wheel, which when released by a signal-box-type lever, could be lowered beneath the vehicle to record mileage in yards, and the apparatus was transferred between successive vans. The vehicle was

One of several AEC Swifts to enter departmental use, ex-SMS 441 became Mobile Recruitment Centre 441R in March 1981 and gained a revised red & white livery. The word 'RECRUITMENT' on the cove panels was often covered over if the vehicle was used for other purposes, though in this instance partially so. The general downturn in the London economy throughout much of the 1980s later made such high-profile recruiting methods unnecessary. *Kim Rennie*

operated by the Road Schedules Department and came complete with a roof-mounted gauge, which could be raised to simulate the profile of a double-deck NS-class bus. Other equipment carried included separate measuring rods for determining the height of bridges and overhanging trees. To assist with surveying, a large map table plus seating was provided. This was stock number CH 3, first registered in 1928 as UC 2300. It was inherited by LT in 1933 and continued in the same role until sale in October 1937.

The LPTB replaced this with 305M; a Morris C-type delivered in December 1936 and originally numbered M 109. Although the Board owned numerous examples of the Morris C, 305M was immediately identifiable by its bus-style body and a larger roof-mounted gauge. When not used on survey duties, 305M could assist with crowd control at special events, to which effect it was fitted with radio and loudspeaker apparatus, and it was based close to Chiswick Works at Turnham Green Garage. Standard dark green livery was carried, and withdrawal occurred in April 1954.

Although passenger journeys had peaked in the 1940s, the development of the New Towns in the 1950s and 1960s meant that the organisation continued to expand into new territories. To facilitate the planning of new services, a replacement route-survey vehicle was purchased. It arrived in December 1953 as 989B, a Bedford CAV 10/12-cwt van. Bodily, the new vehicle was almost identical to a pair of CAV ambulances acquired two months earlier (see later), with the same raised glazed roof section behind the driver to enable staff to stand almost upright in the van. Most unusually, it was finished in plain black and without stock numbers. The only clue to ownership was a small gold 'LONDON TRANSPORT' fleetname on each side, and even these were applied to removable slot-in plates, presumably to allow for the 'covert' surveying of potential new routes. Like 305M, the new van also officiated at major events like the annual Epsom Derby and was radio-fitted. In 1964, the vehicle then in use was quoted as covering 4,500 miles annually, and was at that time involved in the process of re-measuring every route in the Country Area. It lasted until December 1964, by which time a fourth and final survey van had arrived.

This was 1317F, and based on a Ford Thames 400E

van. It was in effect just a standard 12-seat Utilabrake (or minibus in today's parlance) adapted at Chiswick Works to carry the special features mentioned earlier. Normal grey fleet livery was carried, and it appears the fleetname plates were transferred over to it from 989B. Entering service in July 1964, it was the last Ford Thames vehicle of its type in use by the time of disposal in February 1972.

Moving forward a few years, 1983 saw DMS 2559 converted to a mobile survey control unit for LBL. Though not renumbered, it was transferred to the service vehicle fleet, and was fitted out with an upstairs office and lower-deck generator. Repainted upon conversion, it retained the obsolete white upper-deck window surrounds to its red livery. Although LT has made some small forays into penetrating previously un-served areas using smaller buses in recent years, no specialised vehicles have since been allocated to this task. However in 1988, two red-liveried Vauxhall Astra 1300 vans numbered 3285B and 3286B were recorded as being 'route-survey vans' for London Buses. It is unlikely though that it would have been found necessary to equip them with anything other than standard features.

SHELTER CARRIERS

Under the influence of Frank Pick, the LPTB was very keen on a standard house-style. What he expected and indeed obtained was the use of art, architecture and design to create a public transport system that was both functional and aesthetically pleasing. He is famously quoted as saying: 'bus stops should not be mere poles, but the modest representatives of an organisation offering comfort and visual pleasures'. Not only were stations and other buildings built to a specific style, but publicity brochures and posters also had a definite LT 'feel' to them. This insistence on good taste led to the building of a large number of railway stations whose clean design remains acceptable today.

This style affected even the humble bus shelter, and a standardised range was designed for use in London and the Home Counties. Before the war, many shelters were manufactured at Parsons Green and composed of a kit of parts for erection on site. However, afterwards a standard tubular-framed model was designed and this could be transported in one piece to the location. Shelters were erected where there were substantial flows of passengers and therefore on busy sites. Although it was quite simple to erect the component parts in situ, the potential disruption to passengers whilst the building work was in progress meant it was easier to bring the shelters to site in one piece.

To enable these new shelters to be manhandled easily, a low-loading vehicle was required. In this category was 921LT, an AEC Renown chassis-frame/shelter carrier converted from 6-wheel bus LT 951 in October 1948. This ex-LT-class bus had been used to transport engines from scrapped buses back to Chiswick, and was later modified to convey ex-STL chassis-frames between Chiswick and Aldenham as part of the ill-starred SRT project. When made redundant from its original tasks it was realised that the width between the rear wheels allowed an assembled shelter to fit neatly between the wheel-arches. Alterations had already included the removal of most of the bodywork from above the level of the lower deck windowsills, and provision of an open rear to allow unloading. Framing allowed a tarpaulin to cover the front part of the body, and unlike certain other rebuilds, the ex-bus half-cab, front canopy and bonnet were retained. It worked hard in 1953, when it helped remove and then re-install every shelter situated on the Coronation processional route. The shelters were manhandled on and off the vehicle, as no crane was provided, but though bulky and awkward were clearly not too heavy for a small team to cope with.

AEC Renown LT 951 was converted in 1948 to form 921LT, and was one of the very few CDS vehicles to serve in three distinctive roles. It is best remembered as a shelter carrier, when the low height of the ex-bus chassis was ideal for manual loading and unloading in the days before mechanical handling became prevalent. In this instance at Parsons Green, the tubular Q-type shelter must have been destined for a busy location, being double the usual length.
On the wall of the building behind, various enamel signs can be seen undergoing weathering trials.
LT Museum

Right: The second shelter carrier was 1018J, formerly 'unfrozen' STL 2661 and rebuilt in 1954. This was one of the few bus-to-lorry conversions to retain its full overall length, as the relative lightness of post-war shelters enabled the body to be extended over the rear chassis extension. The crew still had to physically manhandle the shelters into position, but the driver now has the benefit of a cab door, a luxury denied when the vehicle was a bus. *Photomatic*

Centre right: When the option of rebuilding ex-buses ceased, LT was forced to look elsewhere for a low-loading vehicle capable of transporting shelters. In 1964, Karrier Bantam tractor unit 1310KB was twinned with a Carrimore trailer numbered C 21. The tractor utilised a longer tipper chassis to allow for a crew-cab. Despite this, in September 1966, some members of staff obviously preferred to ride on the trailer and make rude gestures at the photographer! *A.B. Cross*

In September 1954, another former bus took over the task of transporting shelters. STL 2661 was rebuilt accordingly and reclassified as 1018J. Again, the half-cab was retained, but in this case, a fixed tilt was used instead of tarpaulin sheeting and the vehicle's side panels did not taper down at the rear. The latter were new fittings, unlike those on 921LT, which made use of the old bus bodywork. In order to give the greatest internal clearance, the inner rear wheels were removed and their associated wheel-arches altered. At the same time, a new flat floor was fitted onto the chassis to allow the shelters to be lifted on and off; again without recourse to any mechanical aids.

Six-wheeler 921LT departed in December 1954, shortly after the introduction of replacement 1018J, whilst the latter lasted until October 1961. Both vehicles had been the usual dark green. Between 1961 and 1964 there was no specific shelter carrier, and the work was carried out using the existing low-load trailer pulled by Bedford/Scammell 953B.

Karrier Bantam 1310KB and its associated trailer C 21 were used for this function from July 1964, and 1684F Ford D600 plus trailer K 1 from October 1971. Once again, no crane was provided. As neither was dedicated solely to this purpose, they are described in the section on articulated tractors and trailers. The shelter carriers were always based at Parsons Green and undertook a programmed replacement of stops and shelters. This was regularly interrupted when individual items needed urgent replacement following accident damage. In more recent times shelters have reverted to being assembled from a kit of parts and can be transported by conventional lorries. The whole job is now in the hands of private contractors, some of whose trucks have carried a small white-on-red roundel, together with the slogan 'Working for London Transport Buses'.

TEST-RIGS

A non-CDS vehicle was the test-rig used to evaluate potential routes for operation by the 8ft-wide RTW class. This paired an AEC Regent III chassis with a skeleton mock-up. This had the width and shape of an imaginary bus body 6 inches wider than normal and enclosed a small saloon in which the test crew could ride. Panelling was complete up to lower-deck window-sill level, and the front two window bays were complete here, whilst the upper-deck area above the cab was also in place, allowing a half-cab appearance to be maintained. Elsewhere, a series of interconnecting metal struts enabled the profile of a double-deck bus to be formed. A dummy three-piece front destination box display was provided, seemingly culled from parts of the STL 1056–1613 (non-roofbox) class. For obvious reasons, the wheels were more widely spaced than on a normal RT. As on some other occasions, only the chassis number was used for identification – in this case being 0961037, and livery was light grey with black wings. By 1949, its work had been done, and the chassis subsequently reappeared as RT 2436.

Below: Not strictly a service vehicle was this 8ft-wide test-rig skeleton body in grey livery, built to the same width as the forthcoming RTW class and mounted on 7ft 6in RT chassis. An observers' saloon is provided behind the front bulkhead. In the background of this December 1948 view at Aldenham, two new mobile canteen trailers appear to be nearing completion. *A.B. Cross*

The two Routemaster test-rigs followed existing buses in service in order to replicate normal operating conditions. RM running units were attached to 'slave' bodies and carried sandbags representing the weight of a half-loaded bus. The observers' saloon was fitted behind the driver's cab and contained four seats, a desk and testing equipment. The dull grey livery predated later CDS policy.
A.B. Cross

RT 769 was also partly completed, in this case for use at the Motor Industry Research Establishment proving ground near Nuneaton from October 1948. Again, livery was plain grey, with passenger windows sheeted over with a black material. It moved to Chiswick Works in August 1949 and twelve months later was returned to Park Royal Vehicles, who completed the body in standard bus form.

The test-rig concept returned to London's streets in August 1958 in connection with the development of the Routemaster. Two sets of RM running units were attached to what was basically a bare chassis frame. The body consisted of a driver's half-cab, an observers' or crew-cab behind the driver and a fixed-sided platform. The latter was used to carry bags of sand to simulate the loading and weight of a conventional bus. In order to distribute this evenly, a flat platform for sandbags was provided over the crew compartment, cab and engine; and both areas were covered by tarpaulin (otherwise the weight would increase dramatically if it rained!). The overall appearance resembled a rather cruder grey-painted version of the bus-to-lorry conversions of the 1940s/1950s. The interior of the crew compartment contained four seats, a writing desk and space for testing instruments.

Initially, three rigs were planned, but in the event, only two were proceeded with. The rigs were referred to by their running unit numbers of R2RH002 and R2RH003 and followed normal service buses, stopping and starting at stops when they did, to experience the same wear and tear on components. Unusually, ordinary Central Bus staff, rather than engineers, drove the rigs. This hastened their demise, since the worsening staff shortage meant it became increasingly difficult to find drivers for the vehicles. But in any case, as time passed, more and more new RMs were available to carry out the sort of duties performed by the rigs. The bodies were subsequently removed and the RM running units used to construct new buses. Former test-rig 002 entered service as RM 341 in July 1960, whilst 003 followed in the October of the same year as RM 398. As with the RTW and RT 769 test-rigs, they had not come under the auspices of CDS.

TICKET VANS

A large-scale operation centred on the Tram & Trolleybus Department's Ticket Machine Works at 51–53 Effra Road, Brixton. The London Tramways Company had established its own ticket-printing works at 301–303 Camberwell New Road in 1892, and this was acquired by the LCCT on 1st January 1899, with the work being transferred to 21-23 Belvedere Road, Lambeth between October and November 1910. On 27th July 1927, the LCCT purchased the Effra Road premises, a 38,000 sq ft site formerly owned by Rowntree Limited. The Belvedere Road printing operations were moved to Effra Road from 12th August 1928, and all other ancillary ticket functions, plus other printing work, was gradually transferred there from September 1928 to February 1929.

Another nearby plant in Stockwell Road was involved in maintenance of ticket machines and punches (some of which lasted right through the LCCT-era, and up to about 1954). The LCCT had been the only tram operator to print its own tickets, all other undertakings obtaining their stock from private suppliers (as did bus operator LGOC). The LCCT also designed its own punch, the Type A, which was substantially different from the Bell Punch machines used by Central Buses. Both Effra Road and the Stockwell Road premises were extensively modernised in the years prior to 1933. Partly in view of this, the LPTB decided to retain their services after the take-over. Among the reasons for this was a recognition of the specialised skills held by the works' staff and the quality and lower cost of the items they produced. Indeed, their role was expanded to cater for the other tramway undertakings now absorbed into the new Tram & Trolleybus Department.

The last year of LCC control had seen the works produce 677,000,000 tickets, using 340 tons of white ticket paper. Conductors' boxes were made up daily by specialised staff and contained sets of tickets, a waybill, a ticket punch and, if needed, a cancelling machine. The boxes carried the route and duty numbers, and when ready, were conveyed to their particular depot by van.

The cost of printing, storing, packing, distributing and auditing of these tickets was very high. Also, the (relative) lack of speed of operation by conductors could lead to potential losses through uncollected fares. However, a much simplified fare structure was required before machine-printed tickets could be used. Once a revised fare structure was in place, the famous 'Gibson' ticket machine came into use from 1953. The machine was named after its inventor, a Mr Gibson, who was Superintendent of the Stockwell Punch Works. The servicing of these was carried out in the Supplies Department's workshop in Bowles Road, Old Kent Road (adjacent to Old Kent Road Garage).

Prior to the changeover beginning, the old multi-coloured pre-printed tickets were packed into so-called 'duty boxes' together with a cash sheet. Those destined for Central Buses were prepared in Chiswick Works, whilst satellite ticket offices served the Country Bus and trolleybus fleets. Although the introduction of the Gibsons reduced certain support vehicle movements, others were now necessary to ferry the new machines to and from Old Kent Road for servicing. In March 1955, three vans left the workshop bound for garages using the Gibson. They returned each morning with around a hundred machines (a few from each garage). The Gibsons would be serviced after four months use, during which time each machine had printed around 75,000 tickets. The serviced machines would be returned to garages on the same nightly van runs that collected incoming Gibsons. Other transportation duties involved the four hundred Setright machines used on Green Line coaches.

Old Kent Road's activities were later transferred to Effra Road, after the demise of pre-printed tickets freed-up space within the building. A new feature introduced at the latter site in 1957 was a machine for manufacturing

Gibson ticket rolls. The paper arrived in large reels from a mill in Kent, and was fed into one of four slitting and winding machines able to produce twenty-six rolls in each operation. With 650,000 ticket rolls then being used per month, it is not surprising one lorry was permanently in use supplying each garage in the fleet on a monthly basis. In 1964, 114 staff worked at Effra Road, with a thousand ticket machines being dealt with each week, out of a total of 16,000 then in use. By this time, four night vans were being used in the collection and delivery runs to Central Bus garages (and to a few of the nearer Country Bus sheds). A fifth van was engaged on daytime visits to the remaining Country Area locations, and also delivered Green Line Setrights to Aldgate, Baker Street, Oxford Circus and Victoria (where presumably they would be entrusted to the Green Line 'point' inspector for subsequent transfer by scheduled coach service). The total number of ticket rolls then being produced each week was 152,000 and contained within 750 cartons. LT did not quite sever all links with pre-printed ticket stocks, since these were still carried by conductors for use in emergencies. Another means of dealing with a ticket machine breakdown was by using one of the stand-by Gibsons kept in garages and at some inspectors' points.

In pre-LT days, the LGOC had AEC B-type chassis B 703, 724, 730, 1021, 1397 and 1533 fitted with van bodies and these were used to deliver ticket stocks to the company's garages from the ticket store in Chiswick Works. Some of the earliest recorded LPTB vehicles were ex-LCCT Caledon (Caledon Motors of Glasgow) 5-ton tramway ticket vans numbered 44 and 48 (reg. nos. XB 8087/ 8615). They dated from 1920 and operated from Rye Lane permanent way depot until their sale in 1937. By this time, 127A and 128A, two of the large fleet of Albion KN127s, were in stock as 4-ton tramway ticket vans. They had arrived new as AN 24 and AN 25 in July 1937, and were among many of the type used by LT. The pair were later transferred to catering duties, being sold out of stock between 1952 and 1954.

To replace the B-type vans, five AEC 503 ex-S-type buses were converted in 1928. Numbered as 11S to 15S in 1939, they had initially retained bus stock numbers, and were placed in the new scheme in the same order (i.e.

ex-S 85, 162, 419, 445 and 521). When new in the 1920s, the S-type double-decker was able to carry 54 passengers, a total that was barely improved on for nearly 35 years. The conversion to vans involved the removal of the top deck, the complete re-panelling of the remaining body and the fitting of hinged rear doors, but retained the original bus half-cab and red livery. The former S-type ticket vans were withdrawn in 1940 and offered for use by the ARP Organisation.

Further Albion KN127s entered service as AN 45 to 48 in January 1939 for Central Bus ticket distribution, replacing the ex-S-class at Chiswick. These became 372A to 375A nine months later and had bodies by Cunard of Ealing. They eventually outlasted the earlier Albions, not leaving the fleet until 1956–58. The annual taxation costs of the old S-type vans had been £70 each, as against £30 for the lighter weight Albions, giving the LPTB a saving of £200. The Leyland Cub SKZ1 type was also employed on ticket carriage duties, with 199C, 200C and 201C in use from August/October 1936 (as Nos. 179, 180 and 181) at Rye Lane. Of these 4-ton vans, 200C and 201C were also later reallocated to the Catering Department, in this case from June 1943.

A one-off vehicle from 1937 was a Morris C-type 30-cwt ticket van fitted with a sliding roof. It was first referred to as M110, later becoming 306M. The rear central section of the roof slid forwards to allow heavy items to be lowered in by overhead crane or gantry. Withdrawal of this unusual vehicle was in July 1949, by which time newer types were available.

Post-war saw 838B in use from December 1948, a single Bedford KZ 30-cwt ticket van. The final vehicles listed as being dedicated to ticket use were 809B and 810B of 1949, part of the large batches of Bedford O-series types delivered in the late-1940s to replace time-expired and/or non-standard types. These were of the Bedford OLBC specification and classed as 5-ton vans. With the introduction of the Gibson and its plain paper roll, the need for pre-printed tickets progressively reduced during the 1950s as the old method of fare collection was phased out. Van 809B was retired in January 1959, its companion 810B followed in April 1963, whilst 838B had been withdrawn in April 1960.

This Albion KN127 was bodied by Cunard Motor Bodies of Ealing and used for Central Bus ticket distribution from 1939. AN 48 (later 375A) was externally identical to the Board's Albion catering vans, though no doubt differently racked inside, and was one of four that replaced the ex-S-class conversions. To help drivers to reverse safely, the LPTB stipulated the provision of twin rear-view mirrors long before it became a legal requirement to fit these to the nearside of vehicles. LT Museum

Most ticket vans were indistinguishable from others in general CDS use, but an exception to this was 1542F, a Ford Transit 22-cwt parcel van with sliding doors. The van was based at Effra Road Ticket Machine Works, where it was seen in April 1977.
Julian Bowden-Green

This did not mark the end of CDS involvement in road service fare collection, indeed, far from it. As has already been seen, vans were required to convey conductors' machines to Effra Road for servicing and repair, and to distribute ticket rolls to garages. However such vehicles were no longer specifically identified in fleet lists as 'ticket vans', and use would have been made of the standard van type employed by LT at the time. These included 1956-built Morris LD (as usual, badged 'Austin') 1-ton general freight vans 1042AS to 1045AS, which were based at Effra Road. These were replaced in early-1964 by 1296AS to 1299AS, further Austin/Morris LD 1-ton box vans, though now in grey livery. Ford Thames 7-cwt box vans 1319F and 1321F arrived at Effra Road in September 1964, with a third (1378F) being added in August 1965. One exception to the 'standard van' rule was 1542F, a Ford Transit 22-cwt parcel van with a large coachbuilt body and sliding cab doors, which was in use between January 1970 and August 1980.

Almex and Gibson machines were also used to issue excess fare receipts at certain locations by station foremen, and Roding Valley Station even used a Gibson to produce ordinary tickets for travel. In both cases, repairs and maintenance were carried out at Effra Road. The maintenance of booking office ticket-issuing machines and the associated Automatic Fare Collection (AFC) equipment came under the Chief Signal Engineer, whose department had a separate AFC section based at Telstar House, Eastbourne Terrace, Paddington (design and drawing office) and Lillie Bridge (construction and maintenance). Ordinary Underground tickets were printed by outside firms (e.g. Waterlow & Son, Highgate), but distributed to stations via Effra Road. Though regular supplies were maintained by deliveries throughout the year, a general fare increase would generate a huge number of additional vehicle movements, because most of the existing 'printed stock' became outdated overnight. Eight vans would be employed in restocking ticket offices, with each vehicle serving up to 46 stations per day.

For a number of years, an outstation of Effra Road existed at Swanley, in Kent, but neither establishment survived the introduction of new 'Wayfarer' ticket machines, or the break-up of LBL. Following the introduction of the Underground Ticketing System, LUL tickets are now printed on blank rolls of card by machines, and deliveries of such rolls to stations has been outsourced to private company TranSys.

TRACTORS

From the late-1920s, many manufacturing companies made use of agricultural-style tractors for the internal movement of equipment before the universal adoption of electric towing and fork-lift trucks. The bus companies were no exception to this, and the LPTB inherited and later purchased a number of tractors that were in use until the mid-1960s.

The first batch, numbers 339X to 350X, were ex-LGOC Fordson model Fs and mainly employed in shunting buses around Chiswick Works. To this effect, they were fitted with large matting or rubber-faced buffers fore and aft. These tractors were also regularly sent to Epsom racecourse on the annual Derby Day to assist any buses that became bogged down on grassland. The vehicles, which dated from between 1925 and 1936, varied in

Fordson tractor No. 2 (later 340X) is seen on the Epsom Downs in LGOC days. Its purpose needs no explanation, except to note that the tractor has been fitted with 'strakes' on the solid steel tyres to give it some traction on grass and soil. As well as operating services to and from the Epsom racecourse, other LGOC buses attended the Derby on private hire for use as mobile grandstands. Solid-tyred buses had virtually no grip on the grass and these tractors were invaluable for recovering stranded vehicles.
G. Robbins / A.B. Cross

classification from 1¾-ton to 3¼-ton. All were previously identified in a simple numerical 1 to 12 series and painted light grey. One of the Chiswick tractors towed a small trailer and was used to collect scrap from around the site. Not always based at Chiswick were 339X (Dalston Garage), 342X (Victoria Garage) and 345X (Croydon Garage). For some reason, 347X and 349X exchanged identities in October 1940. Only 343X and 349X were registered, the others operated on trade plates if required. All were fitted with solid-tyred, but internally-sprung, road wheels for factory use, and 345X had the addition of a detachable Detroit sweeper. Withdrawal took place between 1955 and 1960.

The Central Repair Depot at Charlton made use of several tractors over the years, replacing a small Andrew Barclay 0-4-0T steam locomotive (LCCT No. 1). Charlton was not conduit or overhead-equipped, and both passenger and works cars had to be shunted once within the complex. Only one of the Charlton tractors survived long enough to receive a fleet number in the 1939-series. This was 351X, and unlike most of the former LGOC machines, this vehicle was registered (as CUC 192). Withdrawn in 1960, it was fortunately preserved and now forms part of the LT Museum's reserve collection.

Six more Fordson 1¾-ton tractors were acquired second-hand in 1940, numbers 462X, 463X and 464X via W. H. Perry of North Finchley and 465X, 466X and 467X from R. G. Pratt & Co of Sutton. Five of the six ran on trade plates, but 465X gained the registration GYL 408, which came at the end of a batch of 115 LT Guy Arab 'utility' buses. All had large section pneumatic tyres and electric lights, and were specifically purchased for towing trolleybuses around side-street diversions when main roads were blocked by air-raid damage. Tractor 463X had a cab added in March 1942, whilst 466X gained wings and bumpers in September 1953, but all were sold between 1955 and 1961.

No. 600X was unique to LT in being an International Farmall Type-H paraffin model, seeing service between 1941 and 1947. It had originated from Chicago, Illinois, USA and probably came on Lend/Lease. The vehicle had pneumatic tyres and was registered FXT 368 in a block of 400 FXT-prefixed numbers used mainly on STL and 2RT2 buses.

The commonest use of tractors is in agriculture, and

even here, LT had an interest. As part of the wartime 'Dig for Victory' campaign the Government encouraged the cultivation of suitable spare land for food production. LT grew vegetables for staff canteens at a number of locations, including on the path of the planned Northern Line extension to Bushey Heath. Tractors 465X and 600X were used at the Brockley Hill Farm together with Ford V8 open trucks 477F and 479F.

A final batch of standard Fordson E27N tractors was acquired in April 1942. Numbers 626X to 629X were 1¾-ton tractors operating on trade plates at Central and Country garages. Tractor 626X was the last of these in stock, not retired until March 1966. Like most LT tractors, it had carried green livery.

Quite unusual were the Millar or Clark 3-wheel solid-tyred tractors dating from 1921 and 1931, and originally numbered 136 to 142 in the tramway series. Only three survived long enough to receive numbers 354Y, 255Y and 356Y (the former Tramways Nos. 136, 140 and 141). These were small ex-LUT and ex-MET front-tipping dump trucks used for track maintenance. The first was sold in 1937, the last (356Y) not until 1954.

Six second-hand Fordson tractors were acquired in 1940 to tow trolleybuses around side-streets when main roads were blocked due to air-raid damage. To this effect, they carried 'large-section' pneumatic tyres and electric lights. Later dispersed to other duties around the fleet, 1961 saw tractor 463X in use at Charlton Works. *John Gillham*

One of the sadder tasks performed by LT's tractors was the movement of withdrawn tramcars to the scrapyard at Penhall Road, Woolwich. Trade plate-fitted 629X propels one such vehicle on its final journey whilst under the watchful eyes of enthusiasts and other interested parties. Unlike 628X, no mudguards are fitted, whilst the buffers remain unfaced as solid steel. *C. Carter*

Turnover vehicle 1036TV had been RT 106 and spent many years at Stonebridge Park demonstrating the means of righting an overturned bus. Despite its battered appearance here, it must still stand as a tribute to the design of the RT that the body was able to survive such repeated punishment. The livery can be described as grey, but with a liberal addition of rust! John Gillham

AEC Regal IV 1468W was one of four ex-BEA airport coaches converted to mobile uniform issue units. These would remain on-site for a period, being re-supplied daily with new uniforms from Chiswick. Trailers were used to increase carrying-capacity, and bore an outward resemblance to those towed by the BEA Routemasters. A drawback of the units was the one-and-a-half deck design, which severely restricted headroom in places. A.B. Cross

TURNOVER VEHICLES

In December 1955, 'pre-war' RT 106 was converted to a turnover demonstration vehicle to replace earlier LT, ST and STL buses in training breakdown crews in the safe recovery of overturned buses. In those days, larger operators were responsible for righting disabled buses; a business that would today be carried out by specialised contractors or the emergency services. Devoid of glass, 1036TV was in the fleet from June 1956 to March 1971. Livery was at first bus red, later a dirty grey.

Number 1602TV replaced the pre-war RT in September 1970. This had previously been RT 4306, and was the only other ex-bus regularly utilised in this way. It remained in red livery, though gradually deteriorated in appearance to unpainted metal through repeated 'turnovers' at Stonebridge Park Garage. The end came in May 1976, when inflatable air bags were introduced to right overturned buses. Demonstration and training sessions using the new equipment were carried out at both Chiswick Works and Cricklewood Garage and involved various redundant DMS-class buses.

UNIFORM ISSUE UNITS

LT maintained a large clothing store within the Chiswick Works complex, and this was eventually used to kit-out the staff of Central Buses, Country Buses & Coaches, Trams & Trolleybuses and the Underground. Those involved in engineering received overalls from the same site, as did the staff of LT Catering and even the LT Police. In the mid-1960s, 43,500 new uniforms were being issued to the operating grade staff of the road and rail departments. In addition, another 9,000 uniforms were being supplied to new employees joining the service. Existing catering staff were issued with 1,400 protective garments, while another 500 sets were required for the new recruits to this section. Other forms of protective clothing were needed by the engineering disciplines, with 47,000 items of these being distributed to 25,000 workers in depots, garages, offices, stores and works. There were more than 50 types of jacket in use, 80 varied fittings in trousers, plus berets, boots, coats and clogs. To take the humble apron as an example, these ranged from acid-proof, chef's white, butcher's blue-striped, blacksmith's leather, to what were described as 'neat coral-trimmed' designs for waitresses. Associated accessories supplied by the stores included badges, conductors' cash-bags, guards' equipment bags, and even truncheons and hand-cuffs for the BTC Police. The biggest uniform ever supplied was for an LT policeman. He was 6ft 2in tall; a 59in chest and a 47in waist. Each trouser leg was reputedly big enough to accommodate an average-sized man!

Issue for new recruits was traditionally carried out 'over the counter' at Chiswick, but in February 1967, the concept of mobile distribution was launched, with the conversion of four ex-BEA 1½-deck airport coaches. Before this, management would hire a local church hall as a fitting-room and uniforms would be ferried there from Chiswick on a daily basis to supply staff at the local garage or depot (the LGOC using B-type vans for the task). This was a better arrangement as some garages suffered from a lack of space in which the clothing store's staff could work and, for example, it was not popular to take over part of the canteen. Under the new scheme the former BEA vehicles would serve as 'mobile' fitting rooms, though could remain on a site for a week at least, being re-supplied daily from Chiswick.

These distinctive-looking vehicles were based on the same 4RF4 AEC Regal IV chassis used for the RF class, and first introduced in 1952 on the Heathrow – London Waterloo/Cromwell Road service operated by LT on behalf of BEA. MLL 725 and MLL 727 became 1465W and 1466W, whilst MLL 729 and MLL 735 assumed new identities as 1467W and 1468W. In both cases, they used the W-suffix for AEC Regal last allocated in November 1940. The four were modified for their new life at Country Area garages, the first pair being dealt with by North-fleet, the second two north of the river at Hertford. The internal 'half-decks' were removed and replaced by storage bins, serving counters and two changing rooms. The rear luggage-well was used to store spare items, whilst the main body of the vehicle could contain up to 400 pre-packed and pre-addressed uniform parcels (in 1967 there were twenty types of bus uniform in use).

Livery was standard grey, but with the addition of a waist-rail relief band in black, using the moulding originally provided for the first BEA colour scheme. The sides of the vehicles bore the words 'UNIFORM ISSUE UNIT' in black Johnston lettering, plus a black/white 'open' LT roundel of the type first used on the fronts of XMS-class single-deck buses. Capacity was increased by the provision of small 2-wheel trailers, similar but not identical to those used by the 9RM12 Routemasters introduced to replace the 4RF4s on the airport run. It was desirable to segregate used items of clothing from new and the trailers were used to accommodate obsolete items handed-in for return to Chiswick.

For their first years, the units were used exclusively to deliver to LT's 35,000 Central and Country Area bus staff. During that time, the issue of uniforms to Underground employees' was carried out using parcel delivery, normally using standard CDS lorries and vans. Until the late-1970s, delivery also entailed the running of a 'uniform

by senior officers and detectives. These were not part of the LT car pool and were a separate fleet outside CDS control, listed as 'Rolling Stock Assets'.

From 1958, CDS began to supply vehicles to the British Transport Police's LT Area. Over the years, these have included patrol cars, personnel carriers, dog-vans and incident control units. More-specialised work has seen CDS disguise new trucks into a run-down condition for police surveillance work. Today's Distribution Services organisation continues to be responsible for the procurement of cars and vans for what is today the 'London Area' of the BT Police. Though the BTP identify these by A+ [Alpha] L+ [Lima] numbers, they are given their own four-figure designation by CDS (not carried). As an indication of the vestigial LT-connection, tyre pressures can sometimes be seen displayed in the New Johnston typeface.

CIVIL DEFENCE VEHICLES

The wartime ARP organisation had been disbanded in 1946, but was effectively re-formed in 1949 as the Civil Defence Corps (CDC). This was in response to the growing threat being posed by the 'Cold War' with the Soviet Bloc. LT's contribution consisted of its own self-contained section of the Corps, staffed by volunteers from across the combine. As part of this, two successive converted ex-buses were allocated to Civil Defence use. The first was unique as probably the only Q-type bus ever to become a service vehicle for any fleet in the country. The bus involved, 1035CD, was formerly side-engined AEC single-decker Q 75 and found a use as an 8-seat mobile gas unit. This was employed to demonstrate the means of decontamination and protection following such an attack. The unit was painted green/cream and always carried the unofficial stock number Q1035. Converted in August 1952, it was numbered in the CDS series in November 1955 and lasted until 1964.

In December 1960, the London Transport Magazine reported on a major CDC exercise carried out at the LCC's rescue range at Bully Fen, Hackney. In the scenario, a ten-megaton nuclear weapon had been exploded at 'Chiston', seven miles from one of LT's major works. As no local Civil Defence personnel could be spared, all rescue workers had to come from units attached to the Executive's offices, works and depots. Nearly two hundred LT volunteers attended the exercise, travelling by special bus, lorry or van, and units were mobilised from as far afield as Ruislip and Aldenham. Another exercise was late in 1962 at the Yeading rescue range. In this case, the response was to a supposed explosion in a factory storing radio-active material which had led to a hundred people being unaccounted for, and LT teams attending included those from Acton Works, Croydon, Greenwich and Lillie Bridge.

Replacement for the Q came in 1964 with green-liveried 1311CD, previously Country Area Guy Special single-deck bus GS 82. Its LT use may have been prematurely terminated by the Government's decision to stand down the Civil Defence Corps in spring 1968. Independent operator Tillingbourne Valley obviously thought so, since it bought the redundant 1311CD and converted it back to bus use for service in the Guildford area.

The Underground Group had interests in the bus and coach services of the Home Counties through various differing legal arrangements. The East Surrey Traction Company was a subsidiary of LGOC formed in 1911, and operated in Surrey, Sussex and Kent from its own garages at Crawley, East Grinstead and Reigate. It also operated out of the LGOC-owned premises at Chelsham, Dunton Green, Godstone, Leatherhead and Swanley. East Surrey in turn owned the Tunbridge Wells bus company Autocar from 1928. In the north, the Chelmsford-originated National Omnibus & Transport Company similarly operated routes on the LGOC's behalf in Essex, Hertfordshire and Middlesex from garages at Bishop's Stortford, Luton, Romford, Ware and Watford. Meanwhile in Buckinghamshire, the LGOC had a half-share in Amersham & District.

The LGOC had long wanted to complete the ring around London, and on 14th December 1931, the East Surrey board adopted a proposal to assume operational control of National's Hertfordshire activities on behalf on the LGOC. The East Surrey name was now clearly inappropriate and, from 20th January 1932, the company agreed a new title – London General Country Services. Other developments saw the head office of Green Line Coaches Ltd move from 55 Broadway to Reigate in April 1932. In July 1933, LGCS formed the nucleus of LT's Country Buses & Coaches Department. Though the former LGCS head office at Bell Street, Reigate was initially retained, the vast majority of administrative and support functions were soon transferred to 55 Broadway and other central London offices. One consequence of the LPTB Act was the introduction of a green 'Country Area' livery for all buses, replacing the LGCS red inherited from East Surrey.

Although Country Buses had its own main office at Reigate, operations were administered through seven district offices. These were: North (St Albans), North East (Romford, London Road), North West (Watford, later Garston), South (Reigate), South East (Northfleet) and South West (Windsor). The seventh district was 'Central', which housed Green Line Control in Western House (above the old Central London Railway station building at Oxford Circus).

By 1969, LT was effectively unique amongst public transport operators in Great Britain by providing both road and rail services. In view of this, it was structured quite differently from other undertakings. The usual practice was to split administrative functions into three sections – traffic, engineering and accounts. With LT having the three separate operating departments of Central Buses, Country Buses & Coaches and Underground Railways, this would have resulted in much wasteful duplication, with the same tasks being undertaken by three different groups of staff. The answer to this had been to form 'common user' departments able to serve all parts of the organisation. These carried out such activities as accounts, budgeting, estates, legal matters, payrolls, pensions, publicity, recruitment and staff welfare.

When the new National Bus Company subsidiary 'London Country' was created to assume control of Country Buses & Coaches from 1st January 1970, both LT and the NBC recognised the need to disentangle their involvement with the common user departments by that date, or as soon as practicable afterwards. To this effect, a small team of LT/NBC managers had been set up in 1969 to ensure the changeover went as smoothly as possible.

Despite their efforts, much of the new company had to rely on LT for many years to come. Although LCBS was soon running its own advertising and training departments (though it still made use of the Chiswick 'skid pan'), the Effra Road Ticket Machine Works was to be used for

This engine-less hulk had once been RT 1563 and stood at the back of Chelsham Garage as a less than mobile uniform store. One presumes (or hopes) that its engine had been removed to keep another member of the class going.
Jim Blake

another ten years, albeit on a contractual basis, and LCBS Routemasters continued to visit Aldenham for overhaul. An embryonic LCBS Publicity Department was established at Reigate late in 1969 using LT staff. Following the separation in 1970, LCBS produced its own publicity material, which was then posted by LT staff. CDS also continued to serve the infant LCBS for some time remaining responsible for Procurement & Supplies.

The company did not have any form of central overhaul works, a feature then considered essential for any major operator, although some work could be farmed out to fellow NBC subsidiaries in the South East (and the ex-LT types sent to Aldenham). The situation did not really improve until 1976, when LCBS's own engineering and maintenance operation was opened ' Tinsley Green, Crawley.

To quote L. A. Stimpson, London Country's Chief Engineer in 1972: 'In total the Company operates 28 garages, which vary considerably in size, design and age; also they incorporate auxiliary offices, canteens, enquiry offices, workshops, mess rooms, recreation rooms, gardens and plant and equipment. In addition to the garages are bus stations which, although not owned directly by the Company, we have responsibility for their maintenance. Also the headquarters office building, several private dwellings and last but not least, 2,300 bus shelters and 11,000 bus stops. On the formation of the Company it was observed that very little of the property inherited was above standard and much of it was in need of repair and modernisation or would be in the future.'

A total of 18 former-LT service vehicles were transferred to LCBS upon formation, and were as follows:

4 Thames Trader 5-ton half-tilt lorries
   (1148F to 1151F)
2 Thames Trader 7-ton open lorries
   (1217F and 1251F)
4 Thames Trader tree loppers
   (1242F to 1245F)
2 Austin LD 1-ton vans (1333AS and 1452AS)
6 Ford Transit 12-cwt vans (1410F to 1415F) –
   including the first Transit operated by LT (1410F).

None of these was newer than 1966, and 1148F to 1151F dated back to 1960.

The first four were towing lorries and had operated on trade plates until 1970. Following a change in the licensing laws, they were amongst a number of service vehicles given registrations in the AML-H range. The heavier Thames Traders 1217F, 1251F, continued moving engines to and from Chiswick. The vans numbered 1333AS, 1414F, 1415F and 1452F were used for publicity distribution and were manned by LT staff until 1972. In addition, LT Transit 1549F was on loan in the summer of 1970 for the same task. LCBS later put its vans in a new low numbering series, and 1452AS and 1333AS were reclassified 10A and 15A respectively (in 12/72 and 8/73). The smallest vehicles passed to the new organisation were some of the mechanical sweepers. A Lister or Reliance model was still in use at Northfleet Garage circa-1971. As further activities were devolved to LCBS, more vehicles were needed. Thames Trader 5-ton catering vans 1266F and 1269F were acquired from LT in 1971 together with Austin J4-type 12-cwt vans 1341AS, 1392AS and 1393AS. The latter two were later renumbered as 392AS and 393AS. None were to last long with their new owners, and all five had gone by 1972. In addition, four LT service vehicles were loaned to LCBS in 1971. An Austin 12-cwt, was 1340AS, and 1422F, 1438F and 1439F, Ford Anglia 7-cwt vans, 1439F being used only for training. All were returned to LT by June 1972. During its time on hire, 1439F at least carried a green sticker on the cab doors bearing the new LCBS symbol.

On 1st March 1972, LCBS finally assumed responsibility for all the company's publicity posting outside of the GLC area. The other duties included fixing new timetables and replacing damaged or broken glasses and frames. Three small vans were allocated to the Publicity Department. According to the June 1971 issue of London Country Magazine: "To help in the task we have three Austin 'J4' vans – or perhaps a better description would be museum pieces – for all are just about due for retirement. In fact they were so 'clapped' that our Engineering colleagues refused to let them be driven at first without some attention." (Presumably, the culprits were ex-LT 1341AS, 1392AS and 1393AS.) The report ended with the confident statement that: "All-in-all, we are slowly getting the message across that we are now separate from LT, and even that flying polo symbol of ours doesn't look so out of place after over a year."

The first service vehicle delivered direct to LCBS arrived in the first month in the company's operational life, and appropriately took up number '1' in a new series. 1B was a Bedford HAV 8-cwt van and lasted six years. A similar vehicle was 2B from July 1970 and 3B in August 1971. A change of manufacturer was used for 4A, 5A and 6A, three Austin-Morris J4 panel-vans used for publicity and operated from June 1972. Van 4B was a Bedford HA which entered stock in March 1977. As with LT and many operators throughout Europe the Ford Transit was to become the most common van for LCBS. The first examples bought direct were 7F, 8F, 9F and 11F and 14F,

Below: Four of the five LT Thames Trader tree loppers were transferred to LCBS upon its creation. The vehicles were little altered in appearance under the new regime, with only the substitution of a green LC fleetname showing that anything had changed. In 1979, two of the bodies were re-mounted on new Ford D-Series chassis/cabs and became 34F–35F.
Julian Bowden-Green

Bottom: Ford Anglia van 1439F was one of four LT vans loaned to LCBS in 1971. The temporary sticker on the cab door features the new LCBS symbol, something that few of the company's genuine support vehicles ever did. The van's main purpose was for driver-training, which explains the 'L'-plate stuck above the radiator grille.
John Gascoine

London Country established its own heavy recovery capability in 1971–72 with two second-hand AEC Matador breakdown tenders. Tender 583J was acquired from the MoD via a dealer and was based at Garston Garage to serve the Northern Area. Livery was canary yellow with some elements of green as a relief. At this time, a 3-figure fleet number series was in use for the larger LCBS vehicles, though the LT tradition of suffix letters continued. *Phil Picken*

of the Transit 75 specification between 1972 and 1973. Like 4A/4B, another peculiarity surrounds 11F–12F/14F, which were first numbered 10F – 11F/12F, then each moved forward one place to accommodate van 10A (altered from 1452AS), yet it seems there was never a '13' in the fleet! LCBS briefly returned its allegiance to British Leyland with 16A and 17A, two Austin-Morris J4 vans which joined the company in October 1973, and also through successor-model Austin-Morris Sherpa 19A, a 1975 1-ton van. LCBS also made a brief use of the unsuccessful Ford A-series in 1974 and 1975 with 5-ton (gross) lorries 15F and 18F. Larger vehicles were three Ford D550 5-ton stores lorries originally ordered by LT as 1578F, 1579F and 1580F and delivered direct to LCBS in April 1970. Fleet numbers were later amended to 578F to 580F, and this commenced a short-lived three figure series for large HGVs. No. 579F became an HGV-trainer at Reigate from October 1977. Also in this sequence was 581J, a mobile uniform store converted from former lowbridge AEC Regent III RLH 44. The work was carried out by Brewster's Coachworks of Wrotham, and included the removal of all bus seats and the panelling over of the blind apertures, rear platform and many of the windows. A new hinged access door was fitted to the nearside and led to a distribution counter. Forward of this was a fitting room. The upper-deck had hangers for uniform storage, and cupboards for caps and cash-bags were provided on both decks. 581J had originally been built in 1952, so replacement was probably long overdue by 1981. Its final use was as a mobile office at Stevenage Garage, later being secured for preservation. Vehicle 581J was replaced by Leyland National LNB 57. Converted in September 1981, this 1973-built 11.3-metre former bus had its passenger windows panelled over, and was adorned in a non-standard combination of canary yellow and NBC green.

Having inherited no heavy recovery capacity of its own, two second-hand AEC Matador breakdown tenders were acquired by LCBS during 1971–72. The first, 582J, came from the AEC service depot at Southall. This vehicle had been modified with the fitment of a more modern style cab. The second Matador, 583J, came from the MoD via dealer L. W. Vass of Ampthill, and displayed its military origins with the standard Matador cab and large-section cross-country tyres. Livery was yellow with

green relief, and they were based at Garston and Reigate Garages respectively (the Northern and Southern Area head offices). Three more vehicles were listed in this series prior to it being abandoned: 584J, a Ford D550 5-ton stores lorry; 585F, a larger D0910 7-ton stores lorry and 586F, a D550 3-ton example, delivered between 1972 to 1974. Aside from the heavy breakdown tenders, fleet livery had followed LT custom up until this point, with vans and lorries appearing in light grey. The ex-RLH bus, 581J, was an exception and was adorned in the 'Light National Green' used on buses such as the AF, AN and SMA-classes, with yellow 'LONDON COUNTRY' fleetnames between decks and the 'flying polo' symbol at the front. It was later repainted in NBC green with the double-N symbol.

From about 1972 however, almost all service vehicles were delivered in NBC green with white LC fleetnames. Breakdown tenders continued to appear in yellow, whilst various ex-buses carried their own schemes. Another two heavy breakdown tenders were bought second-hand in mid-1976 and started yet another number range! M 1 was a 1967 AEC Matador obtained via Wreckers International (dealer) and allocated to Garston. M 2, an AEC Mercury of 1970, came from the same dealer, and was sent to Reigate (later in use at Northfleet). Both had the Leyland Group Ergomatic cabs and do not appear to have replaced the first two tenders, as 582J and 583J were not withdrawn until 1979 and 1981. M 1 had a large hand-painted shadowed 'LC' name on each side, whilst sister vehicle M 2 carried a green pre-NBC 'LONDON COUNTRY' block fleetname as used on the MB/SM family-types, coupled with the second style of 'double-N' logo (i.e. the symbol red/blue within a white square). At the time, ancillary vehicles were virtually the only types allowed to deviate from the strict NBC corporate identity guidelines.

The first fuel tanker was 5B, a Bedford TK originating from 1968 and entering stock in 1979. Although it did not serve at the same time as van 5A, the re-use of a number was another departure from LT tradition. The vehicle was permanently stationed at Chelsham Garage. In 1976, the two-figure number series was adopted for virtually all new vehicles, regardless of size, and this was to continue in use until the demise of LCBS as a single company in September 1986. As mentioned earlier, the Ford Transit was used as the standard medium-sized van and further vehicles arrived in the coming years: 19F and 20F (1976), 26F to 31F (1978), 36F (1979), 42F, 43F and 44F (1980), 53F and 58F to 61F (1983), 65F (1984), and 69F, 70F and 71F (1985). If a smaller capacity was required, the Ford Escort range was utilised, these being as follows: 37F (1979 – for driver training), 48F and 50F (1982), 56F and 57F (1983) and 64F (1984). Note that number 19F duplicated 19A. Like LT, LCBS settled on the proven D-series range for its lorries. From 1976, these began to be numbered in the common two-figure range (though existing 5xxF vehicles were not renumbered to match). Most were in D0910 dropside format, though known exceptions are listed in greater detail: 19F (D550 – 1976), 21F and 22F (1976), 23F to 26F (stores lorry, 1977), 32F (1978), 37F, 38 and 39F (1979), 40F ('D0710' – 1979), 41F (D0710 – 1980) and 45F (D1311 – 1981). Vehicle 45F was acquired second-hand. After the 'D'-series had been replaced, LCBS stayed loyal to its replacement model, and the following Ford Cargos were operated in dropside form: 46F (1981), 49F, 51F/52F (1982), 54F–55F/62F–63F (1983), 66F (1984) and 67F and 68F (1985).

The D-series was also used as a base for specialised types. The four Thames Trader tree loppers inherited from LT had been built in 1963 and were getting quite long in the tooth by the late-1970s. Two D0710 chassis were given bodies transferred from two of the old Traders and entered stock in March/April 1979 as 34F and 35F. Changes to the old bodies included a new 'Luton head' on the van body to give clearance to allow the D-series cab to tip. As referred to earlier in the main LT section of the book, the new Fords were themselves re-bodied at a later date. A second-hand 1971 AEC Mandator articulated tractor was converted to a master breakdown tender in stock from July 1980, yet only saw two years service as fleet number M 3. Its replacement may have been M 4, a Leyland Marathon recovery truck previously operated by Blue Circle Cement, and which arrived in September 1982. The only other vehicle to use the prefixed-based numbering system was L 1, a 1976 Leyland Clydesdale fuel tanker which was in use by 1983.

Following a long-established tradition, LCBS transferred a number of buses to the service vehicle fleet, all bar one of which retained their bus stock numbers. The year of conversion is given where known: RT 3420 (1972) and 3429 (1977) were used as towing vehicles and retained green livery. RF 79, 556 and 594 were utilised for the same purpose, though repainted in light grey. Several of the RF towing buses also gained areas of canary yellow relief, greatly enhancing their appearance. Around 1978, RFs 125, 175 and 183 were also modified for towing. It is salutary to reflect on just how much of a comparatively small support fleet was devoted to recovery and towing, and demonstrates the level of vehicle reliability experienced during much of the London Country years, with the consequent breakdowns having a serious effect on customer confidence in passenger services. A single-deck bus, RF 647, served as a mobile recruitment bus throughout much of the 1970s. At first carrying standard NBC green livery, but with the addition of cove-mounted fleetnames altered to read: 'LONDON COUNTRY NEEDS YOU'. The almost desperate nature of this plea illustrates the chronic shortage of staff affecting the company throughout most of its existence. By 1977, it had gained a more eye-catching green/white livery scheme and the title of 'Staff employment unit'. Although not strictly a service vehicle, RT 1563 was used as a very immobile uniform store for many years, gently deteriorating whilst dumped at the back of Chelsham Garage with the engine and entire cab area removed.

Green Line Coaches celebrated its diamond jubilee in 1980, and having witnessed the 1979 LT Shillibeer Celebrations from the 'wrong side of the fence', the 10-year old LCBS decided to stage a comprehensive selection of events. These included garage open days, special-liveried coaches and a road-run over part of the original Green

Line route. Leyland National LN 7 had been one of the original 1972 batch, and its 2-door layout made it ideal for conversion to a mobile exhibition and shop. Retaining its fleet number though christened 'InfoMotion', it was a familiar sight in 1980 and for a number of years afterwards. Livery was non-standard as might be expected, though made use of the corporate NBC green/white colours. Redundant Nationals were also to form the basis of two mobile engineering classrooms. LN 1 and LN 3, two of the buses used on the pioneer 'Superbus' routes in Stevenage during the early years of the company, were selected for rebuilding. It is unclear from published sources whether these were ever completed far enough to see use, but the livery application was a pleasant combination of yellow and NBC green.

When the Government decided upon the privatisation of the NBC, the LCBS subsidiary posed a number of problems. It was still very large in comparison to many other bus companies, especially as the politicians probably envisaged a post-privatisation scene populated by competing entrepreneurs, small management buy-out teams and maybe driver co-operatives. With the Conservative Party's professed dislike of monopolies, the idea of handing over the entire LCBS network to one buyer was considered unacceptable. In addition, the 'mint with a hole' operating area had never been a satisfactory arrangement and remained an anomaly created simply by history. Consequently, on 7th September 1986 LCBS ceased to exist and was divided into four new companies: London Country (North West), London Country (North East), London Country (South West) and London Country (South East). The centralised maintenance works at Tinsley Green was established as a separate entity, 'Gatwick Engineering Limited' with services available to the four new operators.

Despite the difficulty in obtaining details of the later LCBS years, the following vehicles are believed to have been on the books at the time of the division: 34F, 35F, 37F, 39F, 41F*, 44F, 46F, 47F*, 48F, 49F, 50F, 51F*, 53F, 54F, 55F, 56F, 57F*, 58F, 59F, 60F, 61F, 62F, 63F*, 64F, 65F, 66F*, 67F*, 68F*, 69F, 70F*, 71F, 72F, L 1, M 1, M 2, M 4, LN 1, LN 3, LN 7, LNB 57*. Vehicles marked * were transferred to Gatwick Engineering Limited.

It is ironic that in recent years, most of the ex-LCBS companies (or their successors) have been acquired by the same large bus group, the very opposite of what was intended by privatisation. Gatwick Engineering Limited was later sold to Frontsource, which also acquired the residual remains of LRT's Bus Engineering Limited at Willesden. Neither site remains in use.

Familiar to enthusiasts for a number of years was Leyland National LN 7, converted as an information centre and shop in 1980 as part of the Green Line golden jubilee. The 2-door layout of LCBS's early Nationals meant that these were more suitable for such a role than later versions. Bearing its green/white livery and new name of 'InfoMotion', LN 7 stands on the piazza outside the LT Museum on 6th June 1982. A.B. Cross

THE USE OF TRADE PLATES

One of the many idiosyncrasies of British motoring law has been the use (and indeed misuse) of trade plates or more correctly 'Trade Licence Plates' by the motor trade. The original purpose of these was to enable new and unregistered vehicles to be driven on public roads without a valid Road Fund Licence for test or demonstration runs, or for new or used vehicles on delivery. Their use and destination had to be recorded in an official register every time they were used.

There were originally two types of trade plate: 'Limited' and 'General'. Both classes were allocated to a user/company, rather than to specific vehicles. Plates were generally composed of three figures and two letters (e.g. 011 GF) depicted in non-standard colours. These were red-on-white for 'Limited' plates, with the 'General' plates reversing this as white on-red. In both cases, shape and size followed ordinary number plate practice. Later changes saw all plates adopt the red-on-white scheme, with further limitations on their use.

The 'General' plates allowed the carriage of goods in conjunction with the owner's motor vehicle business, and trade plates were commonly used on breakdown vehicles. In theory these never carried a load for 'hire or reward', but were used solely in conjunction with the maintenance or recovery of buses and other motor vehicles. Other LT uses were on garage maintenance vehicles like distilled water carriers and some stores lorries, as well as trucks for moving bus batteries, and tyres. The distilled water tankers could run on trade plates when delivering water for buses, but not when delivering to rail depots!

When Aldenham Works was opened, a fleet of buses was introduced to carry workers from their local bus garage, and from Chiswick, to the works' remote location on the outskirts of London. Photographs exist of trade plates in use on buses transporting staff to Aldenham from the Walthamstow area. Trade plates were also used on delicensed buses being transferred between garages. Although LT was very careful with the use of trade plates, the abuse and misuse of them throughout the country was legendary, and hardly what was originally envisaged by the authorities. Abuse by reputable firms was limited, and very often due to mistakes in picking up the wrong plates.

From January 1970, the system became much more tightly regulated to ensure that only very specific categories of concerns could own and use trade plates. Certain service vehicles formerly operating on them were registered at this time using numbers in the then current AML-H range, even though some dated from as far back as 1961! Trade plates continued to be used on bus breakdown tenders and towing lorries, but even these types gained normal licence plates after 1st January 1988, when the regulations were tightened still further. To give LT its due, none of the railway breakdown tenders had ever operated on trade plates, and CDS were to some extent pleased to see the back of them, as they had seriously restricted the flexibility of some of the fleet.

CDS SUPERINTENDENTS

Superintendents (later Distribution Service Managers) of Central Distribution Services since 1949

Geoffrey Fernyhough	... ...	1949 – 1950	Later became MD of LCBS
Tom Courtney	... ...	1950 – 1956	
Peter Rothschild	... ...	1956 – 1960	
Charles Coleshill	... ...	1960 – 1972	
Bryan Constable	... ...	1973 – 1976	
Michael Clark	... ...	1977 – 1993	
Peter Forsdick	... ...	1993 – to date	

PREFIX-LETTER CODES
(From 1933 to 1939)

AN	Albion	F	Ford, Fordson
B	British Ensign	L	Leyland
BD	Bedford	M	Morris, Morris Commercial
C – – L	Leyland Cub	NY	Thornycroft
CH	Chevrolet	P	Tilling Stevens
D	Dennis	TV	Trojan
E	AEC Matador or Monarch	V	Chiswick-built light vans
EN	AEC 506 or YC-type		

Two AEC Mercury tower wagons engage in repairs to bomb-damaged trolleybus overhead. The pair are wearing their wartime 'battledress' of white-edged wings, masked headlamps and brown oxide roofs.

APPENDIX 4

SUFFIX-LETTER CODES

(November 1939 onwards)

Albion … … … … … … A	Morris, Morris Commercial
Austin … … … … … … AS	(later Mercedes-Benz) … … … M
Bedford (later Vauxhall) … … … … B	AEC Militant … … … … … MR
Leyland Cub … … … … … C	Maudslay … … … … … … MY
Civil Defence vehicle … … … … CD	AEC Monarch … … … … … N
Commer … … … … … CM	AEC Matador (later Peugeot) … … … P
Foden and Yorkshire steam vehicles,	AEC Mercury or Marshal … … … Q
Dennis (later Dodge) … … … … D	Mobile crane or road-roller
Dodge … … … … … … DG	(originally Ransomes & Rapier) … … R
ADC 418, (later ERF) … … … … E	Renshaw Lister … … … RN
Ford, Fordson, Fordson Thames … … F	AEC 503 (later Seddon) … … … … S
Guy … … … … … … G	Thornycroft (later Toyota) … … … T
AEC NS-class … … … … … H	Turnover vehicle … … … … … TV
Fiat … … … … … … I	Associated Daimler 802 (ex-LS-class) … U
AEC Regent … … … … … J	Vulcan, Raleigh (later Vauxhall, Volkswagen
Karrier … … … … … K	and Volvo) … … … … … V
Karrier Bantam … … … … … KB	Volkswagen … … … … … … VW
Karrier Gamecock … … … … KG	AEC Regal … … … … … … W
Leyland, Leyland-DAF, Freight Rover … L	4-wheeled tractor … … … … … X
Leyland Titan PD3 … … … … LD	3-wheeled tractor … … … … … Y
Land Rover … … … … … LR	AEC 506 or YC-type … … … … Z
AEC Renown (ex-LT-class) … … … LT	

Index of numbered service vehicles shown in photographs

Front cover upper Amongst the longest lived LT service vehicles were the trolleybus breakdown tenders. Based on Leyland and Albion chassis, the earliest members of the fleet dated from 1936. Ilford depot based 123A, an Albion dating from 1937, lasted in service until 1962. It is seen here in Barkingside High Street about to tow class SA3 trolleybus 1762 back to the depot. David Bradley

Front cover lower Leyland Lynx 1995L and trailer YT28 are seen carrying out one of CDS's more unusual jobs, the 1979 transfer of a 1938 tube stock cab to the new London Transport Museum at Covent Garden. Following as the ensemble passes under the Kilburn station railway bridges is a standard LT Ford Escort Mk2 van. Fred Ivey

Title page Commercial advertising and publicity distribution were activities that had long been centralised in one form or another and required the operation of ancillary vehicles separate from the main passenger-carrying fleet. In pre-LT days, some of the LGOC's Chiswick-built V-class vans were allocated to the task. Here, V 48 is being loaded with posters outside Lambeth North Station. The van's livery is interesting, and appears to be a two-tone scheme together with a silver roof. In addition, the 'UndergrounD' title appears instead of the usual 'General' name. LT Museum

Contents page In the mid-1980s LT purchased a number of pick-up trucks from Ford and Peugeot, many of which were used by garage fitters to attend breakdowns or to collect spares and soon gained local identity transfers. Seen here in Ilford in 1993 is East London's 4205P, a Peugeot 504. The suffix code P was originally allocated to AEC Matador trucks. Colin Lloyd